JAWS

Smashing together, they crush bones and flesh and organs into jelly.

The jaws of a giant killer shark that terrorizes a small holiday resort on Long Island.

Private feuds, lusts and jealousies take second place to a relentless duel, almost unbearable in its suspense and danger . . .

'As engrossing a tale as you're likely to encounter' *Chicago Sun-Times*

Peter Benchley was born in New York City in 1940 and is the son of novelist Nathaniel Benchley and grandson of humorist Robert Benchley. He has worked as a reporter for the *Washington Post*, as associate editor of *Newsweek* and as a speech-writer for the late President Johnson. His stories and articles have appeared in numerous magazines including the *New Yorker* and *National Geographic*.

Jaws is his first novel, his two previous books being a story for children and a book based on his trip round the world. Peter Benchley lives with his wife and two children in Pennington, New Jersey.

JAWS

PETER BENCHLEY

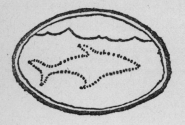

Pan Books London and Sydney

First published in Great Britain 1974 by André Deutsch Ltd
This edition published 1975 by Pan Books Ltd,
Cavaye Place, London SW10 9PG
12th printing 1975
© Peter Benchley 1974
ISBN 0 330 24382 9
Printed in Great Britain by
Cox & Wyman Ltd, London, Reading and Fakenham

For Wendy

Part I

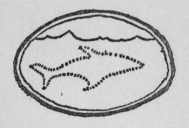

ONE

The great fish moved silently through the night water, propelled by short sweeps of its crescent tail. The mouth was open just enough to permit a rush of water over the gills. There was little other motion: an occasional correction of the apparently aimless course by the slight raising or lowering of a pectoral fin – as a bird changes direction by dipping one wing and lifting the other. The eyes were sightless in the black, and the other senses transmitted nothing extraordinary to the small, primitive brain. The fish might have been asleep, save for the movement dictated by countless millions of years of instinctive continuity: lacking the flotation bladder common to other fish and the fluttering flaps to push oxygen-bearing water through its gills, it survived only by moving. Once stopped, it would sink to the bottom and die of anoxia.

The land seemed almost as dark as the water, for there was no moon. All that separated sea from shore was a long, straight stretch of beach – so white that it shone. From a house behind the grass-splotched dunes, lights cast yellow glimmers on the sand.

The front door to the house opened, and a man and a woman stepped out on to the wooden porch. They stood for a moment staring at the sea, embraced quickly, and scampered down the few steps on to the sand. The man was drunk, and he stumbled on the bottom step. The woman laughed and took his hand, and together they ran to the beach.

'First a swim,' said the woman, 'to clear your head.'

'Forget my head,' said the man. Giggling, he fell backward on to the sand, pulling the woman down with him. They fumbled with each other's clothing, twined limbs around limbs, and thrashed with urgent ardour on the cold sand.

Afterward, the man lay back and closed his eyes. The woman looked at him and smiled. 'Now, how about that swim?' she said.

'You go ahead. I'll wait for you here.'

The woman rose and walked to where the gentle surf washed over her ankles. The water was colder than the night air, for it was only mid-June. The woman called back, 'You're sure you don't want to come?' But there was no answer from the sleeping man.

She backed up a few steps, then ran at the water. At first her strides were long and graceful, but then a small wave crashed into her knees. She faltered, regained her footing, and flung herself over the next waist-high wave. The water was only up to her hips, so she stood, pushed the hair out of her eyes, and continued walking until the water covered her shoulders. There she began to swim – with the jerky, head-above-water stroke of the untutored.

A hundred yards offshore, the fish sensed a change in the sea's rhythm. It did not see the woman, nor yet did it smell her. Running within the length of its body were a series of thin canals, filled with mucus and dotted with nerve endings, and these nerves detected vibrations and signalled the brain. The fish turned towards shore.

The woman continued to swim away from the beach, stopping now and then to check her position by the lights shining from the house. The tide was slack, so she had not moved up or down the beach. But she was tiring, so she rested for a moment, treading water, and then started for shore.

The vibrations were stronger now, and the fish recognized prey. The sweeps of its tail quickened, thrusting the giant body forward with a speed that agitated the tiny phosphorescent animals in the water and caused them to glow, casting a mantle of sparks over the fish.

The fish closed on the woman and hurtled past, a dozen

feet to the side and six feet below the surface. The woman felt only a wave of pressure that seemed to lift her up in the water and ease her down again. She stopped swimming and held her breath. Feeling nothing further, she resumed her lurching stroke.

The fish smelled her now, and the vibrations – erratic and sharp – signalled distress. The fish began to circle close to the surface. Its dorsal fin broke water, and its tail, thrashing back and forth, cut the glassy surface with a hiss. A series of tremors shook its body.

For the first time, the woman felt fear, though she did not know why. Adrenalin shot through her trunk and her limbs, generating a tingling heat and urging her to swim faster. She guessed that she was fifty yards from shore. She could see the line of white foam where the waves broke on the beach. She saw the lights in the house, and for a comforting moment she thought she saw someone pass by one of the windows.

The fish was about forty feet away from the woman, off to the side, when it turned suddenly to the left, dropped entirely below the surface, and with two quick thrusts of its tail, was upon her.

At first, the woman thought she had snagged her leg on a rock or a piece of floating wood. There was no initial pain, only one violent tug on her right leg. She reached down to touch her foot, treading water with her left leg to keep her head up, feeling in the blackness with her left hand. She could not find her foot. She reached higher on her leg, and then she was overcome by a rush of nausea and dizziness. Her groping fingers had found a nub of bone and tattered flesh. She knew that the warm, pulsing flow over her fingers in the chill water was her own blood.

Pain and panic struck together. The woman threw her head back and screamed a guttural cry of terror.

The fish had moved away. It swallowed the woman's limb without chewing. Bones and meat passed down the massive gullet in a single spasm. Now the fish turned again, homing on the stream of blood flushing from the woman's femoral artery, a beacon as clear and true as a lighthouse on a cloudless night. This time the fish attacked from below. It hurtled up under the woman, jaws agape. The great conical head struck her like a locomotive, knocking her up out of the water. The jaws snapped shut around her torso, crushing bones and flesh and organs into a jelly. The fish, with the woman's body in its mouth, smashed down on the water with a thunderous splash, spewing foam and blood and phosphorescence in a gaudy shower.

Below the surface, the fish shook its head from side to side, its serrated triangular teeth sawing through what little sinew still resisted. The corpse fell apart. The fish swallowed, then turned to continue feeding. Its brain still registered the signals of near-by prey. The water was laced with blood and shreds of flesh, and the fish could not sort signal from substance. It cut back and forth through the dissipating cloud of blood, opening and closing its mouth, seining for a random morsel. But by now, most of the pieces of the corpse had dispersed. A few sank slowly, coming to rest on the sandy bottom, where they moved lazily in the current. A few drifted away just below the surface, floating in the surge that ended in the surf.

The man awoke, shivering in the early morning cold. His mouth was sticky and dry, and his wakening belch tasted of Bourbon and corn. The sun had not yet risen, but a line of pink on the eastern horizon told him that daybreak was near. The stars still hung faintly in the lightening sky. The man stood and began to dress. He was annoyed that the woman had not woken him when she went back to the house, and he found it curious that she had left her clothes on the beach. He picked them up and walked to the house.

He tip-toed across the porch and gently opened the screen door, remembering that it screeched when yanked. The living-room was dark and empty, littered with half-empty glasses, ashtrays, and dirty plates. He walked across the living-room, turned right down a hall, past two closed doors. The door to the room he shared with the woman was open, and a bedside light was on. Both beds were made. He tossed the woman's clothes on one of the beds, then returned to the living-room and switched on a light. Both couches were empty.

There were two more bedrooms in the house. The owners slept in one. Two other house guests occupied the other. As quietly as possible, the man opened the door to the first bedroom. There were two beds, each obviously containing only one person. He closed the door and moved to the next room. The host and hostess were asleep on each side of a king-size bed. The man closed the door and went back to his room to find his watch. It was nearly five.

He sat on one bed and stared at the bundle of clothes on the other. He was certain the woman wasn't in the house. There had been no other guests for dinner, so unless she had met someone on the beach while he slept, she couldn't have gone off with anyone. And even if she had, he thought, she probably would have taken at least some of her clothes.

Only then did he permit his mind to consider the possibility of an accident. Very quickly the possibility became a certainty. He returned to the host's bedroom, hesitated for a moment beside the bed, and then softly placed his hand on a shoulder.

'Jack,' he said, patting the shoulder. 'Hey, Jack.'

The man sighed and opened his eyes. 'What?'

'It's me. Tom. I hate like hell to wake you up, but I think we may have a problem.'

'What problem?'

'Have you seen Chrissie?'

'What do you mean, have I seen Chrissie? She's with you.'

'No, she isn't. I mean, I can't find her.'

Jack sat up and turned on a light. His wife stirred and covered her head with a sheet. Jack looked at his watch. 'Jesus Christ. It's five in the morning. And you can't find your date.'

'I know,' said Tom. 'I'm sorry. Do you remember when you saw her last?'

'Sure I remember. She said you were going for a swim, and you both went out on the porch. When did *you* see her last?'

'On the beach. Then I fell asleep. You mean she didn't come back?'

'Not that I saw. At least not before we went to bed, and that was around one.'

'I found her clothes.'

'Where? On the beach?'

'Yes.'

'You looked in the living-room?'

Tom nodded. 'And in the Henkels' room.'

'The Henkels' room!'

Tom blushed. 'I haven't known her that long. For all I know, she could be a little weird. So could the Henkels. I mean, I'm not suggesting anything. I just wanted to check the whole house before I woke you up.'

'So what do you think?'

'What I'm beginning to think,' said Tom, 'is that maybe she had an accident. Maybe she drowned.'

Jack looked at him for a moment, then glanced again at his watch. 'I don't know what time the police in this town go to work,' he said, 'but I guess this is as good a time as any to find out.'

Patrolman Len Hendricks sat at his desk in the Amity police station, reading a detective novel called *Deadly, I'm Yours*. At the moment the phone rang the heroine, a girl named Whistling Dixie, was about to be raped by a motorcycle club. Hendricks let the phone ring until Miss Dixie castrated the first of her attackers with a linoleum knife she had secreted in her hair.

He picked up the phone. 'Amity Police, Patrolman Hendricks,' he said. 'Can I help you?'

'This is Jack Foote, over on Old Mill Road. I want to report a missing person. Or at least I think she's missing.'

'Say again, sir?' Hendricks had served in Vietnam as a radio man, and he was fond of military terminology.

'One of my house guests went for a swim at about one this morning,' said Foote. 'She hasn't come back yet. Her date found her clothes on the beach.'

Hendricks began to scribble on a pad. 'What was the person's name?'

'Christine Watkins.'

'Age?'

'I don't know. Just a second. Say around twenty-five. Her date says that's about right.'

'Height and weight?'

'Wait a minute.' There was a pause. 'We think probably about five-seven, between one twenty and one thirty.'

'Colour of hair and eyes?'

'Listen, Officer, why do you need all this? If the woman's drowned, she's probably going to be the only one you have – at least tonight, right? You don't average more than one drowning around here each night, do you?'

'Who said she drowned, Mr Foote? Maybe she went for a walk.'

'Stark naked at one in the morning? Have you had any reports about a woman walking around naked?'

Hendricks relished the chance to be insufferably cool. 'No, Mr Foote, not yet. But once this summer season starts, you never know what to expect. Last August, a bunch of faggots staged a dance out by the club – a nude dance. Colour of hair and eyes?'

'Her hair is ... oh, dirty blonde, I guess. Sandy. I don't know what colour her eyes are. I'll have to ask her date. No, he says he doesn't know either. Let's say hazel.'

'Okay, Mr Foote. We'll get on it. As soon as we find out anything, we'll contact you.'

Hendricks hung up the phone and looked at his watch. It was 5.10. The chief wouldn't be up for an hour, and Hendricks wasn't anxious to wake him for something as vague as a missing-person report. For all anybody knew, the broad was off humping in the bushes with some guy she met on the beach. On the other hand, if she was washed up somewhere, Chief Brody would want the whole thing taken care of before the body was found by some nanny with a couple of young kids and it became a public nuisance.

Judgement, that's what the chief kept telling him he needed; that's what makes a good cop. And the cerebral challenge of police work had played a part in Hendricks' decision to join the Amity force after he returned from Vietnam. The pay was fair: $9,000 to start, $15,000 after fifteen years, plus fringes. Police work offered security, regular hours, and the chance for some fun – not just thumping unruly kids or collaring drunks, but solving burglaries, trying to catch the occasional rapist (the summer before, a black gardener had raped seven rich white women, not one of whom would appear in court to testify against him), and –

16

on a slightly more elevated plane – the opportunity to become a respected, contributing member of the community. And being an Amity cop was not very dangerous, certainly nothing like working for a metropolitan force. The last duty-related fatality of an Amity policeman occurred in 1957 when an officer had tried to stop a drunk speeding along the Montauk Highway and had been run off the road into a stone wall.

Hendricks was convinced that as soon as he could get sprung from this God-forsaken midnight-to-eight shift, he would start to enjoy his work. For the time being, though, it was a drag. He knew perfectly well why he had the late shift. Chief Brody liked to break in his young men slowly, letting them develop the fundamentals of police work – good sense, sound judgement, tolerance, and politeness – at a time of day when they wouldn't be overtaxed.

The business shift was 8.00 AM to 4.00 PM, and it called for experience and diplomacy. Six men worked that shift. One handled the summertime traffic at the intersection of Main and Water streets. Two patrolled in squad cars. One manned the phones at the station house. One handled the clerical work. And the chief handled the public – the ladies who complained that they were unable to sleep because of the din coming from the Randy Bear or Saxon's, the town's two gin mills; the homeowners who complained that bums were littering the beaches or disturbing the peace; and the vacationing bankers and brokers and lawyers who stopped in to discuss their various plans for keeping Amity a pristine and exclusive summer colony.

Four to midnight was the trouble shift, when the young studs from the Hamptons would flock to the Randy Bear and get involved in a fight or simply get so drunk that they became a menace on the roads; when, very rarely, a couple of predators from Queens would lurk in the dark side streets and mug passersby; and when, about twice a month in the summer, enough evidence having accumulated, the police

17

would feel obliged to stage a pot bust at one of the huge waterfront homes. There were six men on four to midnight, the six largest men on the force, all between thirty and fifty years old.

Midnight to eight was usually quiet. For nine months of the year, peace was virtually guaranteed. The biggest event of the previous winter had been an electrical storm that had set off all the alarms linking the police station to forty-eight of Amity's biggest and most expensive homes. Normally during the summer, the midnight-to-eight shift was manned by three officers. One, however, a young fellow named Dick Angelo, was now taking his two-week leave before the season began to swing. The other was a thirty-year veteran named Henry Kimble, who had chosen the midnight-to-eight shift because it permitted him to catch up on his sleep – he held a daytime job as a bartender at Saxon's. Hendricks tried to raise Kimble on the radio – to get him to take a walk along the beach by Old Mill Road – but he knew the attempt was hopeless. As usual, Kimble was sound asleep in a squad car parked behind the Amity Pharmacy. And so Hendricks picked up the phone and dialled Chief Brody's home number.

Brody was asleep, in that fitful state before waking when dreams rapidly change and there are moments of bleary semiconsciousness. The first ring of the phone was assimilated into his dream – a vision that he was back in high school groping a girl on a stairwell. The second ring snapped the vision. He rolled over and picked up the receiver.

'Yeah?'

'Chief, this is Hendricks. I hate to bother you this early, but—'

'What time is it?'

'Five-twenty.'

'Leonard, this better be good.'

'I think we've got a floater on our hands, Chief.'

'A floater? What in Christ's name is a floater?'

It was a word Hendricks had picked up from his night reading. 'A drowning,' he said, embarrassed. He told Brody about the phone call from Foote. 'I didn't know if you'd want to check it out before people start swimming. I mean, it looks like it's going to be a nice day.'

Brody heaved an exaggerated sigh. 'Where's Kimble?' he said and then added quickly, 'Oh, never mind. It was a stupid question. One of these days I'm going to fix that radio of his so he can't turn it off.'

Hendricks waited a moment, then said, 'Like I said, Chief, I hate to bother . . .'

'Yeah, I know, Leonard. You were right to call. As long as I'm awake, I might as well get up. I'll shave and shower and grab some coffee, and on my way in I'll take a look along the beach in front of Old Mill and Scotch, just to make sure your "floater" isn't cluttering up somebody's beach. Then when the day boys come on, I'll go out and talk to Foote and the girl's date. I'll see you later.'

Brody hung up the phone and stretched. He looked at his wife, lying next to him in the double bed. She had stirred when the phone rang, but as soon as she determined that there was no emergency, she lapsed back into sleep.

Ellen Brody was thirty-six, five years younger than her husband, and the fact that she looked barely thirty was a source of both pride and annoyance to Brody: pride because, since she looked handsome and young and was married to him, she made him seem a man of excellent taste and substantial attraction; annoyance because she had been able to keep her good looks despite the strains of bearing three children, whereas Brody – though hardly fat at six-foot-one and two hundred pounds – was beginning to be concerned about his blood pressure and his thickening middle. Sometimes during the summer, Brody would catch himself gazing with idle lust at one of the young, long-legged girls who pranced around town – their untethered breasts bouncing beneath the thinnest of cotton jerseys. But he never enjoyed the sensation, for it always made him wonder whether Ellen felt the same stirring when she looked at the tanned, slim young men who so perfectly complemented the long-legged girls. And as soon as that thought occurred to him, he felt still worse, for he recognized it as a sign that he was on the unfortunate side of forty and had already lived more than half his life.

Summers were bad times for Ellen Brody, for in summer she was tortured by thoughts she didn't want to think – thoughts of chances missed and lives that could have been. She saw people she had grown up with: prep school classmates now married to bankers and brokers, summering in Amity and wintering in New York, graceful women who stroked tennis balls and enlivened conversations with equal ease, women who (Ellen was convinced) joked among themselves about Ellen Shepherd marrying that policeman because he got her pregnant in the back seat of his 1948 Ford, which had not been the case.

Ellen was twenty-one when she met Brody. She had just finished her junior year at Wellesley and was spending the summer in Amity with her parents – as she had done for the previous eleven summers, ever since her father's advertising agency transferred him from Los Angeles to New York. Although, unlike several of her friends, Ellen Shepherd was hardly obsessed by marriage, she assumed that within a year or two after finishing college she would wed someone from approximately her own social and financial station. The thought neither distressed nor delighted her. She enjoyed the modest wealth her father had earned, and she knew her mother did too. But she was not eager to live a life that was a repetition of her parents'. She was familiar with the petty social problems, and they bored her. She considered herself a simple girl, proud of the fact that in the yearbook for the class of 1953 at Miss Porter's School she was voted Most Sincere.

Her first contact with Brody was professional. She was arrested – or, rather, her date was. It was late at night, and she was being driven home by an extremely drunk young man intent on driving very fast down very narrow streets. The car was intercepted and stopped by a policeman who impressed Ellen with his youth, his looks, and his civility. After issuing a summons, he confiscated the keys to Ellen's date's car and drove them both to their respective homes. The next morning, Ellen was shopping when she found herself next to the police station. As a lark, she walked in and asked the name of the young officer who had been working at about midnight the night before. Then she went home and wrote Brody a thank-you note for being so nice, and she also wrote a note to the chief of police commending young Martin Brody. Brody telephoned to thank her for her thank-you note.

When he asked her out to dinner and the movies on his night off, she accepted out of curiosity. She had scarcely ever talked to a policeman, let alone gone out with one. Brody was nervous, but Ellen seemed so genuinely interested in him and his work that he eventually calmed down enough to have a good time. Ellen found him delightful: strong, simple, kind – sincere. He had been a policeman for six years. He said his ambition was to be chief of the Amity force, to have sons to take duck-shooting in the fall, to save enough money to take a real vacation every second or third year.

They were married that November. Ellen's parents had wanted her to finish college, and Brody had been willing to wait until the following summer, but Ellen couldn't imagine that one more year of college could make any difference in the life she had chosen to lead.

There were some awkward moments during the first few years. Ellen's friends would ask them to dinner or lunch or for a swim, and they would go, but Brody would feel ill at ease and patronized. When they got together with Brody's friends, Ellen's past seemed to stifle fun. People behaved as

21

if they were fearful of committing a *faux pas*. Gradually, as friendships developed, the awkwardness disappeared. But they never saw any of Ellen's old friends any more. Although the shedding of the 'summer people' stigma earned her the affection of the year-round residents of Amity it cost her much that was pleasant and familiar from the first twenty-one years of her life. It was as if she had moved to another country.

Until about four years ago, the estrangement hadn't bothered her. She was too busy, and too happy, raising children to let her mind linger on alternatives long past. But when her last child started school, she found herself adrift, and she began to dwell on memories of how her mother had lived her life once her children had begun to detach from her: shopping excursions (fun because there was enough money to buy all but the most outrageously expensive items), long lunches with friends, tennis, cocktail parties, weekend trips. What had once seemed shallow and tedious now loomed in memory like paradise.

At first she tried to re-establish bonds with friends she hadn't seen in ten years, but all commonality of interest and experience had long since vanished. Ellen talked gaily about the community, about local politics, about her job as a volunteer at the Southampton Hospital – all subjects about which her old friends, many of whom had been coming to Amity every summer for more than thirty years, knew little and cared less. They talked about New York politics, about art galleries and painters and writers they knew. Most conversations ended with feeble reminiscences and speculations about where old friends were now. Always there were pledges about calling each other and getting together again.

Once in a while she would try to make new friends among the summer people she hadn't known, but the associations were forced and brief. They might have endured if Ellen had been less self-conscious about her house, about her husband's job and how poorly it paid. She made sure that everyone she met knew she had started her Amity life on an entirely different plane. She was aware of what she was doing, and she hated herself for it, because in fact she loved her husband deeply, adored her children, and – for most of the year – was quite content with her lot . . .

By now, she had largely given up active forays into the summer community, but the resentments and the longings lingered. She was unhappy, and she took out most of her unhappiness on her husband, a fact that both of them understood but only he could tolerate. She wished she could go into suspended animation for that quarter of every year.

Brody rolled over towards Ellen, raising himself up on one elbow and resting his head on his hand. With his other hand he flicked away a strand of hair that was tickling Ellen's nose and making it twitch. He still had an erection from the remnants of his last dream, and he debated rousing her for a quick bit of sex. He knew she was a slow waker and her early morning moods were more cantankerous than romantic. Still, it would be fun. There had not been much sex in the Brody household recently. There seldom was, when Ellen was in her summer moods.

Just then, Ellen's mouth fell open and she began to snore. Brody felt himself turn off as quickly as if someone had poured ice water on his loins. He got up and went into the bathroom.

It was nearly 6.30 when Brody turned on to Old Mill Road. The sun was well up. It had lost its daybreak red and was turning from orange to bright yellow. The sky was cloudless.

Theoretically, there was a statutory right-of-way between each house, to permit public access to the beach, which could be privately owned only to the mean-high-water mark. But the rights-of-way between most houses were filled with garages or privet hedges. From the road there was no view of the beach. All Brody could see was the tops of the dunes. So every hundred yards or so he had to stop the squad car and walk up a driveway to reach a point from which he could survey the beach.

There was no sign of a body. All he saw on the broad, white expanse was a few pieces of driftwood, a can or two, and a yard-wide belt of seaweed and kelp pushed ashore by the southerly breeze. There was practically no surf, so if a body was floating on the surface it would have been visible. If there is a floater out there, Brody thought, it's floating beneath the surface and I'll never see it till it washes up.

By seven o'clock Brody had covered the whole beach along Old Mill and Scotch roads. The only thing he had seen that struck him as even remotely odd was a paper plate on which sat three scalloped orange rinds – a sign that the summer's beach picnics were going to be more elegant than ever.

He drove back along Scotch Road, turned north towards town on Bayberry Lane, and arrived at the station house at 7.10.

Hendricks was finishing up his paper work when Brody walked in, and he looked disappointed that Brody wasn't dragging a corpse behind him. 'No luck, Chief?' he said.

'That depends on what you mean by luck, Leonard. If you mean did I find a body and if I didn't isn't it too bad, the answer to both questions is no. Is Kimble in yet?'

'No.'

'Well, I hope he isn't asleep. That'd look just dandy having him snoring away in a cop car when people start to do their shopping.'

'He'll be here by eight,' said Hendricks. 'He always is.'

Brody poured himself a cup of coffee, walked into his office and began to flip through the morning papers – the early edition of the New York *Daily News* and the local paper, the Amity *Leader* which came out weekly in the winter and daily in the summer.

Kimble arrived a little before eight, looking, aptly enough, as if he had been sleeping in his uniform, and he had a cup of coffee with Hendricks while they waited for the day shift to appear. Hendricks' replacement came in at eight sharp, and Hendricks was putting on his leather flight jacket and getting ready to leave when Brody came out of his office.

'I'm going out to see Foote, Leonard,' Brody said. 'You want to come along? You don't have to, but I thought you might want to follow up on your . . . floater.' Brody smiled.

'Sure, I guess so,' said Hendricks. 'I got nothing else going today, so I can sleep all afternoon.'

They drove out in Brody's car. As they pulled into Foote's driveway, Hendricks said, 'What do you bet they're all asleep? I remember last summer a woman called at one in the morning and asked if I could come out as early as possible the next morning because she thought some of her jewellery was missing. I offered to go right then, but she said no, she was going to bed. Anyway, I showed up at ten o'clock the next morning and she threw me out. "I didn't mean *this* early," she says.'

'We'll see,' said Brody. 'If they're really worried about this dame, they'll be awake.'

The door opened almost before Brody had finished knocking. 'We've been waiting to hear from you,' said a young man. 'I'm Tom Cassidy. Did you find her?'

'I'm Chief Brody. This is Officer Hendricks. No, Mr Cassidy, we didn't find her. Can we come in?'

'Oh sure, sure. I'm sorry. Go on in the living-room. I'll get the Footes.'

It took less than five minutes for Brody to learn everything he felt he needed to know. Then, as much to seem thorough as from any hope of learning anything useful, he asked to see the missing woman's clothes. He was shown into the bedroom, and he looked through the clothing on the bed.

'She didn't have a bathing suit with her?'

'No,' said Cassidy. 'It's in the top drawer over there. I looked.'

Brody paused for a moment, taking care with his words, then said, 'Mr Cassidy, I don't mean to sound flip or anything, but has this Miss Watkins got a habit of doing strange things ? I mean, like taking off in the middle of the night . . . or walking around naked ?'

'Not that I know of,' said Cassidy. 'But I really don't know her too well.'

'I see,' said Brody. 'Then I guess we'd better go down to the beach again. You don't have to come. Hendricks and I can handle it.'

'I'd like to come, if you don't mind.'

'I don't mind. I just thought you might not want to.'

The three men walked down to the beach. Cassidy showed the policemen where he had fallen asleep – the indentation his body had made in the sand had not been disturbed – and he pointed out where he had found the woman's clothes.

Brody looked up and down the beach. For as far as he could see, more than a mile in both directions, the beach was empty. Clumps of seaweed were the only dark spots on the white sand. 'Let's take a walk,' he said. 'Leonard, you go east as far as the point. Mr Cassidy, let's you and I go west. You got your whistle, Leonard ? Just in case.'

'I've got it,' said Hendricks. 'You care if I take my shoes off ? It's easier walking on the hard sand, I don't want to get them wet.'

'I don't care,' said Brody. 'Technically you're off duty. You can take your pants off if you want. Of course, then I'll arrest you for indecent exposure.'

Hendricks started eastward. The wet sand felt crisp and cool on his feet. He walked with his head down and his hands in his pockets, looking at the tiny shells and tangles of seaweed. A few bugs – they looked like little black beetles – skittered out of his path, and when the wavewash receded, he saw minute bubbles pop above the holes made by sand-worms. He enjoyed the walk. It was a funny thing, he thought, that when you live all your life in a place, you almost never do the things that tourists go there to do – like walk on the beach or go swimming in the ocean. He couldn't remember the last time he went swimming. He wasn't even sure he still owned a bathing suit. It was like something he had heard about New York – that half the people who live in the city never go to the top of the Empire State Building or visit the Statue of Liberty.

Every now and then, Hendricks looked up to see how much closer he was to the point. Once he turned back to see if Brody and Cassidy had found anything. He guessed that they were nearly half a mile away.

As he turned back and started walking again, Hendricks saw something ahead of him, a clump of weed and kelp that seemed unusually large. He was about thirty yards away from the clump when he began to think the weed might be clinging to something.

When he reached the clump, Hendricks bent down to pull some of the weed away. Suddenly he stopped. For a few seconds he stared, frozen rigid. He fumbled in his pants pocket for his whistle, put it to his lips, and tried to blow. Instead, he vomited, staggered back, and fell to his knees.

Snarled within the clump of weed was a woman's head, still attached to shoulders, part of an arm, and about a third of her trunk. The mass of tattered flesh was a mottled blue-grey, and as Hendricks spilled his guts into the sand, he thought – and the thought made him retch again – that the woman's remaining breast looked as flat as a flower pressed in a memory book.

'Wait,' said Brody, stopping and touching Cassidy's arm. 'I think that was a whistle.' He listened, squinting into the morning sun. He saw a black spot on the sand, which he

27

assumed was Hendricks, and then he heard the whistle more clearly. 'Come on,' he said, and the two men began to trot along the sand.

Hendricks was still on his knees when they got to him. He had stopped puking, but his head still hung, mouth open, and his breathing rattled with phlegm.

Brody was several steps ahead of Cassidy, and he said, 'Mr Cassidy, stay back there a second, will you?' He pulled apart some of the weeds, and when he saw what was inside, he felt bile rise in his throat. He swallowed and closed his eyes. After a moment he said, 'You might as well look now, Mr Cassidy, and tell me if it's her or not.'

Cassidy was terrified. His eyes shifted between the exhausted Hendricks and the mass of weed. 'That?' he said, pointing at the weed. Reflexively, he stepped backward. 'That *thing*? What do you mean it's her?'

Brody was still fighting to control his stomach. 'I think,' he said, 'that it may be part of her.'

Reluctantly, Cassidy shuffled forward. Brody held back a piece of weed so Cassidy could get a clear look at the grey and gaping face. 'Oh, my God!' said Cassidy, and he put a hand to his mouth.

'Is it her?'

Cassidy nodded, still staring at the face. Then he turned away and said, 'What happened to her?'

'I can't be sure,' said Brody. 'Offhand, I'd say she was attacked by a shark.'

Cassidy's knees buckled, and as he sank to the sand, he said, 'I think I'm going to be sick.' He put his head down and retched.

The stink of vomit reached Brody almost instantly, and he knew he had lost his struggle. 'Join the crowd,' he said, and he vomited too.

THREE

Several minutes passed before Brody felt well enough to stand, walk back to his car, and call for an ambulance from the Southampton Hospital, and it was almost an hour before the ambulance arrived and the truncated corpse was stuffed into a rubber bag and hauled away.

By eleven o'clock, Brody was back in his office, filling out forms about the accident. He had completed everything but 'cause of death' when the phone rang.

'Carl Santos, Martin,' said the voice of the coroner.

'Yeah, Carl. What have you got for me?'

'Unless you have any reason to suspect a murder, I'd have to say shark.'

'Murder?' said Brody.

'I'm not suggesting anything. All I mean is that it's conceivable – just barely – that some nut could have done this job on the girl with an axe and a saw.'

'I don't think it's a murder, Carl. I've got no motive, no murder weapons, and – unless I want to go off into left field – no suspect.'

'Then it's a shark. And a big bastard, too. Even the screw on an ocean liner wouldn't have done this. It might have cut her in two, but . . .'

'Okay, Carl,' said Brody. 'Spare me the gore. My stomach's none too hot already.'

'Sorry, Martin. Anyway, I'm going to put down shark attack. I'd say that makes the most sense for you too, unless there are . . . you know . . . other considerations.'

'No,' said Brody. 'Not this time. Thanks for calling, Carl.' He hung up, typed 'shark attack' in the 'cause of death' space on the forms, and leaned back in his chair.

The possibility that 'other considerations' might be involved in this case hadn't occurred to Brody. Those considerations were the touchiest part of Brody's job, forcing him constantly to assess the best means of protecting the common weal without compromising either himself or the law.

It was the beginning of the summer season, and Brody knew that on the success or failure of those twelve brief weeks rested the fortunes of Amity for a whole year. A rich season meant prosperity enough to carry the town through the lean winter. The winter population of Amity was about 1,000; in a good summer the population jumped to nearly 10,000. And those 9,000 summer visitors kept the 1,000 permanent residents alive for the whole year.

Merchants – from the owners of the hardware store and the sporting goods store and the two gas stations to the local pharmacist – needed a boom summer to support them through the winter, during which they never broke even. The wives of carpenters, electricians, and plumbers worked during the summer as waitresses or real estate agents, to help keep their families going over the winter. There were only two year-round liquor licences in Amity, so the twelve weeks of summer were critical to most of the restaurants and pubs. Charter fishermen needed every break they could get: good weather, good fishing, and, above all, crowds.

Even after the best of summers, Amity winters were rough. Three of every ten families went on relief. Dozens of men were forced to move for the winter to the north shore of Long Island, where they scratched for work shucking scallops for a few dollars a day.

Brody knew that one bad summer would nearly double the relief rolls. If every house was not rented, there wouldn't be enough work for Amity's blacks, most of whom were gardeners, butlers, bartenders, and maids. And two or three bad summers in a row – a circumstance that, fortunately, hadn't occurred in more than two decades – could create a cycle that could wreck the town. If people didn't have enough money to buy clothes or gas or ample food supplies, if they couldn't afford to have their houses or their appliances repaired, then the merchants and service firms would fail to make enough to tide them over until the next summer. They would close down, and Amity's citizens would start shopping elsewhere. The town would lose tax revenue. Municipal services would deteriorate, and people would begin to move away.

So there was a common, though tacit, understanding in Amity, born of the need to survive. Everyone was expected to do his bit to make sure that Amity remained a desirable summer community. A few years ago, Brody remembered, a young man and his brother had moved into town and set themselves up as carpenters. They came in the spring, when there was enough work preparing houses for summer residents to keep everyone busy, so they were welcomed. They seemed competent enough, and several established carpenters began to refer work to them.

But by midsummer, there were disquieting reports about the Felix Brothers. Albert Morris, the owner of Amity Hardware, let it be known that they were buying cheap steel nails instead of galvanized nails and were charging their customers for galvanized. In a seaside climate, steel nails begin to rust in a few months. Dick Spitzer, who ran the lumberyard, told somebody that the Felixes had ordered a load of low-grade, green wood to use in some cabinets in a house on Scotch Road. The cabinet doors began to warp soon after they were installed. In a bar one night, the elder Felix, Armando, boasted to a drinking buddy that on his current job he was being paid to set supporting studs every sixteen inches but was actually placing them twenty-four inches apart. And the younger Felix, a twenty-one-year-old

31

named Danny with a stubborn case of acne, liked to show his friends erotic books which he bragged he had stolen from the houses he worked in.

Other carpenters stopped referring work to the Felixes, but by then they had built enough of a business to keep them going through the winter. Very quietly, the Amity understanding began to work. At first, there were just a few hints to the Felixes that they had outworn their welcome. Armando reacted arrogantly. Soon, annoying little mishaps began to bother him. All the tyres on his truck would mysteriously empty themselves of air, and when he called for help from the Amity Gulf station, he was told that the air pump was broken. When he ran out of propane gas in his kitchen, the local gas company took eight days to deliver a new tank. His orders for lumber and other supplies were inexplicably mislaid or delayed. In stores where once he had been able to obtain credit he was now forced to pay cash. By the end of October, the Felix Brothers were unable to function as a business, and they moved away.

Generally, Brody's contribution to the Amity understanding – in addition to maintaining the rule of law and sound judgement in the town – consisted of suppressing rumours and, in consultation with Harry Meadows, the editor of the Amity *Leader*, keeping a certain perspective on the rare unfortunate occurrences that qualified as news.

The previous summer's rapes had been reported in the *Leader*, but just barely (as molestations), because Brody and Meadows agreed that the spectre of a black rapist stalking every female in Amity wouldn't do much for the tourist trade. In that case, there was the added problem that none of the women who had told the police they had been raped would repeat their stories to anyone else.

If one of the wealthier summer residents of Amity was arrested for drunken driving, Brody was willing, on a first offence, to book him for driving without a licence, and that charge would be duly reported in the *Leader*. But Brody made sure to warn the driver that the second time he was caught driving under the influence he would be charged, booked, and prosecuted for drunken driving.

Brody's relationship with Meadows was based on a delicate balance. When groups of youngsters came to town from the Hamptons and caused trouble, Meadows was handed every fact – names, ages, and charges lodged. When Amity's own youth made too much noise at a party, the *Leader* usually ran a one-paragraph story without names or addresses, informing the public that the police had been called to quell a minor disturbance on, say, Old Mill Road.

Because several summer residents found it fun to subscribe to the *Leader* year-round, the matter of wintertime vandalism of summer houses was particularly sensitive. For years, Meadows had ignored it – leaving it to Brody to make sure that the homeowner was notified, the offenders punished, and the appropriate repairmen dispatched to the house. But in the winter of 1968 sixteen houses were vandalized within a few weeks. Brody and Meadows agreed that the time had come for a full campaign in the *Leader* against wintertime vandals. The result was the wiring of the forty-eight homes to the police station, which – since the public didn't know which houses were wired and which weren't – all but eliminated vandalism, made Brody's job much easier, and gave Meadows the image of a crusading editor.

Once in a while, Brody and Meadows collided. Meadows was a zealot against the use of narcotics. He was also a man with unusually keen reportorial antennae, and when he sensed a story – one not susceptible to 'other considerations' – he would go after it like a pig after truffles. In the summer of 1971 the daughter of one of Amity's richest families had died off the Scotch Road beach. To Brody, there was no evidence of foul play, and since the family opposed an autopsy, the death was officially listed as drowning.

33

But Meadows had reason to believe that the girl was on drugs and that she was being supplied by the son of a Polish potato farmer. It took Meadows almost two months to get the story, but in the end he forced an autopsy which proved that at the time she drowned the girl had been unconscious from an overdose of heroin. He also tracked down the pusher and exposed a fairly large drug ring operating in the Amity area. The story reflected badly on Amity and worse on Brody, who, because several federal violations were involved in the case, wasn't even able to redeem his earlier insouciance by making an arrest or two. And it won Meadows two regional journalism prizes.

Now it was Brody's turn to press for full disclosure. He intended to close the beaches for a couple of days, to give the shark time to travel far from the Amity shoreline. He didn't know whether or not sharks could acquire a taste for human flesh (as he had heard tigers do), but he was determined to deprive the fish of any more people. This time he wanted publicity, to make people fear the water and stay away from it.

Brody knew there would be a strong argument against publicizing the attack. Like the rest of the country, Amity was still feeling the effects of the recession. So far, the summer was shaping up as a mediocre one. Rentals were up from last year, but they were not 'good' rentals. Many were 'groupers', bands of ten or fifteen young people who came from the city and split the rent on a big house. At least a dozen of the $7,000–$10,000-a-season shore-front houses had not yet been rented, and many more in the $5,000 class were still without leases. Sensational reports of a shark attack might turn mediocrity into disaster.

Still, Brody thought, one death in mid-June, before the crowds come, would probably be quickly forgotten. Certainly it would have less effect than two or three more deaths would. The fish might well have disappeared already, but Brody wasn't willing to gamble lives on the possibility: the odds might be good, but the stakes were prohibitively high.

He dialled Meadows' number. 'Hey, Harry,' he said. 'Free for lunch ?'

'I've been wondering when you'd call,' said Meadows. 'Sure. My place or yours ?'

Suddenly Brody wished he hadn't called at mealtime. His stomach was still groaning, and the thought of food nauseated him. He glanced up at the wall calendar. It was a Thursday. Like all their friends on fixed, tight incomes, the Brodys shopped according to the supermarket specials. Monday's special was chicken, Tuesday's lamb, and so forth through the week. As each item was consumed, Ellen would note it on her list and replace it the next week. The only variables were bluefish and bass, which were inserted in the menu when a friendly fisherman dropped his surplus by the house. Thursday's special was hamburger, and Brody had seen enough chopped meat for one day.

'Yours,' he said. 'Why don't we order out from Cy's ? We can eat in your office.'

'Fine with me,' said Meadows. 'What do you want ? I'll order now.'

'Egg salad, I guess, and a glass of milk. I'll be right there.' Brody called Ellen to tell her he wouldn't be home for lunch.

Harry Meadows was an immense man, for whom the act of drawing breath was exertion enough to cause perspiration to dot his forehead. He was in his late forties, ate too much, chain-smoked cheap cigars, drank bonded Bourbon, and was, in the words of his doctor, the Western world's leading candidate for a huge coronary infarction.

When Brody arrived, Meadows was standing beside his desk, waving a towel at the open window. 'In deference to what your lunch order tells me is a tender stomach,' he said, 'I am trying to clear the air of essence of White Owl.'

'I appreciate that,' said Brody. He glanced around the small, cluttered room, searching for a place to sit.

'Just throw that crap off the chair there,' Meadows said. 'They're just government reports. Reports from the county, reports from the state, reports from the highway commission and the water commission. They probably cost about a million dollars, and from an informational point of view they don't amount to a cup of spit.'

Brody picked up the heap of papers and piled them on top of a radiator. He pulled the chair next to Meadows' desk and sat down.

Meadows rooted around in a large brown paper bag, pulled out a plastic cup and a cellophane-wrapped sandwich, and slid them across the desk to Brody. Then he began to unwrap his own lunch, four separate packages which he opened and spread before himself with the loving care of a jeweller showing off rare gems: a meatball hero, oozing tomato sauce; a plastic carton filled with oily fried potatoes; a dill pickle the size of a small squash; and a quarter of a lemon meringue pie. He reached behind his chair and from a small refrigerator withdrew a sixteen-ounce can of beer. 'Delightful,' he said with a smile as he surveyed the feast before him.

'Amazing,' said Brody, stifling an acid belch. 'Absofuckin-lutely amazing. I must have had about a thousand meals with you, Harry, but I still can't get used to it.'

'Everyone has his little quirks, my friend,' Meadows said as he lifted his sandwich. 'Some people chase other people's wives. Some lose themselves in whisky. I find my solace in nature's own nourishment.'

'That'll be some solace to Dorothy when your heart says, "That's enough, buster, adiós." '

'We've discussed that, Dorothy and I,' said Meadows, filtering the words through a mouthful of bread and meat, 'and we agree that one of the few advantages man has over other animals is the ability to choose the way to bring on his

36

own death. Food may well kill me, but it's also what has made life such a pleasure. Besides, I'd rather go my way than end up in the belly of a shark. After this morning, I'm sure you'll agree.'

Brody was in the midst of swallowing a bit of egg salad sandwich, and he had to force it past a rising gag. 'Don't do that to me,' he said.

They ate in silence for a few moments. Brody finished his sandwich and milk, wadded the sandwich wrapper and stuffed it into the plastic cup. He leaned back and lit a cigarette. Meadows was still eating, but Brody knew his appetite wouldn't be diminished by any discussion. He recalled a time when Meadows had visited the scene of a bloody automobile accident and proceeded to interview police and survivors while sucking on a coconut Popsicle.

'About the Watkins thing,' Brody said. 'I have a couple of thoughts, if you want to hear them.' Meadows nodded. 'First, it seems to me that the cause of death is cut-and-dried. I've already talked to Santos, and—'

'I did, too.'

'So you know what he thinks. It was a shark attack, clear and simple. And if you'd seen the body, you'd agree. There's just me—'

'I did see it.'

Brody was astonished, mostly because he couldn't imagine how anyone who had seen that mess could be sitting there now, licking lemon-pie filling off his fingers. 'So you agree?'

'Yes. I agree that's what killed her. But there are a few things I'm not so sure of.'

'Like what?'

'Like why she was swimming at that time of night. Do you know what the temperature was at around midnight? Sixty. Do you know what the water temperature was? About fifty. You'd have to be out of your mind to go swimming under those conditions.'

37

'Or drunk,' said Brody, 'which she probably was.'

'Maybe. No, you're right – probably. I've checked around a little, and the Footes don't mess with grass or mescalin or any of that stuff. There's one other thing that bothers me, though.'

Brody was annoyed. 'For Christ's sake, Harry, stop chasing shadows. Once in a while, people do die by accident.'

'It's not that. It's just that it's damn funny that we've got a shark around here when the water's still this cold.'

'Is it ? Maybe there are sharks who like cold water. Who knows about sharks ?'

'There are some. There's the Greenland shark, but they never come down this far, and even if they did, they don't usually bother people. Who knows about sharks ? I'll tell you this: At the moment I know a hell of a lot more about them than I did this morning. After I saw what was left of Miss Watkins, I called a young guy I know up at the Woods Hole Oceanographic Institute. I described the body to him, and he said it's likely that only one kind of shark would do a job like that.'

'What kind ?'

'A great white. There are others that attack people, like tigers and hammerheads and maybe even makos and blues, but this fellow Hooper – Matt Hooper – told me that to cut a woman in half like that you'd have to have a fish with a mouth like this' – he spread his hands about three feet apart – 'and the only shark that grows that big *and* attacks people is the great white. There's another name for them.'

'Oh ?' Brody was beginning to lose interest. 'What's that ?'

'Man-eater. Other sharks kill people once in a while, for all sorts of reasons – hunger, maybe, or confusion or because they smell blood in the water. By the way, did the Watkins girl have her period last night ?'

'How the hell would I know ?'

'Just curious. Hooper said that's one way to guarantee yourself an attack if there's a shark around.'

'What did he say about the cold water?'

'That it's quite common for a great white to come into water this cold. Some years ago, a boy was killed by one near San Francisco. The water temperature was fifty-seven.'

Brody sucked a long drag from his cigarette and said, 'You've really done a lot of checking into this, Harry.'

'It seemed to me a matter of – shall we say – common sense and public interest to determine exactly what happened and the chances of it happening again.'

'And did you determine those chances?'

'I did. They're almost non-existent. From what I can gather, this was a real freak accident. According to Hooper, the only thing good about great whites is that they're scarce. There's every reason to believe that the shark that attacked the Watkins girl is long gone. There are no reefs around here. There's no fish-processing plant or slaughterhouse that dumps blood or guts into the water. So there's nothing at all to keep the shark interested.' Meadows paused and looked at Brody, who returned his gaze silently. 'So it seems to me, Martin, that there's no reason to get the public all upset over something that's almost sure not to happen again.'

'That's one way to look at it, Harry. Another is that since it's not likely to happen again, there's no harm in telling people that it did happen this once.'

Meadows sighed. 'Journalistically, you may be right. But I think this is one of those times, Martin, when we have to forget the book and think of what's best for the people. I don't think it would be in the public interest to spread this around. I'm not thinking about the townspeople. They'll know about it soon enough, the ones that don't know already. But what about the people who read the *Leader* in New York or Philadelphia or Cleveland?'

'You flatter yourself.'

'Balls. You know what I mean. And you know what the real estate situation is like around here this summer. We're right on the edge, and other places are, too, like Nantucket and the Vineyard and East Hampton. There are people who still haven't made their summer plans. They know they've got their pick of places this year. There's no shortage of houses for rent ... anywhere. If I run a story saying that a young woman was bitten in two by a monster shark off Amity, there won't be another house rented in this town. Sharks are like axe-murderers, Martin. People react to them with their guts. There's something crazy and evil and uncontrollable about them. If we tell people there's a killer shark around here, we can kiss the summer good-bye.'

Brody nodded. 'I can't argue with that, Harry, and I don't want to tell the people that there *is* a killer shark around here. Look at it from my point of view, just for a second. I won't dispute your odds or anything. You're probably right. That shark has probably gone a hundred miles from here and won't ever show up again. The most dangerous thing out there in the water is probably the undertow. But Harry, there's a chance you're wrong, and I don't think we can take that chance. Suppose – just suppose – we don't say a word, and somebody else gets hit by that fish. What then? My ass is in a sling. I'm supposed to protect people around here, and if I can't protect them from something, the least I can do is warn them that there is a danger. Your ass is in a sling, too. You're supposed to report the news, and there's just no question but that someone killed by a shark is news. I want you to run the story, Harry. I want to close the beaches, just for a couple of days, and just for insurance sake. It won't be a great inconvenience to anybody. There aren't that many people here yet, and the water's cold. If we tell it straight, tell people what happened and why we're doing what we're doing, I think we'll be way ahead.'

Meadows sat back in his chair and thought for a moment.

'I can't speak for your job, Martin, but as far as mine is concerned, the decision has already been made.'

'What does that mean?'

'There won't be any story about the attack in the *Leader*.'

'Just like that.'

'Well, not exactly. It wasn't entirely my decision, though I think that generally I agree with it. I'm the editor of this paper, Martin, and I own a piece of it, but not a big enough piece to buck certain pressures.'

'Such as?'

'I've gotten six phone calls already this morning. Five were from advertisers – one restaurant, one hotel, two real estate firms, and an ice-cream shop. They were most anxious to know whether or not I planned to run a story on the Watkins thing, and most anxious to let me know they felt Amity would best be served by letting the whole thing fade quietly away. The sixth call was from Mr Coleman in New York. Mr Coleman who owns 55 per cent of the *Leader*. It seems Mr Coleman had received a few phone calls himself. He told me there would be no story in the *Leader*.'

'I don't suppose he said whether the fact that his wife is a real estate broker had anything to do with his decision.'

'No,' said Meadows. 'The subject never came up.'

'Figures. Well, Harry, where does that leave us? You're not going to run a story, so as far as the good readers of the *Leader* are concerned, nothing ever happened. I'm going to close the beaches and put up a few signs saying why.'

'Okay, Martin. That's your decision. But let me remind you of something. You're an elected official, right?'

'Just like the President. For four thrill-filled years.'

'Elected officials can be impeached.'

'Is that a threat, Harry?'

Meadows smiled. 'You know better than that. Besides, who am I to be making threats? I just want you to be aware of what you're doing before you tinker with the lifeblood of all those sage and discriminating souls who elected you.'

Brody rose to go. 'Thanks, Harry. I've always heard it's lonely here at the top. What do I owe you for lunch?'

'Forget it. I couldn't take money from a man whose family will soon be begging for food stamps.'

Brody laughed. 'No way. Haven't you heard? The great thing about police work is the security.'

Ten minutes after Brody returned to his office, the intercom buzzer sounded and a voice announced, 'The mayor's here to see you, Chief.'

Brody smiled. The mayor. Not Larry Vaughan, just calling to check in. Not Lawrence Vaughan of Vaughan & Penrose Real Estate, stopping by to complain about some noisy tenants. But Mayor Lawrence P. Vaughan, the people's choice – by seventy-one votes in the last election. 'Send his honour in,' Brody said.

Larry Vaughan was a handsome man, in his early fifties, with a full head of salt-and-pepper hair and a body kept trim by exercise. Though he was a native of Amity, over the years he had developed an air of understated chic. He had made a great deal of money in postwar real estate speculation in Amity, and he was the senior partner (some thought the *only* partner, since no one had ever met or spoken to anyone named Penrose in Vaughan's office) in the most successful agency in town. He dressed with elegant simplicity, in timeless British jackets, button-down shorts, and Weejun loafers. Unlike Ellen Brody, who had descended from summer folk to winter folk and was unable to make the adjustment, Vaughan had ascended smoothly from winter folk to summer folk adjusting each step of the way with grace. He was not one of them, for he was technically a local merchant. So he was never asked to visit them in New York or Palm Beach. But in Amity he moved freely among all but the most aloof members of the summer community, which, of course, did an immense amount of good for his business. He was asked to most of the important summer parties, and he always arrived alone. Very few of his friends knew that he had a wife at home, a simple, adoring woman who spent much of her time doing needlepoint in front of her television set.

Brody liked Vaughan. He didn't see much of him during the summer, but after Labour Day, when things calmed down, Vaughan felt free to shed some of his social scales, and every few weeks he and his wife would ask Brody and Ellen out to dinner at one of the better restaurants in the Hamptons. The evenings were special treats for Ellen, and that in itself was enough to make Brody happy. Vaughan seemed to understand Ellen. He always acted most graciously, treating Ellen as a clubmate and comrade.

Vaughan walked into Brody's office and sat down. 'I just talked to Harry Meadows,' he said.

Vaughan was obviously upset, which interested Brody. He hadn't expected this reaction. 'I see,' he said. 'Harry doesn't waste any time.'

'Where are you going to get the authority to close the beaches?'

'Are you asking me as the mayor or as a real estate broker or out of friendly interest or what, Larry?'

Vaughan pressed, and Brody could see he was having trouble controlling his temper. 'I want to know where you're going to get the authority. I want to know now.'

'Officially, I'm not sure I have it,' Brody said. 'There's something in the code that says I can take whatever actions I deem necessary in the event of an emergency, but I think the selectmen have to declare a state of emergency. I don't imagine you want to go through all that rigmarole.'

'Not a chance.'

'Well, then, unofficially I figure it's my responsibility to keep the people who live here as safe as I can, and at the moment it's my judgement that that means closing the beaches for a couple of days. If it ever came down to cases, I'm not sure I could arrest anyone for going swimming. Unless,' Brody smiled, 'I could make a case of criminal stupidity.'

Vaughan ignored the remark. 'I don't want you to close the beaches,' he said.

'So I see.'

'You know why. The Fourth of July isn't far off, and that's the make-or-break week-end. We'd be cutting our own throats.'

'I know the argument, and I'm sure you know my reasons for wanting to close the beaches. It's not as if I have anything to gain.'

'No. I'd say quite the opposite is true. Look, Martin, this town doesn't need that kind of publicity.'

'It doesn't need any more people killed, either.'

'Nobody else is going to get killed, for God's sake. All you'd be doing by closing the beaches is inviting a lot of reporters to come snooping around where they don't have any business.'

'So? They'd come out here, and when they didn't find anything worth reporting they'd go home again. I don't imagine the New York *Times* has much interest in covering a lodge picnic or a garden-club supper.'

'We just don't need it. Suppose they did find something. There'd be a big to-do that couldn't do anybody any good.'

'Like what, Larry? What could they find out? I don't have anything to hide. Do you?'

'No, of course not. I was just thinking about . . . maybe the rapes. Something unsavoury.'

'Crap,' said Brody. 'That's all past history.'

'Damn it, Martin!' Vaughan paused for a moment, struggling to calm himself. 'Look, if you won't listen to reason, will you listen to me as a friend? I'm under a lot of pressure from

44

my partners. Something like this could be very bad for us.'

Brody laughed. 'That's the first time I've heard you admit you *had* partners, Larry. I thought you ran that shop like an emperor.'

Vaughan was embarrassed, as if he felt he had said too much. 'My business is very complicated,' he said. 'There are times I'm not sure *I* understand what's going on. Do me this favour. This once.'

Brody looked at Vaughan, trying to fathom his motives. 'I'm sorry, Larry, I can't. I wouldn't be doing my job.'

'If you don't listen to me,' said Vaughan, 'you may not have your job much longer.'

'You haven't got any control over me. You can't fire any cop in this town.'

'Not off the force, no. But believe it or not, I do have discretion over the job of chief of police.'

'I don't believe it.'

From his jacket pocket Vaughan took a copy of the corporate charter of the town of Amity. 'You can read it yourself,' he said, flipping through until he found the page he sought. 'It's right here.' He handed the pamphlet across the desk to Brody. 'What it says, in effect, is that even though you were elected to the chief's job by the people, the selectmen have the power to remove you.'

Brody read the paragraph Vaughan had indicated. 'I guess you're right,' he said. 'But I'd love to see what you put down for "good and sufficient cause".'

'I dearly hope it doesn't come to that, Martin. I had hoped this conversation wouldn't even get this far. I had hoped that you would go along, once you knew how I and the selectmen felt.'

'All the selectmen?'

'A majority.'

'Like who?'

'I'm not going to sit here and name names for you. I don't

45

have to. All you have to know is that I have the board behind me, and if you don't do what's right, we'll put someone in your job who will.'

Brody had never seen Vaughan in a mood so aggressively ugly. He was fascinated, but he was also slightly shaken. 'You really do want this, don't you, Larry?'

'I do.' Sensing victory, Vaughan said evenly, 'Trust me, Martin. You won't be sorry.'

Brody sighed. 'Shit,' he said. 'I don't like it. It doesn't smell good. But okay, if it's that important.'

'It's that important.' For the first time since he had arrived, Vaughan smiled. 'Thanks, Martin,' he said, and he stood up. 'Now I have the rather unpleasant task of visiting the Footes.'

'How are you going to keep them from shooting off their mouths to the *Times* or the *News*?'

'I hope to be able to appeal to their public-spiritedness,' Vaughan said, 'just as I appealed to yours.'

'Bull.'

'We do have one thing going for us. Miss Watkins was a nobody. She was a drifter. No family, no close friends. She said she had hitch-hiked East from Idaho. So she won't be missed.'

Brody arrived home a little before five. His stomach had settled down enough to permit him a beer or two before dinner. Ellen was in the kitchen, still dressed in the pink uniform of a hospital volunteer. Her hands were immersed in chopped meat, kneading it into a meat loaf.

'Hello,' she said, turning her head so Brody could plant a kiss on her cheek. 'What was the crisis?'

'You were at the hospital. You didn't hear?'

'No. Today was bathe-the-old-ladies day. I never got off the Ferguson wing.'

'A girl got killed off Old Mill.'

'By what?'

'A shark.' Brody reached into the refrigerator and found a beer.

Ellen stopped kneading meat and looked at him. 'A shark! I've never heard of that around here. You see one once in a while, but they never do anything.'

'Yeah, I know. It's a first for me, too.'

'So what are you going to do?'

'Nothing.'

'Really? Is that sensible? I mean, isn't there anything you can do?'

'Sure, there are some things I could do. Technically. But there's nothing I can actually do. What you and I think doesn't carry much weight around here. The powers-that-be are worried that it won't look nice if we get all excited just because one stranger got killed by a fish. They're willing to take the chance that it was just a freak accident that won't happen again. Or, rather, they're willing to let me take the chance, since it's my responsibility.'

'What do you mean, the powers-that-be?'

'Larry Vaughan, for one.'

'Oh. I didn't realize you had talked to Larry.'

'He came to see me as soon as he heard I planned to close the beaches. He wasn't what you'd call subtle about telling me he didn't want the beaches closed. He said he'd have my job if I did close them.'

'I can't believe that, Martin. Larry isn't like that.'

'I didn't think so, either. Hey, by the way, what do you know about his partners?'

'In the business? I didn't think there were any. I thought Penrose was his middle name, or something like that. Anyway, I thought he owned the whole thing.'

'So did I. But apparently not.'

'Well, it makes me feel better to know you talked to Larry before you made any decision. He tends to take a wider, more

47

over-all view of things than most people. He probably does know what's best.'

Brody felt the blood rise in his neck. He said simply, 'Crap.' Then he tore the metal tab off his beer can, flipped it into the garbage can, and walked into the living-room to turn on the evening news.

From the kitchen Ellen called, 'I forgot to tell you: you had a call a little while ago.'

'Who from?'

'He didn't say. He just said to tell you you're doing a terrific job. It was nice of him to call, don't you think?'

FOUR

For the next few days the weather remained clear and unusually calm. The wind came softly, steadily from the south-west, a gentle breeze that rippled the surface of the sea but made no whitecaps. There was a crispness to the air only at night, and after days of constant sun, the earth and sand had warmed.

Sunday was the twentieth of June. Public schools still had a week or more to run before breaking for the summer, but the private schools in New York had already released their charges. Families who owned summer homes in Amity had been coming out for week-ends since the beginning of May. Summer tenants whose leases ran from 15 June to 15 September had unpacked and, familiar now with where linen closets were, which cabinets contained good china and which the everyday stuff, and which beds were softer than others, were already beginning to feel at home.

By noon, the beach in front of Scotch and Old Mill roads was speckled with people. Husbands lay semicomatose on beach towels, trying to gain strength from the sun before an afternoon of tennis and the trip back to New York on the Long Island Railroad's Cannonball. Wives leaned against aluminium backrests, reading Helen MacInnes and John Cheever and Taylor Caldwell, interrupting themselves now and then to pour a cup of dry vermouth from the Scotch cooler.

Teen-agers lay serried in tight, symmetrical rows, the boys enjoying the sensation of grinding their pelvises into the sand, thinking of pudenda and occasionally stretching their necks to catch a brief glimpse of some, exposed, wittingly or not, by girls who lay on their backs with their legs spread.

These were not Aquarians. They uttered none of the platitudes of peace or pollution, of justice or revolt. Privilege had been bred into them with genetic certainty. As their eyes were blue or brown, so their tastes and consciences were determined by other generations. They had no vitamin deficiencies, no sickle-cell anaemia. Their teeth – thanks either to breeding or to orthodontia – were straight and white and even. Their bodies were lean, their muscles toned by boxing lessons at age nine, riding lessons at twelve, and tennis lessons ever since. They had no body odour. When they sweated, the girls smelled faintly of perfume; the boys smelled simply clean.

None of which is to say that they were either stupid or evil. If their IQs could have been tested *en masse*, they would have shown native ability well within the top ten per cent of all mankind. And they had been, were being, educated, at schools that provided every discipline, including exposure to minority-group sensibilities, revolutionary philosophies, eco- logical hypotheses, political power tactics, drugs, and sex. Intellectually, they knew a great deal. Practically, they chose to know almost nothing. They had been conditioned to believe (or, if not to believe, to sense) that the world was really quite irrelevant to them. And they were right. Nothing touched them – not race riots in places like Trenton, New Jersey, or Gary, Indiana; not the fact that parts of the Missouri River were so foul that the water sometimes caught fire spontaneously; not police corruption in New York or the rising number of murders in San Francisco or revelations that hot dogs contained insect filth and hexachlorophine caused brain damage. They were inured even to the economic spasms that wracked the rest of America. Undulations in the stock markets were nuisances noticed, if at all, as occasions for fathers to bemoan real or fancied extravagances.

Those were the ones who returned to Amity every summer.

The others – and there were some, mavericks – marched and bleated and joined and signed and spent their summer working for acronymic social-action groups. But because they had rejected Amity and, at most, showed up for an occasional Labour Day week-end, they, too, were irrelevant.

The little children played in the sand at the water's edge, digging holes and flinging muck at each other, unconscious and uncaring of what they were and what they would become.

A boy of six stopped skimming flat stones out into the water. He walked up the beach to where his mother lay dozing, and he flopped down next to her towel. 'Hcy, Mom,' he said, limning aimless doodles with his finger in the sand.

His mother turned to look at him, shielding her eyes from the sun. 'What?'

'I'm bored.'

'How can you be bored? It isn't even July.'

'I don't care. I'm bored. I don't have anything to do.'

'You've got a whole beach to play on.'

'I know. But there's nothing to *do* on it. Boy, am I bored.'

'Why don't you go throw a ball?'

'With who? There's nobody here.'

'I see a lot of people. Have you looked for the Harrises? What about Tommy Converse?'

'They're not here. Nobody's here. I sure am bored.'

'Oh, for God's sake, Alex.'

'Can I go swimming?'

'No. It's too cold.'

'How do you know?'

'I know, that's all. Besides, you know you can't go alone.'

'Will you come with me?'

'Into the water? Certainly not.'

'No. I mean just to watch me.'

'Alex, Mom is pooped, absolutely exhausted. Can't you find anything else to do?'

'Can I go out on my raft?'

'Out where?'

'Just out there a little ways. I won't go swimming. I'll just lie on my raft.'

His mother sat up and put on her sunglasses. She looked up and down the beach. A few dozen yards away, a man stood in waist-deep water with a child on his shoulders. The woman looked at him, indulging herself in a quick moment of regret and self-pity that she could no longer shift to her husband the responsibility of amusing their child.

Before she could turn her head, the boy guessed what she was feeling. 'I bet Dad would let me,' he said.

'Alex, you should know by now that that's the wrong way to get me to do anything.' She looked down the beach in the other direction. Except for a few couples in the dim distance, it was empty. 'Oh, all right,' she said. 'Go ahead. But don't go too far out. And don't go swimming.' She looked at the boy and, to show she was serious, lowered her glasses so he could see her eyes.

'Okay,' he said. He stood up, grabbed his rubber raft, and dragged it down to the water. He picked up the raft, held it in front of him, and walked seaward. When the water reached his waist, he leaned forward. A swell caught the raft and lifted it, with the boy aboard. He centred himself so the raft lay flat. He paddled with both arms, stroking smoothly. His feet and ankles hung over the rear of the raft. He moved out a few yards, then turned and began to paddle up and down the beach. Though he didn't notice it, a gentle current carried him slowly offshore.

Fifty yards farther out, the ocean floor dropped precipitously – not with the sheerness of a canyon wall, but from a slope of perhaps ten degrees to more than forty-five degrees. The water was fifteen feet deep where the slope began to change. Soon it was twenty-five, then forty, then fifty feet deep. It levelled off at a hundred feet for about half a mile, then rose in a shoal that neared the surface a mile from shore. Seaward of the shoal, the floor dropped quickly to two hundred feet and then, still farther out, the true ocean depths began.

In thirty-five feet of water, the great fish swam slowly, its tail waving just enough to maintain motion. It saw nothing, for the water was murky with motes of vegetation. The fish had been moving parallel to the shoreline. Now it turned, banking slightly, and followed the bottom gradually upward. The fish perceived more light in the water, but still it saw nothing.

The boy was resting, his arms dangling down, his feet and ankles dipping in and out of the water with each small swell. His head was turned towards shore, and he noticed that he had been carried out beyond what his mother would consider safe. He could see her lying on her towel, and the man and child playing in the wavewash. He was not afraid, for the water was calm and he wasn't really very far from shore – only forty yards or so. But he wanted to get closer; otherwise his mother might sit up, spy him, and order him out of the water. He eased himself back a little bit so he could use his feet to help propel himself. He began to kick and paddle towards shore. His arms displaced water almost silently, but his kicking feet made erratic splashes and left swirls of bubbles in his wake.

The fish did not hear the sound, but rather registered the sharp and jerky impulses emitted by the kicks. They were signals, faint but true, and the fish locked on them, homing. It rose, slowly at first, then gaining speed as the signals grew stronger.

The boy stopped for a moment to rest. The signals ceased. The fish slowed, turning its head from side to side, trying to recover them. The boy lay perfectly still, and the fish passed beneath him, skimming the sandy bottom. Again it turned.

The boy resumed paddling. He kicked only every third or

fourth stroke; kicking was more exertion than steady paddling. But the occasional kicks sent new signals to the fish. This time it needed to lock on them only an instant, for it was almost directly below the boy. The fish rose. Nearly vertical, it now saw the commotion on the surface. There was no conviction that what thrashed above was food, but food was not a concept of significance. The fish was impelled to attack: if what it swallowed was digestible, that was food; if not, it would later be regurgitated. The mouth opened, and with a final sweep of the sickle tail the fish struck.

The boy's last – only – thought was that he had been punched in the stomach. The breath was driven from him in a sudden rush. He had no time to cry out, nor, had he had the time, would he have known what to cry, for he could not see the fish. The fish's head drove the raft out of the water. The jaws smashed together, engulfing head, arms, shoulders, trunk, pelvis, and most of the raft. Nearly half the fish had come clear of the water, and it slid forward and down in a belly-flopping motion, grinding the mass of flesh and bone and rubber. The boy's legs were severed at the hip, and they sank, spinning slowly, to the bottom.

On the beach the man with the child shouted, 'Hey!' He was not sure what he had seen. He had been looking towards the sea, then started to turn his head when an uproar caught his eye. He jerked his head back seaward again, but by then there was nothing to see but the waves made by the splash, spreading outward in a circle. 'Did you see that?' he cried. 'Did you see that?'

'What, Daddy, what?' His child stared up at him, excited.

'Out there! A shark or a whale or something! Something huge!'

The boy's mother, half asleep on her towel, opened her eyes and squinted at the man. She saw him point towards the water and heard him say something to the child, who ran up the beach and stood by a pile of clothing. The man began to run towards the boy's mother, and she sat up. She didn't understand what he was saying, but he was pointing at the water, so she shaded her eyes and looked out to sea. At first, the fact that she saw nothing didn't strike her as odd. Then she remembered, and she said, 'Alex.'

Brody was having lunch: baked chicken, mashed potatoes, and peas. 'Mashed potatoes,' he said as Ellen served him. 'What are you trying to do to me?'

'I don't want you to waste away. Besides, you look good chunky.'

The phone rang. Ellen said, 'I'll get it,' but Brody stood up. That was the way it usually happened. She would say, 'I'll get it,' but he was the one who got it. It was the same when she had forgotten something in the kitchen. She would say, 'I forgot the napkins. I'll get them.' But they both knew he would get up and fetch the napkins.

'No, that's okay,' he said. 'It's probably for me anyway.' He knew the call was probably for her, but the words came reflexively.

'Bixby, Chief,' said the voice from the station house.

'What is it, Bixby?'

'I think you'd better come down here.'

'Why's that?'

'Well, it's like this, Chief . . .' Bixby obviously didn't want to go into details. Brody heard him say something to someone else, then return to the phone. 'I've got this hysterical woman on my hands, Chief.'

'What's she hysterical about?'

'Her kid. Out by the beach.'

A twinge of unease shot through Brody's stomach. 'What happened?'

'It's . . .' Bixby faltered, then said quickly, 'Thursday.'

'Listen, asshole . . .' Brody stopped, for now he understood. 'I'll be right there.' He hung up the phone.

He felt flushed, almost feverish. Fear and guilt and fury blended in a thrust of gut-wrenching pain. He felt at once betrayed and betrayer, deceived and deceiver. He was a criminal forced into crime, an unwilling whore. He had to take the blame, but it was not rightly his. It belonged to Larry Vaughan and his partners, whoever they might be. He had wanted to do the right thing; they had forced him not to. But who were they to force him? If he couldn't stand up to Vaughan, what kind of cop was he? He should have closed the beaches.

Suppose he had. The fish would have gone down the beach – say, to East Hampton – and killed someone there. But that wasn't how it had worked. The beaches had stayed open, and a child had been killed because of it. It was as simple as that. Cause and effect. Brody suddenly loathed himself. And just as suddenly he felt great pity for himself.

'What is it?' asked Ellen.

'A kid just got killed.'

'How?'

'By a goddamn sonofabitch of a shark.'

'Oh no! If you had closed the beaches . . .' She stopped, embarrassed.

'Yeah, I know.'

Harry Meadows was waiting in the parking lot at the rear of the station house when Brody drove up. He opened the passenger-side door of Brody's car and eased his bulk down on to the seat. 'So much for the odds,' he said.

'Yeah. Who's in there, Harry?'

'A man from the *Times*, two from *Newsday*, and one of my people. And the woman. And the man who says he saw it happen.'

'How did the *Times* get hold of it?'

'Bad luck. He was on the beach. So was one of the *Newsday*

guys. They're both staying with people for the week-end. They were on to it within two minutes.'

'What time did it happen?'

Meadows looked at his watch. 'Fifteen, twenty minutes ago. No more.'

'Do they know about the Watkins thing?'

'I don't know. My man does, but he knows enough not to talk. As for the others, it depends on who they've been talking to. I doubt they're on to it. They haven't had any digging time.'

'They'll get on to it, sooner or later.'

'I know,' said Meadows. 'It puts me in a rather difficult position.'

'*You!* Don't make me laugh.'

'Seriously, Martin. If somebody from the *Times* gets that story and files it, it'll appear in tomorrow's paper, along with today's attack, and the *Leader* will look like hell. I'm going to have to use it, to cover myself, even if the others don't.'

'Use it how, Harry? What are you going to say?'

'I don't know yet. As I said, I'm in a rather difficult position.'

'Who are you going to say ordered it hushed up? Larry Vaughan?'

'Hardly.'

'Me?'

'No, no. I'm not going to say anybody ordered it hushed up. There was no conspiracy. I'm going to talk to Carl Santos. If I can put the right words in his mouth, we may all be spared a lot of grief.'

'What about the truth?'

'What about it?'

'What about telling it the way it happened? Say that I wanted to close the beaches and warn people, but the select-men disagreed. And say that because I was too much of a chicken to fight and put my job on the line, I went along with

57

them. Say that all the honchos in Amity agreed there was no point in alarming people just because there was a shark around that liked to eat children.'

'Come on, Martin. It wasn't your fault. It wasn't anybody's. We came to a decision, took a gamble, and lost. That's all there is to it.'

'Terrific. Now I'll just go tell the kid's mother that we're terribly sorry we had to use her son for chips.' Brody got out of the car and started for the back door of the station house. Meadows, slower to extract himself, followed a few paces behind.

Brody stopped. 'You know what I'd like to know, Harry ? Who really made the decision ? You went along with it. I went along with it. I don't think Larry Vaughan was even the actual guy who made the decision. I think he went along with it, too.'

'What makes you think so ?'

'I'm not sure. Do you know anything about his partners in the business ?'

'He doesn't have any real partners, does he ?'

'I'm beginning to wonder. Anyway, fuck it . . . for now.' Brody took another step, and when Meadows still followed him, he said, 'You better go around front, Harry . . . for appearances' sake.'

Brody entered his office through a side door. The boy's mother was sitting in front of the desk, clutching a handkerchief. She was wearing a short robe over her bathing suit. Her feet were bare. Brody looked at her nervously, once again feeling the rush of guilt. He couldn't tell if she was crying, for her eyes were masked by huge, round sunglasses.

A man was standing by the back wall. Brody assumed he was the one who claimed to have witnessed the accident. He was gazing absently at Brody's collection of memorabilia: citations from community-service groups, pictures of Brody with visiting dignitaries. Not exactly the stuff to command much attention from an adult, but staring at it was preferable to risking conversation with the woman.

Brody had never been adept at consoling people, so he simply introduced himself and started asking questions. The woman said she had seen nothing: one moment the boy was there, the next he was gone, 'and all I saw were pieces of his raft.' Her voice was faint but steady. The man described what he had seen or what he thought he had seen.

'So no one actually saw this shark,' Brody said, courting a faint hope in the back of his mind.

'No,' said the man. 'I guess not. But what else could it have been?'

'Any number of things.' Brody was lying to himself as well as to them, testing to see if he could believe his own lies, wondering if any alternative to reality could be made credible. 'The raft could have gone flat and the boy could have drowned.'

'Alex is a good swimmer,' the woman protested. 'Or . . . was . . .'

'And what about the splash?' said the man.

'The boy could have been thrashing around.'

'He never cried out. Not a word.'

Brody realized that the exercise was futile. 'Okay,' he said. 'We'll probably know soon enough, anyway.'

'What do you mean?' said the man.

'One way or another, people who die in the water usually wash up somewhere. If it was a shark, there'll be no mistaking it.' The woman's shoulders hunched forward, and Brody cursed himself for being a clumsy fool. 'I'm sorry,' he said. The woman shook her head and wept.

Brody told the woman and the man to wait in his office, and he walked out into the front of the station house. Meadows was standing by the outer door, leaning against the wall. A young man – the reporter from the *Times*, Brody guessed – was gesturing at Meadows and seemed to be asking questions.

The young man was tall and slim. He wore sandals and a bathing suit and a short-sleeved shirt with an alligator emblem stitched to the left breast, which caused Brody to take an instant, instinctive dislike to the man. In his adolescence Brody had thought of those shirts as badges of wealth and position. All the summer people wore them. Brody badgered his mother until she bought him one – 'a two-dollar shirt with a six-dollar lizard on it,' she said – and when he didn't find himself suddenly wooed by gaggles of summer people, he was humiliated. He tore the alligator off the pocket and used the shirt as a rag to clean the lawn mower with which he earned his summer income. More recently, Ellen had insisted on buying several shifts made by the same manufacturer – paying a premium they could ill afford for the alligator emblem – to help her regain her entrée to her old milieu. To Brody's dismay, one evening he found himself nagging Ellen for buying 'a ten-dollar dress with a twenty-dollar lizard on it.'

Two men were sitting on a bench – the *Newsday* reporters. One wore a bathing suit, the other a blazer and slacks. Meadows' reporter – Brody knew him as Nat something or other – was leaning against the desk, chatting with Bixby. They stopped talking as soon as they saw Brody enter.

'What can I do for you ?' Brody said.

The young man next to Meadows took a step forward and said, 'I'm Bill Whitman, from the New York *Times*.'

'And ?' What am I supposed to do ? Brody thought. Fall on my ass ?

'I was on the beach.'

'What did you see ?'

One of the *Newsday* reporters interrupted: 'Nothing. I was there, too. Nobody saw anything. Except maybe the guy in your office. He says he saw something.'

'I know,' said Brody, 'but he's not sure just what it was he saw.'

The *Times* man said, 'Are you prepared to list this as a shark attack?'

'I'm not prepared to list this as anything, and I'd suggest you don't go listing it as anything, either, until you know a hell of a lot more about it than you do now.'

The *Times* man smiled. 'Come on, Chief, what do you want us to do? Call it a mysterious disappearance? Boy lost at sea?'

It was difficult for Brody to resist the temptation to trade angry ironies with the *Times* reporter. He said, 'Listen, Mr – Whitman, is it? – Whitman. We have no witnesses who saw anything but a splash. The man inside thinks he saw a big silver-coloured thing that he thinks may have been a shark. He says he has never seen a live shark in his life, so that's not what you'd call expert testimony. We have no body, no real evidence that anything violent happened to the boy ... I mean, except that he's missing. It is conceivable that he drowned. It is conceivable that he had a fit or a seizure of some kind and then drowned. And it is conceivable that he was attacked by some kind of fish or animal – or even person, for that matter. All of those things are possible, and until we get ...'

The sound of tyres grinding over gravel in the public parking lot out front stopped Brody. A car door slammed, and Len Hendricks charged into the station house, wearing nothing but a bathing suit. His body had the mottled grey-whiteness of a Styrofoam coffee cup. He stopped in the middle of the floor. 'Chief ...'

Brody was startled by the unlikely sight of Hendricks in a bathing suit – thighs flecked with pimples, genitals bulging in the tight fabric. 'You've been *swimming*, Leonard?'

'There's been another attack!' said Hendricks.

The *Times* man quickly asked, 'When was the first one?'

Before Hendricks could answer, Brody said, 'We were just discussing it, Leonard. I don't want you or anyone else jumping to conclusions until you know what you're talking about. For God's sake, the boy could have drowned.'

'Boy?' said Hendricks. 'What boy? This was a man, an old man. Five minutes ago. He was just beyond the surf, and suddenly he screamed bloody murder and his head went under water and it came up again and he screamed something else and then he went down again. There was all this splashing around, and blood was flying all over the place. The fish kept coming back and hitting him again and again and again. That's the biggest fuckin' fish I ever saw in my whole life, big as a fuckin' station wagon. I went in up to my waist and tried to get to the guy, but the fish kept hitting him.' Hendricks paused, staring at the floor. His breath squeezed out of his chest in short bursts. 'Then the fish quit. Maybe he went away, I don't know. I waded out to where the guy was floating. His face was in the water. I took hold of one of his arms and pulled.'

Brody said, 'And?'

'It came off in my hand. The fish must have chewed right through it, all but a little bit of skin.' Hendricks looked up, his eyes red and filling with tears of exhaustion and fright.

'Are you going to be sick?' said Brody.

'I don't think so.'

'Did you call the ambulance?'

Hendricks shook his head no.

'Ambulance?' said the *Times* reporter. 'Isn't that rather like shutting the barn door after the horse has left?'

'Shut your mouth, smart ass,' said Brody. 'Bixby, call the hospital. Leonard, are you up to doing some work?' Hendricks nodded. 'Then go put on some clothes and find some notices that close the beaches.'

'Do we have any?'

'I don't know. We must. Maybe back in the stock room with those signs that say "This Property Protected by Police." If we don't, we'll have to make some that'll do until we can have some made up. I don't care. One way or another, let's get the goddamn beaches closed.'

Monday morning, Brody arrived at the office a little after seven. 'Did you get it?' he said to Hendricks.

'It's on your desk.'

'Good or bad? Never mind. I'll go see for myself.'

'You won't have to look too hard.'

The city edition of the New York *Times* lay in the centre of Brody's desk. About three-quarters of the way down the right-hand column on page one, he saw the headline:

SHARK KILLS TWO
ON LONG ISLAND

Brody said, 'Shit,' and began to read.

By William F. Whitman
Special to The New York Times

AMITY, L.I. June 20 – A six-year-old boy and a 65-year-old man were killed today in separate shark attacks that occurred within an hour of each other near the beaches of this resort community.

Although the body of the boy, Alexander Kintner, was not found, officials said there was no question that he was killed by a shark. A witness, Thomas Daguerre, of New York, said he saw a large silver-coloured object rise out of the water and seize the boy and his rubber raft and disappear into the water with a splash.

Amity coroner Carl Santos reported that traces of blood found on shreds of rubber later recovered left no doubt that the boy had died a violent death.

At least fifteen persons witnessed the attack on Morris Cater, 65, which took place at approximately 2 PM a quarter of a mile down the beach from where young Kintner was attacked.

Apparently, Mr Cater was swimming just beyond the

surf line when he was suddenly struck from behind. He called out for help, but all attempts to rescue him were in vain.

'I went in up to my waist and tried to get to him,' said Amity police officer Leonard Hendricks, who was on the beach at the time, 'but the fish kept hitting him.'

Mr Cater, a jewellery wholesaler with offices at 1224 Avenue of the Americas, was pronounced dead on arrival at Southampton Hospital.

These incidents are the first documented cases of attacks on bathers on the Eastern Seaboard in more than two decades.

According to Dr David Dieter, an icthyologist at the New York Aquarium at Coney Island, it is logical to assume – but by no means a certainty – that both attacks were the work of one shark.

'At this time of year in these waters,' said Dr Dieter, 'there are very few sharks. It's rare at any time of year for sharks to come so close to the beach. So the chances that two sharks would be off the same beach at virtually the same time – and would each attack someone – are infinitesimal.'

When informed that one witness described the shark that attacked Mr Cater as being 'as large as a station wagon,' Dr Dieter said the shark was probably a 'great white' (*Carcharodon carcharias*), a species known throughout the world for its voraciousness and aggressiveness.

In 1916, he said, a great white killed four bathers in New Jersey on one day – the only other recorded instance of multiple shark-attack fatalities in the United States in this century. Dr Dieter attributed the attacks to 'bad luck, like a flash of lightning that hits a house. The shark was probably just passing by. It happened to be a nice day, and there happened to be people swimming, and he happened to come along. It was pure chance.'

Amity is a summer community on the south shore of Long Island, approximately midway between Bridgehampton and East Hampton, with a wintertime population of 1,000. In the summer, the population increases to 10,000.

Brody finished reading the article and set the paper on the desk. Chance, that doctor said, pure chance. What would he say if he knew about the first attack? Still pure chance? Or would it be negligence, gross and unforgivable? There were three people dead now, and two of them could still be alive, if only Brody had . . .

'You've seen the *Times*,' said Meadows. He was standing in the doorway.

'Yeah, I've seen it. They didn't pick up the Watkins thing.'

'I know. Kind of curious, especially after Len's little slip of the tongue.'

'But you did use it.'

'I did. I had to. Here.' Meadows handed Brody a copy of the Amity *Leader*. The banner headline ran across all six columns of page one: TWO KILLED BY MONSTER SHARK OFF AMITY BEACH. Below that, in smaller type, a subhead: Number of Victims of Killer Fish Rises to Three.

'You sure get your news up high, Harry.'

'Read on.'

Brody read:

Two summer visitors to Amity were brutally slain yesterday by a man-eating shark that attacked them as they frolicked in the chill waters off the Scotch Road beach.

Alexander Kintner, age 6, who lived with his mother in the Goose Neck Lane house owned by Mr and Mrs Richard Packer, was the first to die – attacked from below as he lay on a rubber raft. His body has not been found.

Less than half an hour later, Morris Cater, 65, who was

spending the week-end at the Abelard Arms Inn, was attacked from behind as he swam in the gentle surf off the public beach.

The giant fish struck again and again, savaging Mr Cater as he cried for help. Patrolman Len Hendricks, who by sheer coincidence was taking his first swim in five years, made a valiant attempt to rescue the struggling victim, but the fish gave no quarter. Mr Cater was dead by the time he was pulled clear of the water.

The deaths were the second and third to be caused by shark attack off Amity in the past five days.

Last Wednesday night, Miss Christine Watkins, a guest of Mr and Mrs Foote of Old Mill Road, went for a swim and vanished.

Thursday morning, Police Chief Martin Brody and Officer Hendricks recovered her body. According to coroner Carl Santos, the cause of death was 'definitely and incontrovertibly shark attack.'

Asked why the cause of death was not made public, Mr Santos declined to comment.

Brody looked up from the paper and said, 'Did Santos really decline to comment?'

'No. He said nobody but you and I had asked him about the cause of death, so he didn't feel compelled to tell anybody. As you can see, I couldn't print that response. It would have pinned everything on you and me. I had hoped I could get him to say something like, "Her family requested that the cause of death be kept private, and since there was obviously no crime involved, I agreed," but he wouldn't. I can't say I blame him.'

'So what did you do?'

'I tried to get hold of Larry Vaughan, but he was away for the week-end. I thought he'd be the best official spokesman.'

'And when you couldn't reach him?'
'Read.'

It was understood, however, that Amity police and government officials had decided to withhold the information in the public interest. 'People tend to overreact when they hear about a shark attack,' said one member of the Board of Selection. 'We didn't want to start a panic. And we had an expert's opinion that the odds against another attack were astronomical.'

'Who was your talkative selectman?' asked Brody.
'All of them and none of them,' said Meadows. 'It's basically what they all said, but none of them would be quoted.'
'What about the beaches not being closed? Did you go into that?'
'*You* did.'
'I did?'

Asked why he had not ordered the beaches closed until the marauding shark was apprehended, Chief Brody said, 'The Atlantic Ocean is huge. Fish swim in it and move from place to place. They don't always stay in one area, especially an area like this where there is no food source. What were we going to do? Close the Amity beaches, and people would just drive up to East Hampton and go swimming there. And there's just as good a chance that they'd get killed in East Hampton as in Amity.'

After yesterday's attacks, however, Chief Brody did order the beaches closed until further notice.

'Jesus, Harry,' said Brody, 'you really put it to me. You've got me arguing a case I don't believe, then being proved wrong and *forced* to do what I wanted to do all along. That's a pretty shitty trick.'

67

'It wasn't a trick. I had to have someone give the official line, and with Vaughan away, you were the logical one. You admit that you agreed to go along with the decision, so – reluctantly or not – you supported it. I didn't see any point in airing all the dirty laundry of private disputes.'

'I suppose. Anyway, it's done. Is there anything else I should read in this?'

'No. I just quote Matt Hooper, that fellow from Woods Hole. He says it would be remarkable if we ever have another attack. But he's a little less sure than he was last time.'

'Does he think one fish is doing all this?'

'He doesn't know, of course, but offhand, yes. He thinks it's a big white.'

'I do, too. I mean, I don't know whites from greens or blues, but I think it's one shark.'

'I'm not sure, exactly. Yesterday afternoon I called the Coast Guard out on Montauk. I asked them if they'd noticed a lot of sharks around here recently, and they said they hadn't seen one. Not one so far this spring. It's still early, so that isn't *too* strange. They said they'd send a boat down this way later on and give me a call if they saw anything. I finally called them back. They said they had cruised up and down this area for two hours and hadn't seen a thing. So there sure aren't many sharks around. They also said that when there are sharks around, they're mostly medium-sized, blue sharks – about five to ten feet – and sand sharks that don't generally bother people. From what Leonard said he saw yesterday, this is no medium-sized blue.'

'Hooper said there was one thing we could do,' Meadows said. 'Now that you've got the beaches closed down, we could chum. You know, spread fish guts and goodies like that around in the water. If there's a shark around, he said, that will bring him running.'

'Oh, great. That's what we need, to attract sharks. And what if he shows up? What do we do then?'

'Catch him.'

'With what? My trusty spinning rod?'

'No, a harpoon.'

'A harpoon. Harry, I don't even have a police boat, let alone a boat with harpoons on it.'

'There are fishermen around. They have boats.'

'Yeah, for a hundred and a half a day, or whatever it is.'

'True. But still it seems to me . . .' A commotion out in the hall stopped Meadows in mid-sentence.

He and Brody heard Bixby say, 'I told you, ma'am, he's in conference.' Then a woman's voice said, 'Bullshit! I don't care what he's doing. I'm going in there.'

The sound of running feet – first one pair, then two. The door to Brody's office flew open, and standing in the doorway, clutching a newspaper, tears streaming down her face, was Alexander Kintner's mother.

Bixby came up behind her and said, 'I'm sorry, Chief. I tried to stop her.'

'That's okay, Bixby,' said Brody. 'Come in, Mrs Kintner.'

Meadows stood and offered her his chair, which was the closest one to Brody's desk. She ignored him and walked up to Brody, who was standing behind his desk.

'What can I do . . .'

The woman slapped the newspaper across his face. It didn't hurt Brody so much as startle him – especially the noise, a sharp report that rang deep into his left ear. The paper fell to the floor.

'What about this?' Mrs Kintner screamed. 'What about it?'

'What about what?' said Brody.

'What they say there. That you knew it was dangerous to swim. That somebody had already been killed by that shark. That you kept it a secret.'

Brody didn't know what to say. Of course it was true, all of it, at least technically. He couldn't deny it. And yet he

69

couldn't admit it, either, because it wasn't the whole truth.

'Sort of,' he said. 'I mean yes, it's true, but it's – look, Mrs Kintner . . .' He was pleading with her to control herself until he could explain.

'You killed Alex!' She shrieked the words, and Brody was sure they were heard in the parking lot, on the street, in the centre of the town, in the beaches, all over Amity. He was sure his wife heard them, and his children.

He thought to himself: Stop her before she says anything else. But all he could say was, 'Ssshhh!'

'You did! You killed him!' Her fists were clenched at her sides, and her head snapped forward as she screamed, as if she were trying to inject the words into Brody. 'You won't get away with it!'

'Please, Mrs Kintner,' said Brody. 'Calm down. Just for a minute. Let me explain.' He reached to touch her shoulder and help her to a chair, but she jerked away.

'Keep your fucking hands off me!' she cried. 'You knew. You knew all along, but you wouldn't say. And now a six-year-old boy, a beautiful six-year-old boy, my boy . . .' Tears seemed to pulse from her eyes, and as she quivered in her rage, droplets were cast from her face. 'You knew! Why didn't you tell? Why?' She clutched herself, wrapping her arms around her body as they would be wrapped in a straitjacket, and she looked into Brody's eyes. 'Why?'

'It's . . .' Brody fumbled for words. 'It's a long story.' He felt wounded, incapacitated as surely as if he had been shot. He didn't know if he could explain now. He wasn't even sure he could speak.

'I bet it is,' said the woman. 'Oh, you evil man. You evil, evil man. You . . .'

'Stop it!' Brody's shout was both plea and command. It stopped her. 'Now look, Mrs Kintner, you've got it wrong, all wrong. Ask Mr Meadows.'

Meadows, transfixed by the scene, nodded dumbly.

'Of course he'd say that. Why shouldn't he? He's your pal, isn't he? He probably told you you were doing the right thing.' Her rage was mounting again, flooding, resuscitated by a new burst of emotional amperage. 'You probably decided together. That makes it easier, doesn't it? Did you make money?'

'What?'

'Did you make money from my son's blood? Did someone pay you not to tell what you knew?'

Brody was horrified. 'No! Christ, of course not.'

'Then *why*? Tell me. Tell me why. *I'll* pay you. Just tell me why!'

'Because we didn't think it could happen again.' Brody was surprised by his brevity. That was it, really, wasn't it?

The woman was silent for a moment, letting the words register in her muddled mind. She seemed to repeat them to herself. She said. 'Oh,' then, a second later, 'Jesus.' All of a sudden, as if a switch had been turned somewhere inside her, shutting off power, she had no more self-control. She slumped into the chair next to Meadows and began to weep in gasping, choking sobs.

Meadows tried to calm her, but she didn't hear him. She didn't hear Brody when he told Bixby to call a doctor. And she saw, heard, and felt nothing when the doctor came into the office, listened to Brody's description of what had happened, tried to talk to her, gave her a shot of Librium, led her – with the help of one of Brody's men – to his car, and drove her to the hospital.

When she had left, Brody looked at his watch and said, 'It's not even nine o'clock yet. If ever I felt like I could use a drink . . . wow.'

'If you're serious,' said Meadows, 'I have some Bourbon back in my office.'

'No. If this was any indication of how the rest of the day's going to go, I better not fuck up my head.'

71

'It's hard, but you've got to try not to take what she said too seriously. I mean, the woman was in shock, for one thing.'

'I know, Harry. Any doctor would say she didn't know what she was saying. The trouble is, I'd already thought a lot of the things she was saying. Not in those words, maybe, but the thoughts were the same.'

'Come on, Martin, you know you can't blame yourself.'

'I know. I could blame Larry Vaughan. Or maybe even you. But the point is, the two deaths yesterday could have been prevented. I could have prevented them, and I didn't. Period.'

The phone rang. It was answered in the other room, and a voice on the intercom said, 'It's Mr Vaughan.'

Brody pushed the lighted button, picked up the receiver, and said, 'Hi, Larry. Did you have a nice week-end?'

'Until about eleven o'clock last night,' said Vaughan, 'when I turned on my car radio driving home. I was tempted to call you last night, but I figured you had had a rough enough day without being bothered at that hour.'

'That's one decision I agree with.'

'Don't rub it in, Martin. I feel bad enough.'

Brody wanted to say, 'Do you, Larry?' He wanted to scrape the wound raw, to unload some of the anguish on to someone else: but he knew it was both unfair to attempt and impossible to accomplish, so all he said was, 'Sure.'

'I had two cancellations already this morning. Big leases. Good people. They had already signed, and I told them I could take them to court. They said, go ahead: we're going somewhere else. I'm scared to answer the phone. I still have twenty houses that aren't rented for August.'

'I wish I could tell you different, Larry, but it's going to get worse.'

'What do you mean?'

'With the beaches closed.'

'How long do you think you'll have to keep them closed?'

72

'I don't know. As long as it takes. A few days. Maybe more.'

'You know that the end of next week is the Fourth of July week-end.'

'Sure, I know.'

'It's already too late to hope for a good summer, but we may be able to salvage something – for August, at least – if the Fourth is good.'

Brody couldn't read the tone in Vaughan's voice. 'Are you arguing with me, Larry?'

'No. I guess I was thinking out loud. Or praying out loud. Anyway, you plan to keep the beaches closed until what? Indefinitely? How will you know when that thing's gone away?'

'I haven't had time to think that far ahead. I don't even know why it's here. Let me ask you something, Larry. Just out of curiosity.'

'What?'

'Who are your partners?'

It was a long moment before Vaughan said, 'Why do you want to know? What does that have to do with anything?'

'Like I said, just curiosity.'

'You keep your curiosity for your job, Martin. Let me worry about my business.'

'Sure, Larry. No offence.'

'So what are you going to do? We can't just sit around and hope it will go away. We could starve to death while we waited.'

'I know. Meadows and I were just talking about our options. A fish-expert friend of Harry's says we could try to catch the fish. What would you think about getting up a couple of hundred dollars to charter Ben Gardner's boat for a day or two? I don't know that he's ever caught any sharks, but it might be worth a try.'

'Anything's worth a try, just so we get rid of that thing and go back to making a living. Go ahead. Tell him I'll get the money from somewhere.'

Brody hung up the phone and said to Meadows, 'I don't know why I care, but I'd give my ass to know more about Mr Vaughan's business affairs.'

'Why?'

'He's a very rich man. No matter how long this shark thing goes on, he won't be badly hurt. Sure, he'll lose a little dough, but he's taking all this as if it was life and death – and I don't mean just the town's. His.'

'Maybe he's just a conscientious fellow.'

'That wasn't just conscience talking on the phone just then. Believe me, Harry. I know what conscience is.'

Ten miles south of the eastern tip of Long Island, a chartered fishing boat drifted slowly in the tide. Two wire lines trailed limply aft in an oily slick. The captain of the boat, a tall, spare man, sat on a bench on the flying bridge, staring at the water. Below, in the cockpit, the two men who had chartered the boat sat reading. One was reading a novel, the other the New York *Times*.

'Hey, Quint,' said the man with the newspaper, 'did you see this about the shark that killed those people?'

'I seen it,' said the captain.

'You think we'll run into that shark?'

'Nope.'

'How do you know?'

'I know.'

'Suppose we went looking for him.'

'We won't.'

'Why not?'

'We got a slick goin'. We'll stay put.'

The man shook his head and smiled. 'Boy, wouldn't that be some sport.'

'Fish like that ain't sport,' said the captain.

'How far is Amity from here?'

'Down the coast a ways.'

'Well, if he's around here somewhere, you might run into him one of these days.'

'We'll find one another, all right. But not today.'

FIVE

Thursday morning was foggy – a wet ground fog so thick that it had a taste: sharp and salty. People drove under the speed limit, with their lights on. Around midday, the fog lifted, and puffy cumulus clouds maundered across the sky beneath a high blanket of cirrus. By five in the afternoon, the cloud cover had begun to disintegrate, like pieces fallen from a jigsaw puzzle. Sunlight streaked through the gaps, stabbing shining patches of blue on to the grey-green surface of the sea.

Brody sat on the public beach, his elbows resting on his knees to steady the binoculars in his hands. When he lowered the glasses, he could barely see the boat – a white speck that disappeared and reappeared in the ocean swells. The strong lenses drew it into plain, though jiggly, view. Brody had been sitting there for nearly an hour. He tried to push his eyes, to extend his vision from within to delineate more clearly the outline of what he saw. He cursed and let the glasses drop and hang by the strap around his neck.

'Hey, Chief,' Hendricks said, walking up to Brody.

'Hey, Leonard. What are you doing here?'

'I was just passing by and I saw your car. What are you doing?'

'Trying to figure out what the hell Ben Gardner's doing.'

'Fishing, don't you think?'

'That's what he's being paid to do, but it's the damnedest fishing I ever saw. I haven't seen anything move on that boat in an hour.'

'Can I take a look?' Brody handed him the glasses. Hendricks raised them and looked out to sea. 'Nope, you're right. How long has he been out there?'

'All day, I think. I talked to him last night, and he said he'd be taking off at six this morning.'

'Did he go alone?'

'I don't know. He said he was going to try to get hold of his mate – Danny what's-his-name – but there was something about a dentist appointment. I *hope* to hell he didn't go alone.'

'You want to go see? We've got at least two more hours of daylight.'

'How do you plan to get out there?'

'I'll borrow Chickering's boat. He's got an AquaSport with an eighty-horse Evinrude on it. That'll get us out there.'

Brody felt a shimmy of fear skitter up his back. He was a very poor swimmer, and the prospect of being on top of – let alone in – water above his head gave him what his mother used to call the wimwams: sweaty palms, a persistent need to swallow, and an ache in his stomach – essentially the sensation some people feel about flying. In Brody's dreams, deep water was populated by slimy, savage things that rose from below and shredded his flesh, by demons that cackled and moaned. 'Okay,' he said. 'I don't guess we've got much choice. Maybe by the time we get to the dock he'll already have started in. You go get the boat ready. I'll stop off at headquarters and give his wife a call ... see if he's called in on the radio.'

Amity's town dock was small, with only twenty slips, a fuel dock, and a wooden shack where hot dogs and fried clams were sold in cardboard sleeves. The slips were in a little inlet protected from the open sea by a stone jetty that ran across half the width of the inlet's mouth. Hendricks was standing in the AquaSport, the engine running, and he was chatting with a man in a twenty-five-foot cabin cruiser tied up in the neighbouring slip. Brody walked along the wooden pier and climbed down the short ladder into the boat.

'What did she say?' asked Hendricks.

'Not a word. She's been trying to raise him for half an

77

hour, but she figures he must have turned off the radio.'

'Is he alone?'

'As far as she knows. His mate had an impacted wisdom tooth that had to be taken out today.'

The man in the cabin cruiser said, 'If you don't mind my saying so, that's pretty strange.'

'What is?' said Brody.

'To turn off your radio when you're out alone. People don't do that.'

'I don't know. Ben always bitches about all the chatter that goes on between boats when he's out fishing. Maybe he got bored and turned it off.'

'Maybe.'

'Let's go, Leonard,' said Brody. 'Do you know how to drive this thing?'

Hendricks cast off the bow line, walked to the stern, uncleated the stern line, and tossed it on to the deck. He moved to the control console and pushed a knobbed handle forward. The boat lurched ahead, chugging. Hendricks pushed the handle farther forward, and the engine fired more regularly. The stern settled back, the bow rose. As they made the turn around the jetty, Hendricks pushed the lever all the way forward, and the bow dropped down.

'Planing,' said Hendricks.

Brody grabbed a steel handle on the side of the console. 'Are there any life jackets?' he asked.

'Just the cushions,' said Hendricks. 'They'd hold you up all right, if you were an eight-year-old boy.'

'Thanks.'

What breeze there had been had died, and there was little chop to the sea. But there were small swells, and the boat took them roughly, smacking its wooden prow into each one, recovering with a shudder that unnerved Brody. 'This thing's gonna break apart if you don't slow down,' he said.

Hendricks smiled, relishing his moment of command. 'No

78

worry, Chief. If I slow down, we'll wallow. It'll take us a week to get out there, and your stomach will feel like it's full of squirrels.'

Gardner's boat was about three quarters of a mile from shore. As they drew nearer, Brody could see it bobbing gently in the swells. He could even make out the black letters on the transom: FLICKA.

'He's anchored,' said Hendricks. 'Boy, that's some lot of water to anchor a boat in. We must have more than a hundred feet out here.'

'Swell,' Brody said. 'That's just what I wanted to hear.'

When they were about fifty yards from the *Flicka*, Hendricks throttled down, and the boat settled into a slow side-to-side roll. They closed quickly. Brody walked forward and mounted a platform in the bow. He saw no signs of life. There were no rods in the rod-holders. 'Hey, Ben!' he called. There was no reply.

'Maybe he's below,' said Hendricks.

Brody called again, 'Hey, Ben!' The bow of the AquaSport was only a few feet from the port quarter of the *Flicka*. Hendricks pushed the handle into neutral, then gave it a quick burst of reverse. The AquaSport stopped and, on the next swell, nestled up against the *Flicka*'s gunwale. Brody grabbed the gunwale. 'Hey, Ben!'

Hendricks took a line from the lazaret, walked forward, and made it fast to a cleat on the bow of the AquaSport. He looped the line over the railing of the other boat and tied a crude knot. 'You want to go on board?' he said.

'Yeah.' Brody climbed aboard the *Flicka*. Hendricks followed, and they stood in the cockpit. Hendricks poked his head through the forward hatch. 'You in there, Ben?' He looked around, withdrew his head, and said, 'Not there.'

'He's not on board,' said Brody. 'No two ways about it.'

'What's that stuff?' said Hendricks, pointing to a bucket in the corner of the stern.

Brody walked to the bucket and bent down. A stench of fish and oil filled his nose. The bucket was full of guts and blood. 'Must be chum,' he said. 'Fish guts and other shit. You spread it around in the water and it's supposed to attract sharks. He didn't use much of it. The bucket's almost full.'

A sudden noise made Brody jump. 'Whisky, zebra, echo, two, five, niner,' said a voice crackling over the radio. 'This is the *Pretty Belle*. You there, Jake?'

'So much for that theory,' said Brody. 'He never turned off his radio.'

'I don't get it, Chief. There are no rods. He didn't carry a dinghy, so he couldn't have rowed away. He swam like a fish, so if he fell overboard he would've just climbed back on.'

'You see a harpoon anywhere?'

'What's it look like?'

'I don't know. Like a harpoon. And barrels. Supposedly, you use them as floats.'

'I don't see anything like that.'

Brody stood at the starboard gunwale, gazing into the middle distance. The boat moved slightly, and he steadied himself with his right hand. He felt something strange and looked down. There were four ragged screw holes where a cleat had been. The screws had obviously not been removed by a screwdriver; the wood around the holes was torn. 'Look at this, Leonard.'

Hendricks ran his hand over the holes. He looked to the port side, where a ten-inch steel cleat still sat securely on the wood. 'You imagine that what was here was as big as the one over there?' he said. 'Jesus, what would it take to pull that mother out?'

'Look here, Leonard.' Brody ran his index finger over the outer edge of the gunwale. There was a scar about eight inches long, where the paint had been scraped away and the wood abraded. 'It looks like someone took a file to this wood.'

'Or else rubbed the hell out of it with an awful tight piece of heavy rope.'

Brody walked over the port side of the cockpit and, aimlessly, began to feel his way along the outer edge of the gunwale. 'That's the only place,' he said. When he reached the stern, he leaned on his elbows on the gunwale and gazed down into the water.

For a moment, he stared dumbly at the transom, unseeing. Then a pattern began to take shape, a pattern of holes, deep gouges in the wooden transom, forming a rough semicircle more than three feet across. Next to it was another, similar pattern. And at the bottom of the transom, just at the water line, three short smears of blood. Please, God, thought Brody, not another one. 'Come here, Leonard,' he said.

Hendricks walked to the stern and looked over. 'What?'

'If I hold your legs, you think you can lean over and take a look at those holes down there and try to figure out what made them?'

'What do you think made them?'

'I don't know. But *something*. I want to find out what. Come on. If you can't dope it out in a minute or two, we'll forget about it and go home. Okay?'

'I guess so.' Hendricks lay on the top of the transom. 'Hold me tight, Chief . . . please.'

Brody leaned down and grabbed Hendricks' feet. 'Don't worry,' he said. He took one of Hendricks' legs under each arm and lifted. Hendricks rose, then bent over the transom. 'Okay?' said Brody.

'A little more. Not too much! Jesus, you just dipped my head in the water.'

'Sorry. How's that?'

'Okay, that's it.' Hendricks began to examine the holes. 'What if some shark came along right now?' he grunted. 'He could grab me right out of your hands.'

'Don't think about it. Just look.'

'I'm looking.' In a few moments he said, 'Sonofabitch. Look at that thing. Hey, pull me up. I need my knife.'

'What is it?' Brody asked when Hendricks was back aboard.

Hendricks unfolded the main blade from the body of his pocket knife. 'I don't know,' he replied. 'Some kind of white chip or something, stuck into one of the holes.' Knife in hand, he allowed Brody to lower him over the rail again. He worked briefly, his body twisting from the effort. Then he called: 'Okay. I've got it. Pull.'

Brody stepped backward, hoisting Hendricks over the transom, then lowered Hendricks' feet to the deck. 'Let's see,' he said, holding out his hand. Into Brody's palm Hendricks dropped a triangle of glistening white denticle. It was nearly two inches long. The sides were tiny saws. Brody scraped the tooth against the gunwale, and it cut the wood. He looked out over the water and shook his head. 'My God,' he said.

'It's a tooth, isn't it?' said Hendricks. 'Jesus Christ Almighty. You think the shark got Ben?'

'I don't know what else to think,' said Brody. He looked at the tooth again, then dropped it into his pocket. 'We might as well go. There's nothing we can do here.'

'What do you want to do with Ben's boat?'

'We'll leave it here till tomorrow. Then we'll have someone come get it.'

'I'll drive it back if you want.'

'And leave me to drive the other one? Forget it.'

'We could tow one of them in.'

'No. It's getting dark, and I don't want to have to fool around trying to dock two boats in the dark. This boat'll be all right overnight. Just go check the anchor up front and make sure it's secure. Then let's go. No one's going to need this boat before tomorrow ... especially not Ben Gardner.'

They arrived at the dock in late twilight. Harry Meadows and another man, unknown to Brody, were waiting for them.

'You sure have good antenna, Harry,' Brody said as he climbed the ladder on to the dock.

Meadows smiled, flattered. 'That's my trade, Martin.' He gestured towards the man beside him. 'This is Matt Hooper, Chief Brody.'

The two men shook hands. 'You're the fellow from Woods Hole,' Brody said, trying to get a good look at him in the fading light. He was young – mid-twenties, Brody thought – and handsome: tanned, hair bleached by the sun. He was about as tall as Brody, an inch over six feet, but leaner: Brody guessed 170 pounds, compared to his own 200. A mental reflex scanned Hooper for possible threat. Then, with what Brody recognized as juvenile pride, he determined that if it ever came to a face-off, he could take Hooper. Experience would make the difference.

'That's right,' said Hooper.

'Harry's been tapping your brain long-distance,' Brody said. 'How come you're here?'

Meadows said, 'I called him. I thought he might be able to figure out what's going on.'

'Shit, Harry, all you had to do was ask me,' said Brody. 'I could have told you. You see, there's this fish out there, and . . .'

'You know what I mean.'

Brody sensed his own resentment at the intrusion, the complication that Hooper's expertise was bound to add, the implicit division of authority that Hooper's arrival had created. And he recognized the resentment as stupid. 'Sure, Harry,' he said. 'No problem. It's just been a long day.'

'What did you find out there?' Meadows asked.

Brody started to reach in his pocket for the tooth, but he stopped. He didn't want to go through it all, standing on a dock in near darkness. 'I'm not sure,' he said. 'Come on back to the station and I'll fill you in.'

'Is Ben going to stay out there all night?'

'It looks that way, Harry.' Brody turned to Hendricks, who had finished tying up the boat. 'You going home, Leonard?'

'Yeah. I want to clean up before I go to work.'

Brody arrived at police headquarters before Meadows and Hooper. It was almost eight o'clock. He had two phone calls to make – to Ellen, to see if the dinner leftovers could be reheated or if he should pick up something on the way home, and, the call he dreaded, to Sally Gardner. He called Ellen first: pot roast. It could be reheated. It might taste like a sneaker, but it would be warm. He hung up, checked the phone book for the Gardner number, and dialled it.

'Sally? This is Martin Brody.' Suddenly he regretted having called without thinking the call through. How much should he tell her? Not much, he decided, at least not until he had had a chance to check with Hooper to see if his theory was plausible or absurd.

'Where's Ben, Martin?' The voice was calm, but pitched slightly higher than Brody remembered as normal.

'I don't know, Sally.'

'What do you mean, you don't know? You went out there, didn't you?'

'Yes. He wasn't on the boat.'

'But the boat was there.'

'The boat was there.'

'You went on board? You looked all over it? Even below?'

'Yes.' Then a faint hope. 'Ben didn't carry a dinghy, did he?'

'No. How could he not be there?' The voice was shriller now.

'I . . .'

'Where *is* he?'

Brody caught the tone of incipient hysteria. He wished he had gone to the house in person. 'Are you alone, Sally?'

'No. The kids are here.'

She seemed calmer, but Brody was sure the calm was but

84

a lull before the burst of grief that would come when she realized that the fears with which she had lived every day for the sixteen years Ben had been fishing professionally – closet fears shoved into mental recesses and never uttered because they would seem ridiculous – had come true.

Brody dug at his memory for the ages of the Gardner children. Twelve, maybe; then nine, then about six. What kind of kid was the twelve year old? He didn't know. Who was the nearest neighbour? Shit. Why didn't he think of this before? The Finleys. 'Just a second, Sally.' He called to the officer at the front desk. 'Clements, call Grace Finley and tell her to get her ass over to Sally Gardner's house right now.'

'Suppose she asks why.'

'Just tell her I said to go. Tell her I'll explain later.' He turned back to the phone. 'I'm sorry, Sally. All I can tell you for sure is that we went out to where Ben's boat is anchored. We went on board and Ben wasn't there. We looked all around, downstairs and everything.'

Meadows and Hooper walked into Brody's office. He motioned them to chairs.

'But where could he be?' said Sally Gardner. 'You don't just get off a boat in the middle of the ocean.'

'No.'

'And he couldn't have fallen overboard. I mean, he could have, but he'd get right back in again.'

'Yes.'

'Maybe someone came and took him off in another boat. Maybe the engine wouldn't start and he had to ride with someone else. Did you check the engine?'

'No,' Brody said, embarrassed.

'That's probably it, then.' The voice was subtly lighter, almost girlish, coated with a veneer of hope that, when it broke, would shatter like iced crystal. 'And if the battery was dead, that would explain why he couldn't call on the radio.'

'The radio was working, Sally.'

'Wait a minute. Who's there? Oh, it's you.' There was a pause. Brody heard Sally talking to Grace Finley. Then Sally came back on the line. 'Grace says you told her to come over here. Why?'

'I thought—'

'You think he's dead, don't you? You think he drowned.' The veneer shattered, and she began to sob.

'I'm afraid so, Sally. That's all we can think at the moment. Let me talk to Grace for a minute, will you please?'

A couple of seconds later, the voice of Grace Finley said, 'Yes, Martin?'

'I'm sorry to do this to you, but I couldn't think of anything else. Can you stay with her for a while?'

'All night. I will.'

'That might be a good idea. I'll try to get over later on. Thanks.'

'What happened, Martin?'

'We don't know for sure.'

'Is it that . . . *thing* again?'

'Maybe. That's what we're trying to figure out. But do me a favour, Grace. Don't say anything about a shark to Sally. It's bad enough as it is.'

'All right, Martin. Wait. Wait a minute.' She covered the mouthpiece of the phone with her hand, and Brody heard some muffled conversation. Then Sally Gardner came on the line.

'Why did you do it, Martin?'

'Do what?'

Apparently, Grace Finley tried to take the phone from her hand, for Brody heard Sally say, 'Let me speak, damn you!' Then she said to him, 'Why did you send him? Why Ben?' Her voice wasn't particularly loud, but she spoke with an intensity that struck Brody as hard as if she were yelling.

'Sally, you're—'

86

'This didn't have to happen!' she said. 'You could have stopped it.'

Brody wanted to hang up. He didn't want a repetition of the scene with the Kintner boy's mother. But he had to defend himself. She had to know that it wasn't his fault. How could she blame him? He said, 'Crap! Ben was a fisherman, a good one. He knew the risks.'

'If you hadn't—'

'Stop it, Sally!' Brody let himself stamp on her words. 'Try to get some rest.' He hung up the phone. He was furious, but his fury was confused. He was angry at Sally Gardner for accusing him, and angry at himself for being angry at her. If, she had said. If what? If he had not sent Ben. Sure. And if pigs had wings they'd be eagles. If he had gone himself. But that wasn't his trade. He had sent the expert. He looked up at Meadows. 'You heard.'

'Not all of it. But enough to gather that Ben Gardner has become victim number four.'

Brody nodded. 'I think so.' He told Meadows and Hooper about his trip with Hendricks. Once or twice, Meadows interrupted with a question. Hooper listened, his angular face placid and his eyes – a light, powder blue – fixed on Brody. At the end of his tale, Brody reached into his pants pocket. 'We found this,' he said. 'Leonard dug it out of the wood.' He flipped the tooth to Hooper, who turned it over in his hand.

'What do you think, Matt?' said Meadows.

'It's a white.'

'How big?'

'I can't be sure, but big. Fifteen, twenty feet. That's some fantastic fish.' He looked at Meadows. 'Thanks for calling me,' he said. 'I could spend a whole lifetime around sharks and never see a fish like that.'

Brody asked, 'How much would a fish like that weigh?'

'Five or six thousand pounds.'

Brody whistled. 'Three tons.'

'Do you have any thoughts about what happened?' Meadows asked.

'From what the chief says, it sounds like the fish killed Mr Gardner.'

'How?' said Brody.

'Any number of ways. Gardner might have fallen overboard. More likely, he was pulled over. His leg may have gotten tangled in a harpoon line. He could even have been taken while he was leaning over the stern.'

'How do you account for the teeth in the stern?'

'The fish attacked the boat.'

'What the hell for?'

'Sharks aren't very bright, Chief. They exist on instinct and impulse. The impulse to feed is powerful.'

'But a thirty-foot boat . . .'

'A shark doesn't think. To him it wasn't a boat. It was just something large.'

'And inedible.'

'Not till he'd tried it. You have to understand. There's nothing in the sea this fish would fear. Other fish run from bigger things. That's their instinct. But this fish doesn't run from anything. He doesn't know fear. He might be cautious – say around an even bigger white. But fear – no way.'

'What else do they attack?'

'Anything.'

'Just like that. Anything.'

'Pretty much, yes.'

'Do you have any idea why he's hung around here so long?' said Brody. 'I don't know how much you know about the water here, but . . .'

'I grew up here.'

'You did? In Amity?'

'No, Southampton. I spent every summer there, from grade school through grad school.'

88

'Every *summer*. So you didn't really grow up there.' Brody was groping for something with which to re-establish his parity with, if not superiority to, the younger man, and what he settled for was reverse snobbism, an attitude not uncommon to year-round residents of resort communities. It gave them armour against the contempt they sensed radiating from the rich summer folk. It was an 'I'm all right, Jack' attitude, a social *machismo* that equated wealth with effeteness, simplicity with goodness, and poverty (up to a point) with honesty. And it was an attitude that, in general, Brody found both repugnant and silly. But he had felt threatened by the younger man – he wasn't really sure why – and the sensation was so alien that he had reached for the most convenient carapace, the one Hooper had handed him.

'You're picking nits,' Hooper said testily. 'Okay, so I wasn't born here. But I've spent a lot of time in these waters, and I wrote a paper on this coastline. Anyway, I know what you're getting at, and you're right. This shoreline isn't an environment that would normally support a long stay by a shark.'

'So why is this one staying?'

'It's impossible to say. It's definitely uncharacteristic, but sharks do so many uncharacteristic things that the erratic becomes the normal. Anyone who'd risk money – not to mention his life – on a prediction about what one big shark will do in a given situation is a fool. This shark could be sick. The patterns of his life are so beyond his control that damage to one small mechanism could cause him to disorient and behave strangely.'

'If this is how he acts when he's sick,' said Brody, 'I'd hate to see what he does when he's feeling fine.'

'No. Personally, I don't think he's sick. There are other things that could cause him to stay here – many of them things we'll never understand, natural factors, caprices.'

'Like what?'

'Changes in water temperature or current flow or feeding patterns. As food supplies move, so do the predators. Two summers ago, for example, a completely inexplicable phenomenon took place off the shore of parts of Connecticut and Rhode Island. The whole coastline was suddenly inundated with menhaden – fishermen call them bunker. Huge schools. Millions of fish. They coated the water like an oil slick. There were so many that you could throw a bare hook in the water and reel it in, and more often than not you'd catch a menhaden, so all of a sudden there were masses of bluefish feeding in schools right off the beaches. In Watch Hill, Rhode Island, people were wading into the surf and catching bluefish with rakes. Garden rakes! Just shovelling the fish out of the water. Then the big predators came – big tuna, four, five, six hundred pounds. Deep-sea fishing boats were catching bluefin tuna within a hundred yards of the shore. In harbours sometimes. Then suddenly it stopped. The menhaden went away, and so did the other fish. I spent three weeks down there trying to figure out what was going on. I still don't know. It's all part of the ecological balance. When something tips too far one way or the other, peculiar things happen.'

'But this is even weirder,' said Brody. 'This fish has stayed in one place, in one chunk of water only a mile or two square, for over a week. He hasn't moved up or down the beach. He hasn't touched anybody in East Hampton or Southampton. What is it about Amity?'

'I don't know. I doubt that anyone could give you a good answer.'

Meadows said, 'Minnie Eldridge has the answer.'

'Balls,' said Brody.

'Who's Minnie Eldridge?' asked Hooper.

'The postmistress,' said Brody. 'She says it's God's will, or something like that. We're being punished for our sins.'

Hooper smiled. 'Right now, anyway, that's as good an answer as I've got.'

'That's encouraging,' said Brody. 'Is there anything you plan to do to *get* an answer?'

'There are a few things. I'll take water samples here and in East Hampton. I'll try to find out how other fish are behaving – if anything extraordinary is around, or if anything that should be here isn't. And I'll try to find that shark. Which reminds me, is there a boat available?'

'Yes, I'm sorry to say,' said Brody. 'Ben Gardner's. We'll get you out to it tomorrow, and you can use it at least until we work something out with his wife. Do you really think you can catch that fish, after what happened to Ben Gardner?'

'I didn't say I was going to try to catch it. I don't think I'd want to try that. Not alone, anyway.'

'Then what the hell are you going to do?'

'I don't know. I'll have to play it by ear.'

Brody looked into Hooper's eyes and said, 'I want that fish killed. If you can't do it, we'll find someone who can.'

Hooper laughed. 'You sound like a mobster. "I want that fish killed." So go get a contract out on him. Who are you going to get to do the job?'

'I don't know. What about it, Harry? You're supposed to know everything that goes on around here. Isn't there any fisherman on this whole damn island equipped to catch big sharks?'

Meadows thought for a moment before he spoke. 'There may be one. I don't know much about him, but I think his name is Quint, and I think he operates out of a private pier somewhere around Promised Land. I can find out a little more about him if you like.'

'Why not?' said Brody. 'He sounds like a possible.'

Hooper said, 'Look, Chief, you can't go off half-cocked looking for vengeance against a fish. That shark isn't evil. It's not a murderer. It's just obeying its own instincts. Trying to get retribution against a fish is crazy.'

'Listen you . . .' Brody was growing angry – an anger born

of frustration and humiliation. He knew Hooper was right, but he felt that right and wrong were irrelevant to the situation. The fish was an enemy. It had come upon the community and killed two men, a woman, and a child. The people of Amity would demand the death of the fish. They would need to see it dead before they could feel secure enough to resume their normal lives. Most of all, Brody needed it dead, for the death of the fish would be a catharsis for him. Hooper had touched that nerve, and that infuriated Brody further. But he swallowed his rage and said, 'Forget it.'

The phone rang. 'It's for you, Chief,' said Clements. 'Mr Vaughan.'

'Oh swell. That's just what I need.' He punched the flashing button on the phone and picked up the receiver. 'Yeah, Larry.'

'Hello, Martin. How are you?' Vaughan's voice was friendly, almost effusively so, Brody thought. He's probably had a couple of belts.

'As well as could be expected, Larry.'

'You're working pretty late. I tried to get you at home.'

'Yeah. Well, when you're the chief of police and your constituents are getting themselves killed every twenty minutes, that kind of keeps you busy.'

'I heard about Ben Gardner.'

'What did you hear?'

'That he was missing.'

'News travels pretty fast.'

'Are you sure it was the shark again?'

'Sure? Yeah, I guess so. Nothing else seems to make any sense.'

'Martin, what are you going to *do*?' There was a pathetic urgency in Vaughan's voice.

'That's a good question, Larry. We're doing everything we can right now. We've got the beaches closed down. We've—'

'I'm aware of that, to say the very least.'

'What's that supposed to mean?'

'Have you ever tried to sell healthy people real estate in a leper colony?'

'No, Larry,' Brody said wearily.

'I'm getting cancellations every day. People are walking out on leases. I haven't had a new customer in here since Sunday.'

'So what do you want *me* to do?'

'Well, I thought . . . I mean, what I'm wondering is, maybe we're overreacting to this whole thing.'

'You're kidding. Tell me you're kidding.'

'Hardly, Martin. Now calm down. Let's discuss this rationally.'

'I'm rational. I'm not sure about you, though.'

There was a moment of silence, and then Vaughan said, 'What would you say to opening the beaches, just for the Fourth of July week-end?'

'Not a chance. Not a fucking chance.'

'Now listen . . .'

'No, you listen, Larry. The last time I listened to you, we had two people killed. If we catch that fish, if we kill the sonofabitch, then we'll open the beaches. Until then, forget it.'

'What about nets?'

'What about them?'

'Why couldn't we put steel nets out to protect the beaches? Someone told me that's what they do in Australia.'

He *must* be drunk, Brody thought. 'Larry, this is a straight coastline. Are you going to put nets out along two and a half miles of beaches? Fine. You get the money. I'd say about a million dollars, for openers.'

'What about patrols? We could hire people to patrol up and down the beaches in boats.'

'That's not good enough, Larry. What is it with you, anyway? Are your partners on your ass again?'

'That's none of your damn business, Martin. For God's sake, man, this town is dying!'

'I know it, Larry,' Brody said softly. 'And as far as I know, there's not a damn thing we can do about it. Good night.' He hung up the phone.

Meadows and Hooper rose to leave. Brody walked them to the front door of the station house. As they started out the door, Brody said to Meadows, 'Hey, Harry, you left your lighter inside.' Meadows started to say something, but Brody stepped on his words. 'Come on back inside and I'll give it to you. If you leave it around here overnight, it's likely to disappear.' He waved to Hooper. 'See you.'

When they were back in Brody's office, Meadows took his lighter from his pocket and said, 'I trust you had something to say to me.'

Brody shut the door to his office. 'You think you can find out something about Larry's partners?'

'I guess so. Why?'

'Ever since this thing began, Larry has been on my ass to keep the beaches open. And now, after all that's just happened, he says he wants them open for the Fourth. The other day he said he was under pressure from his partners. I told you about it.'

'And?'

'I think we should know who it is who has enough clout to drive Larry bullshit. I wouldn't care if he wasn't the mayor of this town. But if there are people telling him what to do, I think we ought to know who they are.'

Meadows sighed. 'Okay, Martin. I'll do what I can. But digging around in Larry Vaughan's affairs isn't my idea of fun.'

'There's not a whole hell of a lot that is fun these days, is there?'

Brody walked Meadows to the door, then went back to his desk and sat down. Vaughan had been right about one thing, he thought: Amity was showing all the signs of imminent death. It wasn't just the real estate market, though its sickness was as contagious as smallpox. Evelyn Bixby, the wife of one of Brody's officers, had lost her job as a real estate agent and was working as a waitress in a hash house on Route 27.

Two new boutiques that were scheduled to open the next day had put off their debuts until July 3, and the proprietors of both made a point of calling on Brody to tell him that if the beaches weren't open by then, they wouldn't open their stores at all. One of them was already looking at a site for rent in East Hampton. The sporting goods store had posted signs announcing a clearance sale – a sale that normally took place over the Labour Day week-end. The only good thing about the Amity economy, as far as Brody was concerned, was that Saxon's was doing so badly that it laid off Henry Kimble. Now that he didn't have his bartending job, he slept during the day and could occasionally survive through a shift of police work without a nap.

Beginning on Monday morning – the first day the beaches were closed – Brody had posted two officers on the beaches. Together, they had had seventeen confrontations with people who insisted on swimming. One was with a man named Robert Dexter, who claimed a constitutional right to swim off his own beach and who allowed his dog to terrorize the officer on duty, until the cop pulled his pistol and threatened to shoot the dog. Another dust-up took place on the public beach, when a New York lawyer started reading the United States Constitution to a policeman and a multitude of cheering youths.

Still, Brody was convinced that – so far, at least – no one had gone swimming.

On Wednesday, two kids had rented a skiff and rowed about three hundred yards offshore, where they spent an hour ladling blood, chicken guts, and duck heads overboard. A passing fishing boat spotted them and called Brody via the marine operator. Brody called Hooper, and together they went in *Flicka* and towed the boys to shore. In the skiff the boys had a flying gaff attached to two hundred yards of clothesline, secured to the prow by a square knot. They said they planned to hook the shark with the gaff and go for a 'Nantucket sleigh ride'. Brody told them that if they ever tried the stunt again, he'd arrest them for attempted suicide.

There had been four reports of shark sightings. One had turned out to be a floating log. Two, according to the fisherman who followed up the reports, were schools of jumping bait fish. And one, as far as anyone could tell, was a flat nothing.

On Tuesday evening, just at dusk, Brody had received an anonymous phone call telling him that a man was dumping shark bait into the water off the public beach. It turned out to be not a man, but a woman dressed in a man's raincoat – Jessie Parker, one of the clerks at Walden's Stationery Store. At first she denied throwing anything into the water, but then she admitted that she had tossed a paper bag into the surf. It contained three empty vermouth bottles.

'Why didn't you throw them in the garbage?' Brody had asked.

'I didn't want the garbage man to think I'm a heavy drinker.'

'Then why didn't you throw them in someone else's garbage?'

'That wouldn't be nice,' she said. 'Garbage is . . . sort of private, don't you think?'

Brody told her that from now on, she should take her empty bottles, put them in a plastic bag, put that bag in a brown paper bag, then smash the bottles with a hammer until they were ground up. Nobody would ever know they had been bottles.

Brody looked at his watch. It was after nine, too late to pay a visit to Sally Gardner. He hoped she was asleep. Maybe

Grace Finley had given her a pill or a glass of whisky to help her rest. Before he left the office, he called the Coast Guard station at Montauk and told the duty officer about Ben Gardner. The officer said he would dispatch a patrol boat at first light to search for the body.

'Thanks,' said Brody. 'I hope you find it before it washes up.' Brody was suddenly appalled at himself. 'It' was Ben Gardner, a friend. What would Sally say if she heard Brody refer to her husband as 'it'? Fifteen years of friendship wiped out, forgotten. There was no more Ben Gardner. There was only an 'it' that should be found before it became a gory nuisance.

'We'll try,' said the officer. 'Boy, I feel for you guys. You must be having a hell of a summer.'

'I only hope it isn't our last,' said Brody. He hung up, turned out the light in his office, and walked out to his car.

As he turned into his driveway, Brody saw the familiar blue-grey light shining from the living-room windows. The boys were watching television. He walked through the front door, flipped off the outside light, and poked his head into the dark living-room. The oldest boy, Billy, lay on the couch, leaning on an elbow. Martin, the middle son, age twelve, lounged in an easy chair, his shoeless feet propped up on the coffee table. Eight-year-old Sean sat on the floor, his back against the couch, stroking a cat in his lap. 'How goes it?' said Brody.

'Good, Dad,' said Bill, without shifting his gaze from the television.

'Where's your mom?'

'Upstairs. She said to tell you your dinner's in the kitchen.'

'Okay. Not too late, Sean, huh? It's almost nine-thirty.'

'Okay, Dad,' said Sean.

Brody went into the kitchen, opened the refrigerator, and took out a beer. The remains of the pot roast sat on the kitchen table in a roasting pan, surrounded by a scum of congealed gravy. The meat was brownish-grey and stringy. 'Dinner?' said Brody to himself. He checked the icebox for sandwich makings. There was some hamburger, a package of chicken legs, a dozen eggs, a jar of pickles, and twelve cans of soda pop. He found a piece of American cheese, dried and curled with age, and he rolled it into a ball and popped it into his mouth. He debated heating up the pot roast, then said aloud, 'The hell with it.' He found two pieces of bread, spread mustard on them, took a carving knife from a magnetic board on the wall, and sliced a thick slab of roast. He dropped the meat on one of the pieces of bread, scattered a few pickles on top of it, covered it with the other piece of bread, and mashed the sandwich down with the heel of his hand. He put it on a plate, picked up his beer, and climbed the stairs to his bedroom.

Ellen was sitting up in bed, reading *Cosmopolitan*. 'Hello,' she said. 'A tough day? You didn't say anything on the phone.'

'A tough day. That's about all we're having these days. You heard about Ben Gardner? I wasn't really positive when I talked to you.' He put the plate and the beer on the dresser and sat on the edge of the bed to remove his shoes.

'Yes. I got a call from Grace Finley asking if I knew where Dr Craig was. His service wouldn't say, and Grace wanted to give Sally a sedative.'

'Did you find him?'

'No. But I had one of the boys take some Seconol over to her.'

'What's Seconol?'

'Sleeping pills.'

'I didn't know you were taking sleeping pills.'

'I don't, often. Just every now and then.'

'Where did you get them?'

'From Dr Craig, when I went to him last time about my nerves. I told you.'

'Oh.' Brody tossed his shoes into a corner, stood up, and took off his trousers, which he folded neatly over the back of a chair. He took off his shirt, put it on a hanger, and hung it in the closet. In T-shirt and undershorts he sat down on the bed and began to eat his sandwich. The meat was dry and flaky. All he could taste was mustard.

'Didn't you find the roast?' said Ellen.

Brody's mouth was full, so he nodded.

'What's that you're eating, then?'

He swallowed. 'The roast.'

'Did you heat it up?'

'No. I don't mind it like this.'

Ellen made a face and said, 'Yech.'

Brody ate in silence, as Ellen aimlessly turned the pages of her magazine. After a few moments, she closed the magazine, put it in her lap, and said, 'Oh dear.'

'What's the matter?'

'I was just thinking about Ben Gardner. It's so horrible. What do you think Sally will do?'

'I don't know,' said Brody. 'I worry about her. Have you ever talked money with her?'

'Never. But there can't be much. I don't think her children have had new clothes in a year, and she's always saying that she'd give anything to be able to afford meat more than once a week, instead of having to eat the fish Ben catches. Will she get social security?'

'I'd think so, but it won't amount to much. There's welfare.'

'Oh, she couldn't,' said Ellen.

'You wait. Pride is something she won't be able to afford. Now there won't even be the fish any more.'

'Is there anything we can do?'

'Personally? I don't see how. We're not exactly in fat city ourselves. But there may be something the town can do. I'll talk to Vaughan about it.'

'Have you made any progress?'

'You mean about catching that damn thing? No. Meadows called that oceanographer friend of his down from Woods Hole, so he's here. Not that I see what good he's going to do.'

'What's he like?'

'He's all right, I guess. He's young, a decent-looking guy. He's a bit of a know-it-all, but that's not surprising. He seems to know the area pretty well.'

'Oh? How so?'

'He said he was a summer kid in Southampton. Spent all his summers there.'

'Working?'

'I don't know, living with the parents probably. He looks to be the type.'

'What type?'

'Rich. Good family. The Southampton summer type. You ought to know it, for God's sake.'

'Don't get angry. I was just asking.'

'I'm not angry. I just said you ought to know the type, that's all. I mean you're the type yourself.'

Ellen smiled. 'I used to be. But now I'm just an old lady.'

'That's a crock,' Brody said. 'Nine out of ten of the summer broads in this town can't do what you can for a bathing suit.' He was happy to see her fishing for compliments, and happy to give them to her. This was one of their ritual preludes to sex, and the sight of Ellen in bed made Brody yearn for sex. Her hair hung down to her shoulders on both sides of her head, then tucked inward in a curl. Her night-gown was cut so deeply in front that both her breasts were visible, all but the nipples, and was so diaphanous that Brody was sure he could actually see the dark flesh of the nipples. 'I'm going to brush my teeth,' he said. 'I'll be right back.'

When he returned from the bathroom, he was tumescent. He walked to the dresser to turn out the light.

'You know,' Ellen said, 'I think we should give the boys tennis lessons.'

'What for? Have they said they want to play tennis?'

'No. Not in so many words. But it's a good sport for them to know. It will help them when they're grown-up. It's an entrée.'

'To what?'

'To the people they should know. If you play tennis well, you can walk into a club anywhere and get to know people. Now's the time they should be learning.'

'Where are they going to get lessons?'

'I was thinking of the Field Club.'

'As far as I know, we're not members of the Field Club.'

'I think we could get in. I still know a few people who are members. If I asked them, I'll bet they'd propose us.'

'Forget it.'

'Why?'

'Number one, we can't afford it. I bet it costs a thousand bucks to join, and then it's at least a few hundred a year. We haven't got that kind of money.'

'We have savings.'

'Not for tennis lessons, for Christ sake! Come on, let's drop it.' He reached for the light.

'It would be good for the boys.'

Brody let his hand fall to the top of the dresser. 'Look, we're not tennis people. We wouldn't feel right there. *I* wouldn't feel right there. They don't want us there.'

'How do you know? We've never tried.'

'Just forget it.' He switched off the light, walked over to the bed, pulled back the covers, and slid in beside Ellen. 'Besides,' he said, nuzzling her neck, 'there's another sport I'm better at.'

'The boys are awake.'

'They're watching television. They wouldn't know it if a bomb went off up here.' He kissed her neck and began to rub his hand in circles on her stomach, moving higher with each rotation.

Ellen yawned. 'I'm so sleepy,' she said. 'I took a pill before you came home.'

Brody stopped rubbing. 'What the hell for?'

'I didn't sleep well last night, and I didn't want to wake up if you came home late. So I took a pill.'

'I'm going to throw those goddamn pills away.' He kissed her cheek, then tried to kiss her mouth but caught her in mid-yawn.

'I'm sorry,' she said. 'I'm afraid it won't work.'

'It'll work. All you have to do is help a little.'

'I'm so tired. But you go ahead if you want. I'll try to stay awake.'

'Shit,' said Brody. He rolled back to his side of the bed. 'I'm not very big on screwing corpses.'

'That was uncalled-for.'

Brody didn't reply. He lay on his back, staring at the ceiling and feeling his erection dwindle. But the pressure inside him was still there, a dull ache in his groin.

A moment later, Ellen said, 'What's Harry Meadows' friend's name?'

'Hooper.'

'Not David Hooper.'

'No. I think his name is Matt.'

'Oh. I went out with a David Hooper a long, long time ago. I remember . . .' Before she could finish the sentence, her eyes shut, and soon she slipped into the deep breathing of sleep.

A few blocks away, in a small clapboard house, a black man sat at the foot of his son's bed. 'What story do you want to read?' he said.

'I don't want to read a story,' said the boy, who was seven. 'I want to *tell* a story.'

'Okay. What'll we tell one about?'

'A shark. Let's tell one about a shark.'

The man winced. 'No. Let's tell one about . . . a bear.'

'No, a shark. I want to know about sharks.'

'You mean a once-upon-a-time story?'

'Sure. Like, you know, once upon a time there was a shark that ate people.'

'That's not a very nice story.'

'Why do sharks eat people?'

'I guess they get hungry. I don't know.'

'Do you bleed if a shark eats you?'

'Yes,' said the man. 'Come on. Let's tell a story about another kind of animal. You'll have nightmares if we tell about a shark.'

'No, I won't. If a shark tried to eat me, I'd punch him in the nose.'

'No shark is going to try to eat you.'

'Why not? If I go swimming I bet one would. Don't sharks eat black people?'

'Now stop it! I don't want to hear any more about sharks.' The man lifted a pile of books from the bedside table. 'Here. Let's read *Peter Pan*.'

Part 2

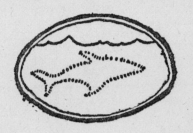

SIX

On her way home Friday noon, after a morning of volunteer work at the Southampton Hospital, Ellen stopped at the post office to buy a roll of stamps and get the mail. There was no home mail delivery in Amity. In theory, only special delivery mail was brought to the door – any door within a mile radius of the post office; in fact, even special delivery mail (except that clearly labelled as sent by the Federal Government) was kept at the post office until someone called for it.

The post office was a small, square building on Teal Street, just off Main. It had 500 mailboxes, 340 of which were rented to Amity's permanent residents. The other 160 were allotted to summer people, according to the whims of the post-mistress, Minnie Eldridge. Those people she liked were permitted to rent boxes for the summer. Those she didn't like had to wait in line at the counter. Since she refused to rent a box to any summer person on a year-round basis, summer people never knew from one year to the next whether or not they would have a mailbox when they arrived in June.

It was generally assumed that Minnie Eldridge was in her early seventies, and that she had somehow convinced the authorities in Washington that she was well under compulsory retirement age. She was small and frail-looking, but deceptively strong, able to hustle packages and cartons nearly as quickly as the two young men who worked in the post office with her. She never spoke about her past or her private life. The only common knowledge about her was that she had been born in Nantucket Island and had left sometime soon after World War I. She had been in Amity for as long as anyone living could remember, and she considered herself not only a native, but also the resident expert on the history of the town. She needed no prodding at all to embark on a discourse about Amity's eponym, a seventeenth-century woman named Amity Hopewell who had been convicted of witchcraft, and she took pleasure in reciting the list of major events in the town's past: the landing of some British troops during the Revolution in an ill-fated attempt to outflank a Colonial force (the Britons lost their way and wandered aimlessly back and forth across Long Island); the fire in 1823 that destroyed every building except the town's only church; the wreck of a rum-running ship in 1921 (the ship was eventually refloated, but by then all the cargo off-loaded to make the ship lighter had vanished); the hurricane of 1938, and the widely reported (though never fully ascertained) landing of three German spies on the Scotch Road beach in 1942.

Ellen and Minnie made each other nervous. Ellen sensed that Minnie didn't like her, and she was right. Minnie felt uneasy with Ellen because she couldn't catalogue her. Ellen was neither summer folk nor winter folk. She hadn't earned her year-round mailbox, she had married it.

Minnie was alone in the post office, sorting mail, when Ellen arrived.

'Morning, Minnie,' Ellen said.

Minnie looked up at the clock over the counter and said, 'Afternoon.'

'Could I have a roll of eights, please?' Ellen put a five-dollar bill and three ones on the counter.

Minnie pushed a few more letters into boxes, set down her bundle, and walked to the counter. She gave Ellen a roll of stamps and dropped the bills into a drawer. 'What's Martin think he's going to do about that shark?' she said.

'I don't know. I guess they'll try to catch it.'

'Canst thou draw out leviathan with a hook?'

'I beg your pardon?'

'Book of Job,' said Minnie. 'No mortal man's going to catch that fish.'

'Why do you say that?'

'We're not meant to catch it, that's why. We're being readied.'

'For what?'

'We'll know when the time comes.'

'I see,' Ellen put the stamps in her purse. 'Well, maybe you're right. Thanks, Minnie.' She turned and walked towards the door.

'There'll be no mistaking it,' Minnie said to Ellen's back.

Ellen walked to Main Street and turned right, past a boutique and an antique shop. She stopped at Amity Hardware and went inside. There was no immediate response to the tinkle of the bell that the door struck as she opened it. She waited for a few seconds, then called, 'Albert?'

She walked to the back of the store, to an open door that led to the basement. She heard two men talking below.

'I'll be right up,' called the voice of Albert Morris. 'Here's a whole box of them,' Morris said to the other man. 'Look through and see if you find what you want.'

Morris came to the bottom of the stairs and started up – slowly and deliberately, one step at a time, holding on to the banister. He was in his early sixties, and he had had a heart attack two years earlier.

'Cleats,' he said when he reached the top of the stairs.

'What?' said Ellen.

'Cleats. Fella wants cleats for a boat. Size he's looking for, he must be the captain of a battleship. Anyway, what can I do for you?'

'The rubber nozzle in my kitchen sink is all cracked. You know, the kind with the switch for spraying. I want to get a new one.'

'No problem. They're up this way.' Morris led Ellen to a

cabinet in the middle of the store. 'This what you had in mind?' He held up a rubber nozzle.

'Perfect.'

'Eighty cents. Charge or cash?'

'I'll pay you for it. I don't want you to have to write up a slip just for eighty cents.'

'Written 'em a lot smaller 'n that,' said Morris. 'I could tell you stories that'd set your ears to ringing.'

They walked across the narrow store to the cash register, and as he rang up the sale on the register, Morris said, 'Lots of people upset about this shark thing.'

'I know. You can't blame them.'

'They think the beaches oughta be opened up again.'

'Well, I . . .'

'You ask me, I think they're full of – pardon the expression – bull. I think Martin's doing right.'

'I'm glad to know that, Albert.'

'Maybe this new fella can help us out.'

'Who's that?'

'This fish expert from up Massachusetts.'

'Oh, yes. I heard he was in town.'

'He's right here.'

Ellen looked around and saw no one. 'What do you mean?'

'Down cellar. He's the one wants the cleats.'

Just then, Ellen heard footsteps on the stairs. She turned and saw Hooper coming through the door, and she suddenly felt a surge of girlish nervousness, as if she were seeing a beau she hadn't seen in years. The man was a stranger, yet there was something familiar about him.

'I found them,' said Hooper, holding up two large stainless-steel cleats. He walked over to the counter, smiled politely at Ellen, and said to Morris, 'These'll do fine.' He put the cleats on the counter and handed Morris a twenty-dollar bill.

Ellen looked at Hooper, trying to define her reminiscence. She hoped Albert Morris would introduce them, but he seemed to have no intention of doing so. 'Excuse me,' she said to Hooper, 'but I have to ask you something.'

Hooper looked at her and smiled again – a pleasant, friendly smile that softened the sharpness of his features and made his light blue eyes shine. 'Sure,' he said. 'Ask away.'

'You aren't by any chance related to David Hooper, are you?'

'He's my older brother. Do you know David?'

'Yes,' said Ellen. 'Or rather, I used to. I went out with him a long time ago. I'm Ellen Brody. I used to be Ellen Shepherd. Back then, I mean.'

'Oh, sure. I remember you.'

'You don't.'

'I do. No kidding. I'll prove it to you. Let me see . . . You wore your hair shorter then, sort of a pageboy. You always wore a charm bracelet. I remember that because it had a big charm that looked like the Eiffel Tower. And you always used to sing that song – what was it called? – "Shiboom," or something like that. Right?'

Ellen laughed. 'My heavens, you have quite a memory. I'd forgotten that song.'

'It's screwy the things that impress kids. You went out with David for what – two years?'

'Two summers,' Ellen said. 'They were fun. I hadn't thought about them much in the past few years.'

'Do you remember me?'

'Vaguely. I'm not sure. I remember David had a younger brother. You must have been about nine or ten then.'

'About that; David's ten years older than I am. Another thing I remember: Everybody called me Matt. I thought it sounded grown-up. But you called me Matthew. You said it sounded more dignified. I was probably in love with you.'

'Oh?' Ellen reddened, and Albert Morris laughed.

'At one time or another,' said Hooper, 'I fell in love with all the girls David went out with.'

'Oh.'

Morris handed Hooper his change, and Hooper said to Ellen, 'I'm going down to the dock. Can I drop you anywhere?'

'Thank you. I have a car.' She thanked Morris, and, with Hooper behind her, walked out of the store. 'So now you're a scientist,' she said when they were outside.

'Kind of by accident. I started out as an English major. But then I took a course in marine biology to satisfy my science requirement, and – bingo! – I was hooked.'

'On what? The ocean?'

'No. I mean, yes and no. I was always crazy about the ocean. When I was twelve or thirteen, my idea of a big time was to take a sleeping-bag down to the beach and spend the night lying in the sand listening to the waves, wondering where they had come from and what fantastic things they had passed on the way. What I got hooked on in college was fish, or, to be really specific, sharks.'

Ellen laughed. 'What an awful thing to fall in love with. It's like having a passion for rats.'

'That's what most people think,' said Hooper. 'But they're wrong. Sharks have everything a scientist dreams of. They're beautiful – God, how beautiful they are! They're like an impossibly perfect piece of machinery. They're as graceful as any bird. They're as mysterious as any animal on earth. No one knows for sure how long they live or what impulses – except for hunger – they respond to. There are more than two hundred and fifty species of shark, and every one is different from every other one. Scientists spend their lives trying to find answers about sharks, and as soon as they come up with a nice, pat generalization, something shoots it down. People have been trying to find an effective shark repellant for over two thousand years. They've never found one that really works. He stopped, looked at Ellen, and smiled. 'I'm sorry. I don't mean to lecture. As you can see, I'm an addict.'

'And as *you* can see,' said Ellen, 'I don't know what I'm talking about. I imagine you went to Yale.'

'Of course. Where else? For four generations, the only male in our family who didn't go to Yale was an uncle of mine who got thrown out of Andover and ended up at Miami or Ohio. After Yale, I went to graduate school at the University of Florida. And after that, I spent a couple of years chasing sharks around the world.'

'That must have been interesting.'

'For me it was paradise. It was like giving an alcoholic the keys to a distillery. I tagged sharks in the Red Sea and dived with them off Australia. The more I learned about them, the more I knew I didn't know.'

'You dived with them?'

Hooper nodded. 'In a cage mostly, but sometimes not. I know what you must think. A lot of people think I've got a death wish – my mother in particular. But if you know what you're doing, you can reduce the danger to almost nil.'

'You must be the world's greatest living shark expert.'

'Hardly,' Hooper said with a laugh. 'But I'm trying. The one trip I missed out on, the one I would have given anything to go on, was Peter Gimbel's trip. It was made into a movie. I dream about that trip. They were in the water with two great whites, the same kind of shark that's here now.'

'I'm just as glad you didn't go on that trip,' said Ellen. 'You probably would have tried to see what the view was like from inside one of the sharks. But tell me about David. How is he?'

'He's okay, all things considered. He's a broker in San Francisco.'

'What do you mean, "all things considered"?'

'Well, he's on his second wife. His first wife was – maybe you know this – Patty Fremont.'

'Sure. I used to play tennis with her. She sort of inherited David from me. That's a nice way of putting it.'

'That lasted three years, until she latched on to someone with a family business and a house in Antibes. So David went and found himself a girl whose father is the majority stockholder in an oil company. She's nice enough, but she's got the IQ of an artichoke. If David had any sense, he would have known when he had it good and he would have held on to you.'

Ellen blushed and said softly, 'You're nice to say it.'

'I'm serious. That's what I'd have done if I'd been him.'

'What did you do? What lucky girl finally got you?'

'None, so far. I guess there are girls around who just don't know how lucky they could be.' Hooper laughed. 'Tell me about yourself. No, don't. Let me guess. Three children. Right?'

'Right. I didn't realize it showed that much.'

'No, no. I don't mean that. It doesn't show at all. Not at all. Your husband is – let's see – a lawyer. You have an apartment in town and a house on the beach in Amity. You couldn't be happier. And that's exactly what I'd wish for you.'

Ellen shook her head, smiling. 'Not quite. I don't mean the happiness part, the rest. My husband is the police chief in Amity.'

Hooper let the surprise show in his eyes for only an instant. Then he smacked himself on the forehead and said, 'What a dummy I am! Of course. Brody. I never made the connection. That's great. I met your husband last night. He seems like quite a guy.'

Ellen thought she detected a flicker of irony in Hooper's voice, but then she told herself, Don't be stupid – you're making things up. 'How long will you be here?' she said.

'I don't know. That depends on what happens with this fish. As soon as he leaves, I'll leave.'

'Do you live in Woods Hole?'

'No, but not far away. In Hyannisport. I have a little house on the water. I have a thing about being near the water. If I get more than ten miles inland, I begin to feel claustrophobic.'

'You live all alone?'

'All alone. It's just me and about a hundred million dollars' worth of stereo equipment and a million books. Hey, do you still dance?'

'Dance?'

'Yeah. I just remembered. One of the things David used to say was that you were the best dancer he ever went out with. You won a contest, didn't you?'

The past – like a bird long locked in a cage and suddenly released – was flying at her, swirling around her head, showering her with longing. 'A samba contest,' she said. 'At the Beach Club. I'd forgotten. No, I don't dance any more. Martin doesn't dance, and even if he did, I don't think anyone plays that kind of music any more.'

'That's too bad, David said you were terrific.'

'That was a wonderful night,' Ellen said, letting her mind float back, picking out the tiny memories. 'It was a Lester Lanin band. The Beach Club was covered with crêpe paper and balloons. David wore his favourite jacket – red silk.'

'I have it now,' said Hooper. 'I inherited *that* from *him*.'

'They played all those wonderful songs. "Mountain Greenery" was one. He could two-step so well. I could barely keep up with him. The only thing he wouldn't do was waltz. He said waltzes made him dizzy. Everybody was so tanned. I don't think there was any rain all summer long. I remember I chose a yellow dress for that night because it went with my tan. There were two contests, a Charleston that Susie Kendall and Chip Fogarty won. And the samba contest. They played "Brazil" in the finals, and we danced as if our lives depended on it. Bending sideways and backward like crazy people. I thought I was going to collapse when it was over. You know what we won for first prize? A canned chicken. I kept it in my room until it got so old it began to swell and Daddy made me throw it away.' Ellen smiled. 'Those were fun times. I try not to think about them too much.'

'Why?'

'The past always seems better when you look back on it than it did at the time. And the present never looks as good as it will in the future. It's depressing if you spend too much time reliving old joys. You think you'll never have anything as good again.'

'It's easy for me to keep my mind off the past.'

'Really? Why?'

'It just wasn't too great, that's all. David was the first-born. I was pretty much of an afterthought. I think my purpose in life was to keep the parents' marriage together. And I failed. That's pretty crummy when you fail at the first thing you're supposed to accomplish. David was twenty when the parents got divorced. I wasn't even eleven. And the divorce wasn't exactly amiable. The few years before it weren't too amiable, either. It's the old story – nothing special – but it wasn't a lot of fun. I probably make too much of it. Anyway, I look forward to a lot of things. I don't look back a lot.'

'I suppose that's healthier.'

'I don't know. Maybe if I had a terrific past, I'd spend all my time living in it. But ... enough of that. I should get down to the dock. You're sure I can't drop you anywhere.'

'Positive, thank you. My car's just across the street.'

'Okay. Well ...' Hooper held out his hand. 'It's been really great to see you again, and I hope I'll see you before I go.'

'I'd like that,' said Ellen, shaking his hand.

'I don't suppose I could get you out on a tennis court late some afternoon.'

Ellen laughed. 'Oh my. I haven't held a tennis racket in my hand since I can't remember when. But thanks for asking.'

'Okay. Well, see you.' Hooper turned and trotted the few yards down the block to his car, a green Ford Pinto.

Ellen stood and watched as Hooper started the car,

manoeuvred out of the parking space, and pulled out into the street. As he drove past her, she raised her hand to her shoulder and waved, tentatively, shyly. Hooper stuck his left hand out of the car window and waved. Then he turned the corner and was gone.

A terrible, painful sadness clutched at Ellen. More than ever before, she felt that her life – the best part of it, at least, the part that was fresh and fun – was behind her. Recognizing the sensation made her feel guilty, for she read it as proof that she was an unsatisfactory mother, an unsatisfied wife. She hated her life, and hated herself for hating it. She thought of a line from a song Billy played on the stereo: 'I'd trade all my tomorrows for a single yesterday.' Would she make a deal like that? She wondered. But what good was there in wondering? Yesterdays were gone, spinning ever farther away down a shaft that had no bottom. None of the richness, none of the delight, could ever be retrieved.

A vision of Hooper's smiling face flashed across her mind. Forget it, she told herself. That's stupid. Worse. It's self-defeating.

She walked across the street and climbed into her car. As she pulled out into the traffic, she saw Larry Vaughan standing on the corner. God, she thought, he looks as sad as I feel.

SEVEN

The week-end was as quiet as the week-ends in the late fall. With the beaches closed, and with the police patrolling them during the daylight hours, Amity was practically deserted. Hooper cruised up and down the shore in Ben Gardner's boat, but the only signs of life he saw in the water were a few schools of baitfish and one small school of bluefish. By Sunday night, after spending the day off East Hampton – the beaches there were crowded, and he thought there might be a chance the shark would appear where people were swimming – he told Brody he was ready to conclude that the fish had gone back to the deep.

'What makes you think so?' Brody had asked.

'There's not a sign of him,' said Hooper. 'And there are other fish around. If there was a big white in the neighbourhood, everything else would vanish. That's one of the things divers say about whites. When they're around, there's an awful stillness in the water.'

'I'm not convinced,' said Brody. 'At least not enough to open the beaches. Not yet.' He knew that after an uneventful week-end there would be pressure – from Vaughan, from other real-estate agents, from merchants – to open the beaches. He almost wished Hooper had seen the fish. That would have been a certainty. Now there was nothing but negative evidence, and to his policeman's mind that was not enough.

On Monday afternoon, Brody was sitting in his office when Bixby announced a phone call from Ellen.

'I'm sorry to bother you,' she said, 'but I wanted to check something with you. What would you think about giving a dinner-party?'

'What for?'

'Just to have a dinner-party. We haven't had one in years. I can't even remember when our last one was.'

'No,' said Brody. 'Neither can I.' But it was a lie. He remembered all too well their last dinner-party: three years ago, when Ellen was in the midst of her crusade to re-establish her ties with the summer community. She had asked three summer couples. They were nice enough people, Brody recalled, but the conversations had been stiff, forced, and uncomfortable. Brody and his guests had searched each other for any common interest or experience, and they had failed. So after a while, the guests had fallen back on talking among themselves, self-consciously polite about including Ellen whenever she said something like, 'Oh, I remember him!' She had been nervous and flighty, and after the guests had left, after she had done the dishes and said twice to Brody, '*Wasn't* that a nice evening!' she had shut herself in the bathroom and wept.

'Well, what do you think?' said Ellen.

'I don't know. I guess it's all right, if you want to do it.' Who are you going to invite?'

'First of all, I think we should have Matt Hooper.'

'What for? He eats over at the Abelard, doesn't he? It's all included in the price of the room.'

'That's not the point, Martin. You know that. He's alone in town, and besides, he's very nice.'

'How do you know? I didn't think you knew him.'

'Didn't I tell you? I ran into him in Albert Morris's on Friday. I'm *sure* I mentioned it to you.'

'No, but never mind. It doesn't make any difference.'

'It turns out he's the brother of the Hooper I used to know. He remembered a lot more about me than I did about him. But he *is* a lot younger.'

'Uh-huh. When are you planning this shindig for?'

'I was thinking about tomorrow night. And it's not going

to be a shindig. I simply thought we could have a nice, small party with a few couples. Maybe six or eight people altogether.'

'Do you think you can get people to come on that short notice?'

'Oh, yes. Nobody does anything during the week. There are a few bridge parties, but that's about all.'

'Oh,' said Brody. 'You mean summer people.'

'That's what I had in mind. Matt would certainly feel at ease with them. What about the Baxters? Would they be fun?'

'I don't think I know them.'

'Yes, you do, silly. Clem and Cici Baxter. She was Cici Davenport. They live out on Scotch. He's taking some vacation now. I know because I saw him on the street this morning.'

'Okay. Try them if you want.'

'Who else?'

'Somebody I can talk to. How about the Meadows?'

'But he already knows Harry.'

'He doesn't know Dorothy. She's chatty enough.'

'All right,' said Ellen. 'I guess a little local colour won't hurt. And Harry does know everything that goes on around here.'

'I wasn't thinking about local colour,' Brody said sharply. 'They're our friends.'

'I know. I didn't mean anything.'

'If you want local colour, all you have to do is look in the other side of your bed.'

'I *know*. I said I was sorry.'

'What about a girl?' said Brody. 'I think you should try to find some nice young thing for Hooper.'

There was a pause before Ellen said, 'If you think so.'

'I don't really care. I just thought he might enjoy himself more if he had someone his own age to talk to.'

'He's not *that* young, Martin. And we're not *that* old. But all right. I'll see if I can think of somebody who'd be fun for him.'

'I'll see you later,' Brody said, and he hung up the phone. He was depressed, for he saw something ominous in this dinner party. He couldn't be sure, but he believed – and the more he thought about it, the stronger the belief became – that Ellen was launching another campaign to re-enter the world he had taken her from, and this time she had a lever with which to jimmy her way in: Hooper.

The next evening, Brody arrived home a little after five. Ellen was setting the dinner-table in the dining-room. Brody kissed her on the cheek and said, 'Boy, it's been a long time since I've seen that silver.' It was Ellen's wedding silver, a gift from her parents.

'I know. It took me hours to polish it.'

'And will you look at this?' Brody picked up a tulip wine glass. 'Where did you get these?'

'I bought them at the Lure.'

'How much?' Brody set the glass down on the table.

'Not much,' she said, folding a napkin and placing it neatly beneath a dinner fork and salad fork.

'How much?'

'Twenty dollars. But that was for a whole dozen.'

'You don't kid around when you throw a party.'

'We didn't have any decent wine glasses,' she said defensively. 'The last of our old ones broke months ago, when Sean tipped over the sideboard.'

Brody counted the places set around the table. 'Only six?' he said. 'What happened?'

'The Baxters couldn't make it. Cici called. Clem had to go into town on some business, and she thought she'd go with him. They're spending the night.' There was a fragile lilt to her voice, a false insouciance.

'Oh,' said Brody. 'Too bad.' He dared not show that he was pleased. 'Who'd you get for Hooper, some nice young chick?'

'Daisy Wicker. She works for Gibby at the Bibelot. She's a nice girl.'

'What time are people coming?'

'The Meadows and Daisy at seven-thirty. I asked Matthew for seven.'

'I thought his name was Matt.'

'Oh, that's just an old joke he reminded me of. Apparently, I used to call him Matthew when he was young. The reason I wanted him to come early was so the kids would have a chance to get to know him. I think they'll be fascinated.'

Brody looked at his watch. 'If people aren't coming till seven-thirty, that means we won't be eating till eight-thirty or nine. I'll probably starve to death before then. I think I'll grab a sandwich.' He started for the kitchen.

'Don't stuff yourself,' said Ellen. 'I've got a delicious dinner coming.'

Brody sniffed the kitchen aromas, eyed the clutter of pots and packages, and said, 'What are you cooking?'

'It's called butterfly lamb,' she said. 'I hope I don't do something stupid and botch it.'

'Smells good,' said Brody. 'What's this stuff by the sink? Should I throw it out and wash the pot?'

From the living-room Ellen said, 'What stuff?'

'The stuff in the pot.'

'What – omigod!' she said, and she hurried into the kitchen. 'Don't you dare throw it out.' She saw the smile on Brody's face. 'Oh, you rat.' She slapped him on the rear. 'That's gazpacho. Soup.'

'Are you sure it's still okay?' he teased. 'It looks all slimy.'

'That's what it's supposed to look like, you clot.'

Brody shook his head. 'Old Hooper's going to wish he ate at the Abelard.'

'You're a beast,' she said. 'Wait till you taste it. You'll change your tune.'

'Maybe. If I live long enough.' He laughed and went to the

refrigerator. He rummaged around and found some bologna and cheese for a sandwich. He opened a beer and started for the living-room. 'I think I'll watch the news for a while and then go shower and change,' he said.

'I put clean clothes out for you on the bed. You might shave, too. You have a hideous five o'clock shadow.'

'Good God, who's coming to dinner – Prince Philip and Jackie Onassis?'

'I just want you to look nice, that's all.'

At 7.05, the door bell rang, and Brody answered it. He was wearing a blue madras shirt, blue uniform slacks, and black cordovans. He felt crisp and clean. Spiffy, Ellen had said. But when he opened the door for Hooper, he felt, if not rumpled, at least outclassed. Hooper wore bell-bottom blue-jeans, Weejun loafers with no socks, and a red Lacoste shirt with an alligator on the breast. It was the uniform of the young and rich in Amity.

'Hi,' said Brody. 'Come in.'

'Hi,' said Hooper. He extended his hand, and Brody shook it.

Ellen came out of the kitchen. She was wearing a long batik skirt, slippers, and a blue silk blouse. She wore the string of cultured pearls Brody had given her as a wedding present. 'Matthew,' she said. 'I'm glad you could come.'

'I'm glad you asked me,' Hooper said, shaking Ellen's hand. 'I'm sorry I don't look more respectable, but I didn't bring anything down with me but working clothes. All I can say for them is that they're clean.'

'Don't be silly,' said Ellen. 'You look wonderful. The red goes beautifully with your tan and your hair.'

Hooper laughed. He turned and said to Brody, 'Do you mind if I give Ellen something?'

'What do you mean?' Brody said. He thought to himself, give her what? A kiss? A box of chocolates? A punch in the nose?

'A present. It's nothing, really. Just something I picked up.'

'No, I don't mind,' said Brody, still perplexed that the question should have been asked.

Hooper dug into the pocket of his jeans and pulled out a small package wrapped in tissue. He handed it to Ellen. 'For the hostess,' he said, 'to make up for my grubby clothes.'

Ellen tittered and carefully unwrapped the paper. Inside was what seemed to be a charm, or perhaps a necklace pendant, an inch or so across. 'It's lovely,' she said. 'What is it?'

'It's a shark tooth,' said Hooper. 'A tiger-shark tooth, to be more specific. The casing's silver.'

'Where did you get it?'

'In Macao. I passed through there a couple of years ago on a project. There was a little back-street store, where an even littler Chinese man spent his whole life polishing shark teeth and moulding the silver caps to hold the rings. I couldn't resist them.'

'Macao,' said Ellen. 'I don't think I could place Macao on a map if I had to. It must have been fascinating.'

Brody said, 'It's near Hong Kong.'

'Right,' said Hooper. 'In any event, there's supposed to be a superstition about these things, that if you keep it with you you'll be safe from shark bite. Under the present circumstances, I thought it would be appropriate.'

'Completely,' said Ellen. 'Do you have one?'

'I have one,' said Hooper, 'but I don't know how to carry it. I don't like to wear things around my neck, and if you carry a shark tooth in your pants pocket, I've found you run two real risks. One is that you'll get stabbed in the leg, and the other is that you'll end up with a gash in your pants. It's like carrying an open-blade knife around in your pocket. So in my case, practicality takes precedence over superstition, at least while I'm on dry land.'

Ellen laughed and said to Brody, 'Martin, could I ask a favour? Would you run upstairs and get that thin silver chain out of my jewellery box? I'll put Matthew's shark tooth on right now.' She turned to Hooper and said, 'You never know when you might meet a shark at dinner.'

Brody started up the stairs, and Ellen said, 'Oh, and Martin, tell the boys to come down.'

As he rounded the corner at the top of the stairs, Brody heard Ellen say, 'It *is* such fun to see you again.'

Brody walked into the bedroom and sat down on the edge of the bed. He took a deep breath and clenched and unclenched his right fist. He was fighting anger and confusion, and he was losing. He felt threatened, as if an intruder had come into his home, possessing subtle, intangible weapons he could not cope with: looks and youth and sophistication and, above all, a communion with Ellen born in a time which, Brody knew, Ellen wished had never ended. Where previously he had felt Ellen was trying to use Hooper to impress other summer people, now he felt she was trying to impress Hooper herself. He didn't know why. Maybe he was wrong. After all, Ellen and Hooper had known each other long ago. Perhaps he was making too much of two friends simply trying to get to know one another again. Friends? Christ, Hooper had to be ten years younger than Ellen, or almost. What kind of friends could they have been? Acquaintances. Barely. So why was she putting on her supersophisticated act? It demeaned her, Brody thought; and it demeaned Brody that she should try, by posturing, to deny her life with him.

'Fuck it,' he said aloud. He stood up, opened a dresser drawer, and rooted through it until he found Ellen's jewellery box. He took out the silver chain, closed the drawer, and walked into the hall. He poked his head into the boys' rooms and said, 'Let's go, troops,' and then he walked downstairs.

Ellen and Hooper were sitting at opposite ends of the couch, and as Brody walked into the living-room, he heard Ellen say, 'Would you rather that I not call you Matthew?'

Hooper laughed and said, 'I don't mind. It does sort of bring back memories, and despite what I said the other day, there's nothing wrong with that.'

The other day? Brody thought. In the hardware store? That must have been some conversation. 'Here,' he said to Ellen, handing her the chain.

'Thank you,' she said. She unclasped the pearls and tossed them on to the coffee table. 'Now, Matthew, show me how this should go.' Brody picked the string of pearls off the table and put them in his pocket.

The boys came downstairs single file, all dressed neatly in sports shirts and slacks. Ellen snapped the silver chain around her neck, smiled at Hooper, and said, 'Come here, boys. Come meet Mr Hooper. This is Billy Brody. Billy's fourteen.' Billy shook hands with Hooper. 'And this is Martin Junior. He's twelve. And this is Sean. He's nine ... almost nine. Mr Hooper is an oceanographer.'

'An Ichthyologist, actually,' said Hooper.

'What's that?' said Martin Junior.

'A zoologist who specializes in fish life.'

'What's a zoologist?' asked Sean.

'I know that,' said Billy. 'That's a guy who studies animals.'

'Right,' said Hooper. 'Good for you.'

'Are you going to catch the shark?' asked Martin.

'I'm going to try to find him,' said Hooper. 'But I don't know. He may have gone away already.'

'Have you ever caught a shark?'

'Yes, but not one as big as this.'

Sean said, 'Do sharks lay eggs?'

'That young man,' said Hooper, 'is a good question, and a very complicated one. Not like a chicken, if that's what you mean. But yes, some sharks do have eggs.'

Ellen said, 'Give Mr Hooper a chance, boys.' She turned to Brody. 'Martin, could you make us a drink?'

'Sure,' said Brody. 'What'll it be?'

'A gin and tonic would be fine for me,' said Hooper. 'What about you, Ellen?'

'Let's see. What would be good. I think I'll just have some vermouth on the rocks.'

'Hey, Mom,' said Billy, 'what's that around your neck?'

'A shark tooth, dear. Mr Hooper gave it to me.'

'Hey, that's really cool. Can I look?'

Brody went into the kitchen. The liquor was kept in a cabinet over the sink. The door was stuck. He tugged at the metal handle, and it came off in his hand. Without thinking, he pegged it into the garbage pail. From a drawer he took a screwdriver and pried open the cabinet door. Vermouth. What the hell was the colour of the bottle? Nobody ever drank vermouth on the rocks. Ellen's drink when she drank, and that was rarely, was rye and ginger. Green. There it was, way in the back. Brody grabbed the bottle, twisted off the cap, and sniffed. It smelled like one of those cheap, fruity wines the winos bought for sixty-nine a pint.

Brody made the two drinks, then fashioned a rye and ginger for himself. By habit, he began to measure the rye with a shot glass, but then he changed his mind and poured until the glass was a third full. He topped it off with ginger ale, dropped in a few ice cubes, and reached for the two other glasses. The only convenient way to carry them in one hand was to grip one with the thumb and last three fingers of his hand and then support the other against the first by sticking his index finger down the inside of the glass. He took a slug of his own drink and went back into the living-room.

Billy and Martin had crowded on to the couch with Ellen and Hooper. Sean was sitting on the floor. Brody heard Hooper say something about a pig, and Martin said, 'Wow!'

'Here,' said Brody, handing the forward glass – the one with his finger in it – to Ellen.

'No tip for you, my man,' she said. 'It's a good thing you decided against a career as a waiter.'

Brody looked at her, considered a series of rude remarks, and settled for, 'Forgive me, Duchess.' He handed the other glass to Hooper and said, 'I guess this is what you had in mind.'

'That's great. Thanks.'

'Matt was just telling us about a shark he caught,' said Ellen. 'It had almost a whole pig in it.'

'No kidding,' said Brody, sitting in a chair opposite the couch.

'And that's not all, Dad,' said Martin. 'There was a roll of tar paper, too.'

'And a human bone,' said Sean.

'I said it looked like a human bone,' said Hooper. 'There was no way to be sure at the time. It might have been a beef rib.'

Brody said, 'I thought you scientists could tell those things right on the spot.'

'Not always,' said Hooper. 'Especially when it's only a piece of a bone like a rib.'

Brody took a long swallow of his drink and said, 'Oh.'

'Hey, Dad,' said Billy. 'You know how a porpoise kills a shark?'

'With a gun?'

'No, man. It butts him to death. That's what Mr Hooper says.'

'Terrific,' said Brody, and he drained his glass. 'I'm going to have another drink. Anybody else ready?'

'On a week night?' said Ellen. 'My.'

'Why not? It's not every night we throw a no-kidding, go-to-hell dinner-party.' Brody started for the kitchen but was stopped by the ringing of the doorbell. He opened the door and saw Dorothy Meadows, short and slight, dressed, as usual, in a dark blue dress and a single strand of pearls.

Behind her was a girl Brody assumed was Daisy Wicker – a tall, slim girl with long, straight hair. She wore slacks and sandals and no makeup. Behind her was the unmistakable bulk of Harry Meadows.

'Hello, there,' said Brody. 'Come on in.'

'Good evening, Martin,' said Dorothy Meadows. 'We met Miss Wicker as we came into the driveway.'

'I walked,' said Daisy Wicker. 'It was nice.'

'Good, good. Come on in. I'm Martin Brody.'

'I know. I've seen you driving your car. You must have an interesting job.'

Brody laughed, 'I'd tell you all about it, except it would probably put you to sleep.'

Brody led them into the living-room and turned them over to Ellen for introduction to Hooper. He took orders – Bourbon on the rocks for Harry, club soda with a twist of lemon for Dorothy, and a gin and tonic for Daisy Wicker. But before he fixed their drinks, he made a fresh one for himself, and he sipped it as he prepared the others. By the time he was ready to return to the living-room, he had finished about half his drink, so he poured in a generous splash of rye and a dash more ginger ale.

He took Dorothy's and Daisy's drinks first, and returned to the kitchen for Meadows' and his own. He was taking one last swallow before rejoining the company, when Ellen came into the kitchen.

'Don't you think you better slow down?' she said.

'I'm fine,' he said. 'Don't worry about me.'

'You're not being exactly gracious.'

'I'm not? I thought I was being charming.'

'Hardly.'

He smiled at her and said, 'Tough shit,' and as he spoke, he realized she was right: he had better slow down. He walked into the living-room.

The children had gone upstairs. Dorothy Meadows sat on

the couch next to Hooper and was chatting with him about his work at Woods Hole. Meadows, in the chair opposite the couch, listened quietly. Daisy Wicker was standing alone, on the other side of the room, by the fireplace, gazing about with a subdued smile on her face. Brody handed Meadows his drink and strolled over next to Daisy.

'You're smiling,' he said.

'Am I ? I didn't notice.'

'Thinking of something funny ?'

'No. I guess I was just interested. I've never been in a policeman's house before.'

'What did you expect ? Bars on the windows ? A guard at the door ?'

'No, nothing. I was just curious.'

'And what have you decided ? It looks just like a normal person's house, doesn't it ?'

'I guess so. Sort of.'

'What does that mean ?'

'Nothing.'

'Oh.'

She took a sip of her drink and said, 'Do you like being a policeman ?'

Brody couldn't tell whether or not there was hostility in the question. 'Yes,' he said. 'It's a good job, and it has a purpose to it.'

'What's the purpose ?'

'What do you think ?' he said, slightly irritated. 'To uphold the law.'

'Don't you feel alienated ?'

'Why the hell should I feel alienated ? Alienated from what ?'

'From the people. I mean, the only thing that justifies your existence is telling people what not to do. Doesn't that make you feel freaky ?'

For a moment, Brody thought he was being put on, but the

girl never smiled or smirked or shifted her eyes from his. 'No, I don't feel freaky,' he said. 'I don't see why I should feel any more freaky than you do, working at the whatchamacallit.'

'The Bibelot.'

'Yeah. What do you sell there anyway?'

'We sell people their past. It gives them comfort.'

'What do you mean, their past?'

'Antiques. They're bought by people who hate their present and need the security of their past. Or if not theirs, someone else's. Once they buy it, it becomes theirs. I bet that's important to you, too.'

'What, the past?'

'No, security. Isn't that supposed to be one of the heavy things about being a cop?'

Brody glanced across the room and noticed that Meadows' glass was empty. 'Excuse me,' he said. 'I have to tend to the other guests.'

'Sure. Nice talking to you.'

Brody took Meadows' glass and his own into the kitchen. Ellen was filling a bowl with Tortilla chips.

'Where the hell did you find that girl?' he said. 'Under a rock?'

'Who? Daisy? I told you, she works at the Bibelot.'

'Have you ever talked to her?'

'A little. She seems very nice and bright.'

'She's a spook. She's just like some of the kids we bust who start smart-mouthing us in the station.' He made a drink for Meadows, then poured another for himself. He looked up and saw Ellen staring at him.

'What's the matter with you?' she said.

'I guess I don't like strange people coming into my house and insulting me.'

'Honestly, Martin. I'm sure there was no insult intended. She was probably just being frank. Frankness is in these days, you know.'

131

'Well, if she gets any franker with me, she's gonna be out, I'll tell you that.' He picked up the two drinks and started for the door.

Ellen said, 'Martin . . .' and he stopped. 'For my sake . . . please.'

'Don't worry about a thing. Everything'll be fine. Like they say in the commercials, *calm down*.'

He refilled Hooper's drink and Daisy Wicker's without refilling his own. Then he sat down and nursed his drink through a long story Meadows was telling Daisy. Brody felt all right – pretty good, in fact – and he knew that if he didn't have anything more to drink before dinner, he'd be fine.

At 8.30, Ellen brought the soup plates out from the kitchen and set them around the table. 'Martin,' she said, 'would you open the wine for me while I get everyone seated?'

'Wine?'

'There are three bottles in the kitchen. A white in the ice-box and two reds on the counter. You may as well open them all. The reds will need time to breathe.'

'Of course they will,' Brody said as he stood up. 'Who doesn't?'

'Oh, and the *tire-bouchin* is on the counter next to the red.'

'The what?'

Daisy Wicker said, 'It's *tire-bouchon*. The corkscrew.'

Brody took vengeful pleasure in seeing Ellen blush, for it relieved him of some of his own embarrassment. He found the corkscrew and went to work on the two bottles of red wine. He pulled one cork cleanly, but the other crumbled as he was withdrawing it, and pieces slipped into the bottle. He took the bottle of white out of the refrigerator, and as he uncorked it he tangled his tongue trying to pronounce the name of the wine: Montrachet. He arrived at what seemed to him an acceptable pronunciation, wiped the bottle dry with a dishtowel, and took it into the dining-room.

Ellen was seated at the end of the table nearest the kitchen.

Hooper was at her left, Meadows at her right. Next to Meadows, Daisy Wicker, then an empty space for Brody at the far end of the table, and, opposite Daisy, Dorothy Meadows.

Brody put his left hand behind his back and, standing over Ellen's right shoulder, poured her a glass of wine. 'A glass of Mount Ratchet,' he said. 'Very good year, 1970. I remember it well.'

'Enough,' said Ellen, tipping the mouth of the bottle up. 'Don't fill the glass all the way.'

'Sorry,' said Brody, and he filled Meadows' glass next.

When he had finished pouring the wine, Brody sat down. He looked at the soup in front of him. Then he glanced furtively around the table and saw that the others were actually eating it: it wasn't a joke. So he took a spoonful. It was cold, and it didn't taste anything like soup, but it wasn't bad.

'I love gazpacho,' said Daisy, 'but it's such a pain to make that I don't have it very often.'

'Mmmm,' said Brody, spooning another mouthful of soup. 'Do you have it very often?'

'No,' he said. 'Not too often.'

'Have you ever tried a G and G?'

'Can't say as I have.'

'You ought to try one. Of course, you might not enjoy it since it's breaking the law.'

'You mean eating this thing is breaking the law? How? What is it?'

'Grass and gazpacho. Instead of herbs, you sprinkle a little grass over the top. Then you smoke a little, eat a little, smoke a little, eat a little. It's really wild.'

It was a moment before Brody realized what she was saying, and even when he understood, he didn't answer right away. He tipped his soup bowl towards himself, scooped out the last little bit of soup, drained his wine glass in one draught, and wiped his mouth with his napkin. He looked at Daisy, who was smiling sweetly at him, and at Ellen, who was smiling at something Hooper was saying.

'It really is,' said Daisy.

Brody decided to be low-keyed – avuncular and none the less annoyed, but low-keyed, so as not to upset Ellen. 'You know,' he said, 'I don't find . . .'

'I bet Matt's tried one.'

'Maybe he has. I don't see what that . . .'

Daisy raised her voice and said, 'Matt, excuse me.' The conversation at the other end of the table stopped. 'I was just curious. Have you ever tried a G and G? By the way, Mrs Brody, this is terrific gazpacho.'

'Thank you,' said Ellen. 'But what's a G and G?'

'I tried one once,' said Hooper. 'But I was never really into that.'

'You must tell me,' Ellen said. 'What is it?'

'Matt'll tell you,' said Daisy, and just as Brody turned to say something to her, she leaned over to Meadows and said, 'Tell me more about the water table.'

Brody stood up and began to clear away the soup bowls. As he walked into the kitchen, he felt a slight rush of nausea and dizziness, and his forehead was sweating. But by the time he put the bowls into the sink, the feeling had passed.

Ellen followed him into the kitchen and tied an apron around her waist. 'I'll need some help carving,' she said.

'Okeydoke,' said Brody, and he searched through a drawer for a carving knife and fork. 'What did you think of that?'

'Of what?'

'That G and G business. Did Hooper tell you what it is?'

'Yes. That was pretty funny, wasn't it? I must say, it sounds tasty.'

'How would you know?'

'You never know what we ladies do when we get together over at the hospital. Here, carve.' With a two-tine serving

134

fork, she hefted the lamb on to the carving board. 'Slices about three-quarters of an inch thick, if you can, the way you'd slice a steak.'

That Wicker bitch was right about one thing, Brody thought as he slashed the meat: I sure as shit feel alienated right now. A slab of meat fell away, and Brody said, 'Hey, I thought you said this was lamb.'

'It is.'

'It isn't even done. Look at that.' He held up the piece he had sliced. It was pink and, towards the middle, almost red.

'That's the way it's supposed to be.'

'Not if it's lamb, it isn't. Lamb's supposed to be cooked through, well done.'

'Martin, believe me. It's all right to cook a butterfly lamb sort of medium. I promise you.'

Brody raised his voice. 'I'm not gonna eat raw lamb!'

'Ssshhh! For God's sake. Can't you keep your voice down?'

Brody said in a hoarse whisper, 'Then put the goddamn thing back till it's done.'

'It's done!' said Ellen. 'If you don't want to eat it, don't eat it, but that's the way I'm going to serve it.'

'Then cut it yourself.' Brody dropped the knife and fork on the carving board, picked up the two bottles of red wine, and left the kitchen.

'There'll be a short delay,' he said as he approached the table, 'while the cook kills our dinner. She tried to serve it as it was, but it bit her on the leg.' He raised a bottle of wine over one of the clean glasses and said, 'I wonder why you're not allowed to serve red wine in the same glass the white wine was.'

'The tastes,' said Meadows, 'don't complement each other.'

'What you're saying is, it'll give you gas.' Brody filled the six glasses and sat down. He took a sip of wine, said, 'Good,' then took another sip and another. He refilled his glass.

Ellen came in from the kitchen carrying the carving board. She set it on the sideboard next to a stack of plates. She returned to the kitchen and came back, carrying two vegetable dishes. 'I hope it's good,' she said. 'I haven't tried it before.'

'What is it?' asked Dorothy Meadows. 'It smells delicious.'

'Butterfly lamb. Marinated.'

'Really? What's in the marinade?'

'Ginger, soy sauce, a whole bunch of things.' She put a thick slice of lamb, some asparagus and summer squash on each plate, and passed the plates to Meadows, who sent them down and around the table.

When everyone had been served and Ellen had sat down, Hooper raised his glass and said, 'A toast to the chef.'

The others raised their glasses, and Brody said, 'Good luck.'

Meadows took a bite of meat, chewed it, savoured it, and said, 'Fantastic. It's like the tenderest of sirloins, only better. What a splendid flavour.'

'Coming from you, Harry,' said Ellen, 'that's a special compliment.'

'It's delicious,' said Dorothy. 'Will you promise to give me the recipe? Harry will never forgive me if I don't give this to him at least once a week.'

'He better rob a bank,' said Brody.

'But it is delicious, Martin, don't you think?'

Brody didn't answer. He had started to chew a piece of meat when another wave of nausea hit him. Once again sweat popped out on his forehead. He felt detached, as if his body were controlled by someone else. He sensed panic at the loss of motor control. His fork felt heavy, and for a moment he feared it might slip from his fingers and clatter on to the table. He tripped it with his fist and held on. He was sure his tongue wouldn't behave if he tried to speak. It was the wine. It had to be the wine. With greatly exaggerated precision, he reached forward to push his wine glass away from

136

him. He slid his fingers along the tablecloth to minimize the chances of knocking over the glass. He sat back and took a deep breath. His vision blurred. He tried to focus his eyes on a painting above Ellen's head, but he was distracted by the image of Ellen talking to Hooper. Every time she spoke she touched Hooper's arm – lightly, but, Brody thought, intimately, as if they were sharing secrets. He didn't hear what anyone was saying. The last thing he remembered hearing was, 'Don't you think?' How long ago was that? Who had said it? He didn't know. He looked at Meadows, who was talking to Daisy. Then he looked at Dorothy and said thickly, 'Yes.'

'What did you say, Martin?' She looked up at him. 'Did you say something?'

He couldn't speak. He wanted to stand and walk out to the kitchen, but he didn't trust his legs. He'd never make it without holding on to something. Just sit still, he told himself. It'll pass.

And it did. His head began to clear. Ellen was touching Hooper again. Talk and touch, talk and touch. 'Boy, it's hot,' he said. He stood up and walked, carefully but steadily, to a window and tugged it open. He leaned on the sill and pressed his face against the screen. 'Nice night,' he said. He straightened up. 'I think I'll get a glass of water.' He walked into the kitchen and shook his head. He turned on the cold-water tap and rubbed some water on his brow. He filled a glass and drank it down, then refilled it and drank that down. He took a few deep breaths, went back into the dining-room, and sat down. He looked at the food on his plate. Then he suppressed a shiver and smiled at Dorothy.

'Any more, anybody?' said Ellen. 'There's plenty here.'

'Indeed,' said Meadows. 'But you'd better serve the others first. Left to my own devices, I'd eat the whole thing.'

'And you know what you'd be saying tomorrow,' said Brody.

'What's that?'

Brody lowered his voice and said gravely, 'I can't believe I ate the *whole* thing.'

Meadows and Dorothy laughed, and Hooper said, in a high falsetto whine, 'No, Ralph, *I* ate it.' Then even Ellen laughed. It was going to be all right.

By the time dessert was served – coffee ice cream in a pool of crème de cacao – Brody was feeling well. He had two helpings of ice cream, and he chatted amiably with Dorothy. He smiled when Daisy told him a story about lacing the stuffing of last Thanksgiving's turkey with marijuana.

'My only worry,' said Daisy, 'was that my maiden aunt called Thanksgiving morning and asked if she could come for dinner. The turkey was already made and stuffed.'

'So what happened?' said Brody.

'I tried to sneak her some turkey without stuffing, but she made a point of asking for it, so I said what the heck and gave her a big spoonful.'

'And?'

'By the end of the meal she was giggling like a little girl. She even wanted to dance. To *Hair* yet.'

'It's a good thing I wasn't there,' said Brody. 'I would have arrested you for corrupting the morals of a maiden.'

They had coffee in the living-room, and Brody offered drinks, but only Meadows accepted. 'A tiny brandy, if you have it,' he said.

Brody looked at Ellen, as if to ask, do we have any? 'In the cupboard, I think,' she said.

Brody poured Meadows' drink and thought briefly of pouring one for himself. But he resisted, telling himself, Don't press your luck.

At a little after ten, Meadows yawned and said, 'Dorothy, I think we had best take our leave. I find it hard to fulfil the public trust if I stay up too late.'

'I should go, too,' said Daisy. 'I have to be at work at

eight. Not that we're selling very much these days.'

'You're not alone, my dear,' said Meadows.

'I know. But when you work on commission, you really feel it.'

'Well, let's hope the worst is over. From what I gather from our expert here, there's a good chance the leviathan has left.' Meadows stood up.

'A chance,' said Hooper. 'I hope so.' He rose to go. 'I should be on my way, too.'

'Oh, don't go!' Ellen said to Hooper. The words came out much stronger than she had intended. Instead of a pleasant request, they sounded a shrill plea. She was embarrassed, and she added quickly, 'I mean, the night is young. It's only ten.'

'I know,' said Hooper. 'But if the weather's any good tomorrow, I want to get up early and get out into the water. Besides, I have a car and I can drop Daisy off on my way home.'

Daisy said, 'That would be fun.' Her voice, as usual, was without tone or colour, suggesting nothing.

'The Meadows can drop her,' Ellen said.

'True,' said Hooper, 'but I really should go so I can get up early. But thanks for the thought.'

They said their good-byes at the front door – perfunctory compliments, redundant thanks. Hooper was the last to leave, and when he extended his hand to Ellen, she took it in both of hers and said, 'Thank you *so* much for my shark tooth.'

'You're welcome. I'm glad you like it.'

'And thank you for being so nice to the children. They were fascinated to meet you.'

'So was I. It was a little weird, though. I must have been about Sean's age when I knew you before. You haven't changed much at all.'

'Well, *you've* certainly changed.'

'I hope so. I'd hate to be nine all my life.'

139

'We'll see you again before you go?'

'Count on it.'

'Wonderful.' She released his hand. He said a quick good night to Brody and walked to his car.

Ellen waited at the door until the last of the cars had pulled out of the driveway, then she turned off the outside light. Without a word, she began to pick up the glasses, coffee cups, and ashtrays from the living-room.

Brody carried a stack of dessert dishes into the kitchen, set them on the sink, and said, 'Well, that was all right.' He meant nothing by the remark, and sought nothing more than rote agreement.

'No thanks to you,' said Ellen.

'What?'

'You were awful.'

'I was?' He was genuinely surprised at the ferocity of her attack. 'I know I got a little queasy there for a minute, but I didn't think—'

'All evening, from start to finish, you were awful.'

'That's a lot of crap!'

'You'll wake the children.'

'I don't give a damn. I'm not going to let you stand there and work out your own hang-ups by telling me I'm a shit.'

Ellen smiled bitterly. 'You see? There you go again.'

'*Where* do I go again? What are you talking about?'

'I don't want to talk about it.'

'Just like that. You don't want to talk about it. Look . . . okay, I was wrong about the goddamn meat. I shouldn't have blown my stack. I'm sorry. Now . . .'

'I said I don't want to talk about it!'

Brody was ready for a fight, but he backed off, sober enough to realize that his only weapons were cruelty and innuendo, and that Ellen was close to tears. And tears, whether shed in orgasm or in anger, disconcerted him. So he said only, 'Well, I'm sorry about that.' He walked out of the kitchen and climbed the stairs.

In the bedroom, as he was undressing, the thought occurred to him that the cause of all the unpleasantness, the source of the whole mess, was a fish: a mindless beast that he had never seen. The ludicrousness of the thought made him smile.

He crawled into bed and, almost simultaneous with the touch of his head to the pillow, fell into a dreamless sleep.

A boy and his date sat drinking beer at one end of the long mahogany bar in the Randy Bear. The boy was eighteen, the son of the pharmacist at the Amity Pharmacy.

'You'll have to tell him sometime,' said the girl.

'I know. And when I do, he's gonna go bullshit.'

'It wasn't your fault.'

'You know what he'll say? It must have been my fault. I must have done something, or else they would have kept me and canned somebody else.'

'But they fired a lot of kids.'

'They kept a lot, too.'

'How did they decide who to keep?'

'They didn't say. They just said they weren't getting enough guests to justify a big staff, so they were letting some of us go. Boy, my old man is gonna go right through the roof.'

'Can't he call them? He must know somebody there. I mean, if he says you really need the money for college . . .'

'He wouldn't do it. That'd be begging.' The boy finished his beer. 'There's only one thing I can do. Deal.'

'Oh, Michael, don't do that. It's too dangerous. You could go to jail.'

'That's quite a choice, isn't it?' the boy said acidly. 'College or jail.'

'What would you tell your father?'

'I don't know. Maybe I'll tell him I'm selling belts.'

EIGHT

Brody awoke with a start, jolted by a signal that told him something was wrong. He threw his arm across the bed to touch Ellen. She wasn't there. He sat up and saw her sitting in the chair by the window. Rain splashed against the window-panes, and he heard the wind whipping through the trees.

'Lousy day, huh?' he said. She didn't answer, continuing to stare fixedly at the drops sliding down the glass. 'How come you're up so early?'

'I couldn't sleep.'

Brody yawned. 'I sure didn't have any trouble.'

'I'm not surprised.'

'Oh, boy. Are we starting in again?'

Ellen shook her head. 'No. I'm sorry. I didn't mean anything.' She seemed subdued, sad.

'What's the matter?'

'Nothing.'

'Whatever you say.' Brody got out of bed and went into the bathroom.

When he had shaved and dressed, he went down to the kitchen. The boys were finishing their breakfast, and Ellen was frying an egg for him. 'What are you guys gonna do on this crummy day?' he said.

'Clean lawnmowers,' said Billy, who worked during the summer for a local gardener. 'Boy, do I hate rainy days.'

'And what about you two?' Brody said to Martin and Sean.

'Martin's going to the Boys' Club,' said Ellen, 'and Sean's spending the day at the Santos's.'

'And you?'

'I've got a full day at the hospital. Which reminds me: I won't be home for lunch. Can you get something downtown?'

'Sure. I didn't know you worked a full day Wednesdays.'

'I don't usually. But one of the other girls is sick, and I said I'd fill in.'

'Oh.'

'I'll be back by suppertime.'

'Fine.'

'Do you think you could drop Sean and Martin off on your way to work? I want to do a little shopping on my way to the hospital.'

'No problem.'

'I'll pick them up on my way home.'

Brody and the two younger children left first. Then Billy, wrapped from head to foot in foul-weather gear, bicycled off to work.

Ellen looked at the clock on the kitchen wall. It was a few minutes to eight. Too early? Maybe. But better to catch him now, before he went off somewhere and the chance was lost. She held her right hand out in front of her and tried to steady the fingers, but they quivered uncontrollably. She smiled at her nervousness and whispered to herself, 'Some swinger you'd make.' She went upstairs to the bedroom, sat on the bed, and picked up the green phone book. She found the number for the Abelard Arms Inn, put her hand on the phone, hesitated for a moment, then picked up the receiver and dialled the number.

'Abelard Arms.'

'Mr Hooper's room, please. Matt Hooper.'

'Just a minute, please. Hooper. Here it is. Four-oh-five. I'll ring it for you.'

Ellen heard the phone ring once, then again. She could hear her heart beating, and she saw the pulse throb in her right wrist. Hang up, she told herself. Hang up. There's time.

'Hello?' said Hooper's voice.

'Oh.' She thought, Good God, suppose he's got Daisy Wicker in the room with him.

'Hello?'

Ellen swallowed and said, 'Hi. It's me ... I mean it's Ellen.'

'Oh, hi.'

'I hope I didn't wake you.'

'No. I was just getting ready to go downstairs and have some breakfast.'

'Good. It's not a very nice day, is it?'

'No, but I don't really mind. It's a luxury for me to be able to sleep this late.'

'Can you ... will you be able to work today?'

'I don't know. I was just trying to figure that out. I sure can't go out in the boat and hope to get anything done.'

'Oh.' She paused, fighting the dizziness that was creeping up on her. Go ahead, she told herself. Ask the question. 'I was wondering ...' No, be careful; ease into it. 'I wanted to thank you for the beautiful charm.'

'You're welcome. I'm glad you like it. But I should be thanking you. I had a good time last night.'

'I did ... we did, too. I'm glad you came.'

'Yes.'

'It was like old times.'

'Yes.'

Now, she said to herself. Do it. The words spilled from her mouth. 'I was wondering, if you can't do any work today, I mean if you can't go out in the boat or anything, I was wondering if ... if there was any chance you'd like to ... if you're free for lunch.'

'Lunch?'

'Yes. You know, if you have nothing else to do, I thought we might have some lunch.'

144

'We? You mean you and the chief and me?'

'No, just you and I. Martin usually has lunch at his desk. I don't want to interfere with your plans or anything. I mean, if you've got a lot of work to do . . .'

'No, no. That's okay. Heck, why not? Sure. What did you have in mind?'

'There's a wonderful place up in Sag Harbour. Banner's. Do you know it?' She hoped he didn't. She didn't know it, either, which meant that no one there would know her. But she had heard that it was good and quiet and dark.

'No, I've never been there,' said Hooper. 'But Sag Harbour. That's quite a hike for lunch.'

'It's not bad, really, only about fifteen or twenty minutes. I could meet you there whenever you like.'

'Any time's all right with me.'

'Around twelve-thirty, then?'

'Twelve-thirty it is. See you then.'

Ellen hung up the phone. Her hands were still shaking, but she felt elated, excited. Her senses seemed alive and incredibly keen. Every time she drew a breath she savoured the smells around her. Her ears jingled with a symphony of tiny house sounds – creaks and rustles and thumps. She felt more intensely feminine than she had in years – a warm, wet feeling both delicious and uncomfortable.

She went into the bathroom and took a shower. She shaved her legs and under her arms. She wished she had bought one of those feminine hygiene deodorants she had seen advertised, but, lacking that, she powdered herself and daubed cologne behind her ears, inside her elbows, behind her knees, on her nipples, and on her genitals.

There was a full-length mirror in the bedroom, and she stood before it, examining herself. Were the goods good enough? Would the offering be accepted? She had worked to keep in shape, to preserve the smoothness and sinuousness of youth. She could not bear the thought of rejection.

The goods were good. The lines in her neck were few and barely noticeable. Her face was unblemished and unscarred. There were no droops or sags or pouches. She stood straight and admired the contours of her breasts. Her waist was slim, her belly flat – the reward for endless hours of exercise after each child. The only problem, as she assessed her body critically, was her hips, by no stretch of anyone's imagination were they girlish. They signalled motherhood. They were, as Brody once said, breeder's hips. The recollection brought a quick flash of remorse, but excitement quickly nudged it aside. Her legs were long and – below the pad of fat on her rear – slender. Her ankles were delicate, and her feet – with the toenails neatly pruned – were perfect enough to suit any pediphile.

She dressed in her hospital clothes. From the back of her closet she took a plastic shopping bag, into which she put a pair of bikini underpants, a bra, a neatly folded lavender summer dress, a pair of low-heeled pumps, a can of spray deodorant, a plastic bottle of bath powder, a toothbrush and a tube of toothpaste. She carried the bag to the garage, tossed it into the back seat of her Volkswagen beetle, backed out of the driveway, and drove to the Southampton Hospital.

The dull drive increased the fatigue she had been feeling for hours. She had not slept all night. She had first lain in bed, then sat by the window, struggling with all the twistings of emotion and conscience, desire and regret, longing and recrimination. She didn't know exactly when she had decided on the manifestly rash, dangerous plan. She had been thinking about it – and trying not to think about it – since the day she first met Hooper. She had weighed the risks and, somehow, calculated that they were worth taking, though she was not entirely sure what she could gain from the adventure. She knew she wanted change, almost any change. She wanted to be assured and reassured that she was desirable – not just to her husband, for she had grown complacent about that, but to the people she saw as her real peers, the people among whom she still numbered herself. She felt that without some remedy, the part of herself that she most cherished would die. Perhaps the past could never be revived. But perhaps it could be recalled physically as well as mentally. She wanted an injection, a transfusion of the essence of her past, and she saw Matt Hooper as the only possible donor. The thought of love never entered her mind. Nor did she want or anticipate a relationship either profound or enduring. She sought only to be serviced, restored.

She was grateful that the work assigned her when she arrived at the hospital demanded concentration and conversation, for it prevented her from thinking. She and another volunteer changed the bedding of the elderly patients for whom the hospital community was a surrogate – and, in some cases, final – home. She had to remember the names of children in distant cities, had to fashion new excuses for why they hadn't written. She had to feign recollection of the plots of television shows and speculate on why such-and-such a character had left his wife for a woman who was patently an adventuress.

At 11.45, Ellen told the supervisor of volunteers that she didn't feel well. Her thyroid was acting up again, she said, and she was getting her period. She thought she'd go lie down for a while in the staff lounge. And if a nap didn't help, she said, she'd probably go home. In fact, if she wasn't back on the job by 1.30 or so, the supervisor could assume she had gone home. It was an explanation that she hoped was vague enough to discourage anyone from actively looking for her.

She went into the lounge, counted to twenty, and opened the door a crack to see if the corridor was empty. It was; most of the staff were in, or on their way to, the cafeteria on the other side of the building. She stepped into the corridor, closed the door softly behind her, and hurried around a corner and out a side door of the hospital that led to the staff parking lot.

She drove most of the way to Sag Harbour, then stopped at a gas station. When the tank was full and the gas paid for, she asked to use the ladies' room. The attendant gave her the key, and she pulled her car around to the side of the station, next to the ladies' room door. She opened the door, but before going into the ladies' room she returned the key to the attendant. She walked to her car, removed the plastic bag from the back seat, entered the ladies' room, and pushed the button that locked the door.

She stripped, and standing on the cold floor in her bare feet, looking at her reflection in the mirror above the sink, she felt a thrill of risk. She sprayed deodorant under her arms and on her feet. She took the clean underpants from the plastic bag and stepped into them. She shook a little powder into each cup of the bra and put it on. She took the dress from the bag, unfolded it, checked it for wrinkles, and slipped it over her head. She poured powder into each of her shoes, brushed off the bottom of each foot with a paper towel, and put on the shoes. Then she brushed her teeth and combed her hair, stuffed her hospital clothes into the plastic bag, and opened the door. She looked both ways, saw that no one was watching her, then stepped out of the ladies' room, tossed the bag into the car, and got in.

As she drove out of the gas station, she hunched down in her seat so the attendant, if he should chance to notice her, would not see that she had changed clothes.

It was 12.15 when she arrived at Banner's, a small steak-and-seafood restaurant on the water in Sag Harbour. The parking lot was in the rear, for which she was grateful. On the off-chance that someone she knew might drive down the street in Sag Harbour, she didn't want her car in plain view.

One reason she had picked Banner's was that it was known as a favourite night-time restaurant for yachtsmen and summer people, which meant that it probably had little luncheon trade. And it was expensive, which made it almost certain that no year-round residents, no local tradesmen, would go there for lunch. Ellen checked her wallet. She had nearly fifty dollars – all the emergency cash she and Brody kept in the house. She made a mental note of the bills: a twenty, two tens, a five, and three ones. She wanted to replace exactly what she had taken from the coffee can in the kitchen closet.

There were two other cars in the parking lot, a Chevrolet Vega and a bigger car, tan. She remembered that Hooper's car was green and that it was named after some animal. She got out of her car and walked into the restaurant, holding her hands over her head to protect her hair from the light rain.

The restaurant was dark, but because the day was gloomy it took her eyes only a few seconds to adjust. There was only one room, with a bar on the right as she walked in and about twenty tables in the centre. The left-hand wall was lined with eight booths. The walls were dark wood, decorated with bull-fight and movie posters.

A couple – in their late twenties, Ellen guessed – were having a drink at a table by the window. The bartender, a young man with a Vandyke beard and a button-down shirt, sat by the cash register reading the New York *Daily News*. They were the only people in the room. Ellen looked at her watch. Almost 12.30.

The bartender looked up and said, 'Hi. Can I help you?'

Ellen stepped to the bar. 'Yes . . . yes. In a minute. But first I'd like . . . can you tell me where the ladies' room is?'

'End of the bar, turn right. First down on your left.'

'Thank you.' Ellen walked quickly down the length of the bar, turned right, and went into the ladies' room.

She stood in front of the mirror and held out her right hand. It trembled, and she clenched it into a fist. Calm down, she said to herself. You have to calm down or it's no use. It's lost. She felt that she was sweating, but when she put a hand inside her dress and felt her armpit, it was dry. She combed her hair and surveyed her teeth. She remembered something a boy she had once gone out with had said: Nothing turns my stomach faster than seeing a girl with a big piece of crud between her teeth. She looked at her watch: 12.35.

She went back into the restaurant and looked around. Just the same couple, the bartender, and a waitress standing at the bar, folding napkins.

The waitress saw Ellen come around the corner of the bar, and she said, 'Hello. May I help you?'

'Yes. I'd like a table, please. For lunch.'

'For one?'

'No. Two.'

'Fine,' said the waitress. She put down a napkin, picked up a pad, and walked Ellen to a table in the middle of the room. 'Is this all right?'

'No. I mean, yes. It's fine. But I'd like to have that table in the corner booth, if you don't mind.'

'Sure,' said the waitress. 'Any table you like. We're not exactly full.' She led Ellen to the table, and Ellen slipped into the booth with her back to the door. Hooper would be able to find her. If he came. 'Can I get you a drink?'

'Yes. A gin and tonic, please.' When the waitress left the table, Ellen smiled. It was the first time since her wedding that she had had a drink during the day.

The waitress brought the drink, and Ellen drank half of it immediately, eager to feel the relaxing warmth of alcohol. Every few seconds, she checked the door and looked at her watch. He's not going to come, she thought. It was almost 12.45. He got cold feet. He's scared of Martin. Maybe he's scared of me. What will I do if he doesn't come? I guess I'll have some lunch and go back to work. He's got to come! He can't do this to me.

'Hello.'

The word startled Ellen. She hopped in her seat and said, 'Oh!'

Hooper slid into the seat opposite her and said, 'I didn't mean to scare you. And I'm sorry I'm late. I had to stop for gas, and the station was jammed. The traffic was terrible. And so much for my excuses. I should have left more time. I *am* sorry.' He looked into her eyes and smiled.

She looked down at her glass. 'You don't have to apologize. I was late myself.'

The waitress came to the table. 'Can I get you a drink?' she said to Hooper.

He noticed Ellen's glass and said, 'Oh, sure. I guess so. If you are. I'll have a gin and tonic.'

'I'll have another one,' said Ellen. 'This one's almost finished.'

The waitress left, and Hooper said, 'I don't normally drink at lunch.'

'Neither do I.'

'After about three drinks I say stupid things. I never did hold my liquor very well.'

Ellen nodded. 'I know the feeling. I tend to get sort of...'

'Impetuous? So do I.'

'Really? I can't imagine you getting impetuous. I thought scientists weren't ever impetuous.'

Hooper smiled and said histrionically, 'It may seem, madam, that we are wed to our test tubes. But beneath the icy exteriors there beat the hearts of some of the most brazen, raunchy people in the world.'

Ellen laughed. The waitress brought the drinks and left two menus on the edge of the table. They talked – chatted really – about old times, about people they had known and what those people were doing now, about Hooper's ambitions in icthyology. They never mentioned the shark or Brody or Ellen's children. It was an easy, rambling conversation, which suited Ellen. Her second drink loosened her up, and she felt happy and in command of herself.

She wanted Hooper to have another drink, and she knew he was not likely to take the initiative and order one. She picked up one of the menus, hoping that the waitress would notice the movement, and said, 'Let me see. What looks good?'

Hooper picked up the other menu and began to read, and after a minute or two, the waitress strolled over to the table. 'Are you ready to order?'

'Not quite yet,' said Ellen. 'It all looks good. Are you ready, Matthew?'

'Not quite,' said Hooper.

'Why don't we have one more drink while we're looking?'

'Both?' said the waitress.

Hooper seemed to ponder for a moment. Then he nodded his head and said, 'Sure. A special occasion.'

They sat in silence, reading the menus. Ellen tried to assess how she felt. Three drinks would be a fairly heavy load for her to carry, and she wanted to make sure she didn't get fuzzy-headed or fuzzy-tongued. What was that saying, about alcohol increasing the desire but taking away from the performance? But that's just with men, she thought. I'm glad I don't have to worry about *that*. But what about him? Suppose he can't . . . Is there anything I can do? But that's silly. Not on two drinks. It must take five or six or seven. A man has to be incapacitated. But not if he's scared. Does he look scared? She peeked over the top of her menu and looked at Hooper. He didn't look nervous. If anything, he looked slightly perplexed.

'What's the matter?' she said.

He looked up. 'What do you mean?'

'Your eyebrows were all scrunched up. You looked confused.'

'Oh, nothing. I was just looking at the scallops, or what

they claim are scallops. The chances are they're flounder, cut up with a cookie cutter.'

The waitress brought their drinks and said, 'Ready?'

'Yes,' said Ellen. 'I'll have the shrimp cocktail and the chicken.'

'What kind of dressing would you like on your salad? We have French, Roquefort, Thousand Island, and oil and vinegar.'

'Roquefort, please.'

Hooper said, 'Are these really bay scallops?'

'I guess so,' said the waitress. 'If that's what it says.'

'All right. I'll have the scallops, and French dressing on the salad.'

'Anything to start?'

'No,' said Hooper, raising his glass. 'This'll be fine.'

In a few minutes, the waitress brought Ellen's shrimp cocktail. When she had left, Ellen said, 'Do you know what I'd love? Some wine.'

'That's a very interesting idea,' Hooper said, looking at her. 'But remember what I said about impetuousness. I may become irresponsible.'

'I'm not worried.' As Ellen spoke, she felt a blush crawl up her cheeks.

'Okay, but first I better check the treasury.' He reached in his back pocket for his wallet.

'Oh, no. This is my treat.'

'Don't be silly.'

'No, really, I asked you to lunch.' She began to panic. It had never occurred to her that he might insist on paying. She didn't want to annoy him by sticking him with a big bill. On the other hand, she didn't want to seem patronizing, to offend his virility.

'I know,' he said. 'But I'd like to take *you* to lunch.'

Was this a gambit? She couldn't tell. If it was, she didn't want to refuse it, but if he was just being polite . . . 'You're sweet,' she said, 'but . . .'

'I'm serious. Please.'

She looked down and toyed with the one shrimp remaining on her plate. 'Well . . .'

'I know you're only being thoughtful,' Hooper said, 'but don't be. Didn't David ever tell you about our grandfather ?'

'Not that I remember. What about him ?'

'Old Matt was known – and not very affectionately – as the Bandit. If he was alive today, I'd probably be at the head of the pack calling for his scalp. But he isn't, so all I had to worry about was whether to keep the bundle of money he left me or give it away. It wasn't a very difficult moral dilemma. I figure I can spend it as well as anyone I'd give it to.'

'Does David have a lot of money, too ?'

'Yes. That's one of the things about him that's always baffled me. He's got enough to support himself and any number of wives for life. So why did he settle on a meatball for a second wife ? Because she has more money than he does. I don't know. Maybe money doesn't feel comfortable unless it's married to money.'

'What did your grandfather do ?'

'Railroads and mining. Technically, that is. Basically, he was a robber baron. At one point he owned most of Denver. He was the landlord of the whole red-light district.'

'That must have been profitable.'

'Not as much as you'd think,' Hooper said with a laugh. 'From what I hear, he liked to collect his rent in trade.'

That might be a gambit, Ellen thought. What should she say ? 'That's supposed to be every schoolgirl's fantasy,' she ventured playfully.

'What is ?'

'To be a . . . you know, a prostitute. To sleep with a whole lot of different men.'

'Was it yours ?'

Ellen laughed, hoping to cover her blush. 'I don't remember if it was exactly that,' she said. 'But I guess we all have fantasies of one kind or another.'

Hooper smiled and leaned back in his chair. He called the waitress over and said, 'Bring us a bottle of cold Chablis, would you please?'

Something's happened, Ellen thought. She wondered if he could sense – smell? like an animal – the invitation she had extended. Whatever it was, he had taken the offensive. All she had to do was avoid discouraging him.

The food came, followed a moment later by the wine. Hooper's scallops were the size of marshmallows. 'Flounder,' he said after the waitress had left. 'I should have known.'

'How can you tell?' Ellen asked. Immediately she wished she hadn't said anything. She didn't want to let the conversation drift.

'They're too big, for one thing. And the edges are too perfect. They were obviously cut.'

'I suppose you could send them back.' She hoped he wouldn't, a quarrel with the waitress could spoil their mood.

'I might,' said Hooper, and he grinned at Ellen. 'Under different circumstances.' He poured Ellen a glass of wine, then filled his own and raised it for a toast. 'To fantasies,' he said. 'Tell me about yours.' His eyes were a bright, liquid blue, and his lips were parted in a half smile.

Ellen tittered. 'Oh, mine aren't very interesting. I imagine they're just your old run-of-the-mill fantasies.'

'There's no such thing,' said Hooper. 'Tell me.' He was asking, not demanding, but Ellen felt that the game she had started demanded that she answer.

'Oh, you know,' she said. Her stomach felt warm, and the back of her neck was hot. 'Just the standard things. Rape, I guess, is one.'

'How does it happen?'

She tried to think, and she remembered the times when, alone, she would let her mind wander and conjure the carnal images. Usually she was in bed, often with her husband asleep beside her. Sometimes she found that, without knowing it, she had been rubbing her hand over her vagina, caressing herself.

'Different ways,' she said.

'Name one.'

'Sometimes I'm in the kitchen in the morning, after everybody has left, and a workman from one of the houses next door comes to my back door. He wants to use the phone or have a glass of water.' She stopped.

'And then?'

'I let him in the door and he threatens to kill me if I don't do what he wants.'

'Does he hurt you?'

'Oh no. I mean, he doesn't stab me or anything.'

'Does he hit you?'

'No. He just . . . rapes me.'

'Is it fun?'

'Not at first. It's scary. But then, after a while, when he's . . .'

'When he's got you all . . . ready.'

Ellen's eyes moved to his, reading the remark for humour, irony, or cruelty. She saw none. Hooper ran his tongue over his lips and leaned forward until his face was only a foot or so from hers.

Ellen thought: The door's open now; all you have to do is walk through it. She said, 'Yes.'

'Then it's fun.'

'Yes.' She shifted in her seat, for the recollection was becoming physical.

'Do you ever have an orgasm?'

'Sometimes,' she said. 'Not always.'

'Is he big?'

'Tall? Not . . .'

They had been speaking very softly, and now Hooper

lowered his voice to a whisper. 'I don't mean tall. Is he . . .
you know . . . big?'

'Usually,' said Ellen, and she chuckled. 'Huge.'

'Is he black?'

'No. I've heard that some women have fantasies about
being raped by black men but I never have.'

'Tell me another one.'

'Oh no,' she said, laughing. 'Now it's your turn.'

They heard footsteps and turned to see the waitress
approaching their table. 'Is everything all right?' she said.

'Fine,' Hooper said curtly. 'Everything's fine.' The
waitress left.

Ellen whispered, 'Do you think she heard?'

Hooper leaned forward. 'Not a chance. Now tell me
another one.'

It's going to happen, Ellen thought, and she felt suddenly
nervous. She wanted to tell him why she was behaving this
way, to explain that she didn't do this all the time. He probably thinks I'm a whore. Forget it. Don't get sappy or you'll
ruin it. 'No,' she said with a smile. 'It's your turn.'

'Mine are usually orgies,' he said. 'Or at least threesies.'

'What are threesies?'

'Three people. Me and two girls.'

'Greedy. What do you do?'

'It varies. Everything imaginable.'

'Are you . . . big?' she said.

'Bigger every minute. What about you?'

'I don't know. Compared to what?'

'To other women. Some women have really tight ones.'

Ellen giggled. 'You sound like a comparison-shopper.'

'Just a conscientious consumer.'

'I don't know how I am,' she said. 'I haven't anything to
compare it to.' She looked down at her half-eaten chicken,
and she laughed.

'What's funny?' he asked.

157

'I was just wondering,' she said, and her laughter built. 'I was just wondering if – oh, Lord, I'm getting a pain in my side – if chickens have . . .'

'Of course!' said Hooper. 'But talk about a tightie!'

They laughed together, and when the laughter faded, Ellen impulsively said, 'Let's make a fantasy.'

'Okay. How do you want to start?'

'What would you do to me if we were going to . . . you know.'

'That's a very interesting question,' he said with mock gravity. 'Before considering the what, however, we'd have to consider the where. I suppose there's always my room.'

'Too dangerous. Everybody knows me at the Abelard. Anywhere in Amity would be too dangerous.'

'What about your house?'

'Lord, no. Suppose one of my children came home. Besides . . .'

'I know. No desecrating the conjugal sheets. Okay, where else?'

'There must be motels between here and Montauk. Or even better, between here and Orient Point.'

'Fair enough. Even if there's not, there's always the car.'

'In broad daylight? You *do* have wild fantasies.'

'In fantasies, anything is possible.'

'All right. That's settled. So what would you do?'

'I think we should proceed chronologically. First of all, we'd leave here in one car. Probably mine, because it's least known. And we'd come back later to pick up yours.'

'Okay.'

'Then, while we were driving along . . . no, even before that, before we left here, I'd send you into the ladies' room and tell you to take off your panties.'

'Why?'

'So I could . . . explore you while we're on the road. Just to keep the motors running.'

'I see,' she said, trying to seem matter-of-fact. She felt hot, flushed, and sensed that her mind was floating somewhere apart from her body. She was a third person listening to the conversation. She had to fight to keep from shifting on the leatherette bench. She wanted to squirm back and forth, to move her thighs up and down. But she was afraid of leaving a stain on the seat.

'Then,' said Hooper, 'while we were driving along, you might be sitting on my right hand and I'd be giving you a massage. Maybe I'd have my fly open. Maybe not, though, because you might get ideas, which would undoubtedly cause me to lose control, and *that* would probably cause a massive accident that would leave us both dead.'

Ellen started to giggle again, imagining the sight of Hooper lying by the side of the road, stiff as a flagpole, and herself lying next to him, her dress bunched up around her waist and her vagina yawning open, glistening wet, for the world to see.

'We'd try to find a motel,' said Hooper, 'where the rooms are either in separate cabins or at least not butted right up against each other, wall to wall.'

'Why?'

'Noise. The walls are usually made of Kleenex and spit, and we wouldn't want to be inhibited by the thought of a shoe salesman in the next room pressing his ear to the wall and getting his kicks listening to us.'

'Suppose you couldn't find a motel like that.'

'We would,' said Hooper. 'As I said, in a fantasy anything is possible.'

Why does he keep saying that? Ellen thought. He can't really be playing a word game, working up a fantasy he has no intention of fulfilling. Her mind scrambled for a question to keep the conversation alive. 'What name would you register us under?'

'Ah yes. I'd forgotten. These days I can't conceive of any-one getting up tight about something like this, but you're right: we should have a name, just in case we ran into an old-fashioned innkeeper. How about Mr and Mrs Al Kinsey. We could say we were on an extended field trip for research.'

'And we'd tell him we'd send him an autographed copy of our report.'

'We'd dedicate it to him!'

They both laughed, and Ellen said, 'What about after we registered?'

'Well, we'd drive to wherever our room was, scout around to see if anyone seemed to be in the rooms near by – unless we had a cabin to ourselves – and then go inside.'

'And then?'

'That's when our options broaden. I'd probably be so turned on that I'd grab you, let you have it – maybe on the bed, maybe not. That time would be my time. Your time would come later.'

'What do you mean?'

'The first time would be out of control – a slam-bam-thank-you-ma'am deal. After that, I'd have more control, and the second time I could prepare you.'

'How would you do that?'

'With delicacy and finesse.'

The waitress was approaching the table, so they sat back and stopped talking.

'Will there be anything else?'

'No,' said Hooper. 'Just the check.'

Ellen assumed that the waitress would return to the bar to total the bill, but she stood at the table, scribbling and carrying her ones. Ellen slid to the edge of the seat and said as she stood up, 'Excuse me. I want to powder my nose before we go.'

'I know,' said Hooper, smiling.

'You do?' said the waitress as Ellen passed her. 'Boy, that's what marriage will do for you. I hope nobody ever knows me that well.'

*　　*　　*

Ellen arrived home a little before 4.30. She went upstairs, into the bathroom, and turned on the water in the tub. She took off all her clothes and stuffed them into the laundry hamper, mixing them with the clothes already in the hamper. She looked in the mirror and examined her face and neck. No marks.

After her bath, she powdered herself, brushed her teeth, and gargled with mouthwash. She went into the bedroom, put on a fresh pair of underpants and a nightgown, pulled back the bedclothes and climbed into bed. She closed her eyes, hoping that sleep would pounce upon her.

But sleep could not overpower a memory that kept sliding into her mind. It was a vision of Hooper, eyes wide and staring – but unseeing – at the wall as he approached climax. The eyes seemed to bulge until, just before release, Ellen had feared they might actually pop out of their sockets. Hooper's teeth were clenched, and he ground them the way people do during sleep. From his voice there came a gurgling whine, whose tone rose higher and higher with each frenzied thrust. Even after his obvious, violent climax, Hooper's countenance had not changed. His teeth were still clenched, his eyes still fixed on the wall, and he continued to pump madly. He was oblivious of the being beneath him, and when, perhaps a full minute after his climax, Hooper still did not relax, Ellen had become afraid – of what, she wasn't sure, but the ferocity and intensity of his assault seemed to her a pursuit in which she was only a vehicle. After a while, she had tapped him on the back and said softly, 'Hey, I'm here too,' and in a moment his eyelids closed and his head dropped to her shoulder. Later, during their subsequent coupling, Hooper had been more gentle, more controlled, less detached. But the fury of the first encounter still lingered disturbingly in Ellen's mind.

Finally, her mind gave in to fatigue, and she fell asleep.

Almost instantly, it seemed, she was awakened by a voice

that said, 'Hey there, are you okay?' She opened her eyes and saw Brody sitting on the end of the bed.

She yawned. 'What time is it?'

'Almost six.'

'Oh-oh. I've got to pick up Sean. Phyllis Santos must be having a fit.'

'I got him,' said Brody. 'I figured I'd better, once I couldn't reach you.'

'You tried to reach me?'

'A couple of times. I tried you at the hospital at around two. They said they thought you'd come home.'

'That's right. I did. I felt awful. My thyroid pills aren't doing what they should. So I came home.'

'Then I tried to reach you here.'

'My, it must have been important.'

'No, it was nothing important. If you must know, I was calling to apologize for whatever I did that got you upset last night.'

A twinge of shame struck Ellen, but it passed, and she said, 'You're sweet, but don't worry. I'd already forgotten about it.'

'Oh,' said Brody. He waited a moment to see if she was going to say anything else, and when it was clear she wasn't, he said, 'So where were you?'

'I told you, here!' The words came out more harshly than she had intended. 'I came home and went to bed, and that's where you found me.'

'And you didn't hear the phone? It's right there.' Brody pointed to the bed table near the other side of the bed.

'No, I . . .' She started to say she had turned the phone off, but then she remembered that this particular phone couldn't be turned off all the way. 'I took a pill. The moaning of the damned won't wake me after I've taken one of those pills.'

Brody shook his head. 'I really am going to throw those damn things down the john. You're turning into a junkie.' He stood and went into the bathroom.

Ellen heard him flip up the toilet seat and begin to urinate – a loud, powerful, steady stream that went on and on and on. She smiled. Until today she had assumed Brody was some kind of urinary freak; he could go for almost a day without urinating. Then, when he did pee, he seemed to pee for ever. Long ago, she had concluded that his bladder was the size of a watermelon. Now she knew that huge bladder capacity was simply a male trait. Now, she said to herself, I am a woman of the world.

'Have you heard from Hooper?' Brody called over the noise of the endless stream.

Ellen thought for a moment about her response, then said, 'He called this morning, just to say thank you. Why?'

'I tried to get hold of him today, too. Around midday and a couple of times during the afternoon. The hotel said they didn't know where he was. What time did he call here?'

'Just after you left for work.'

'Did he say what he was going to be doing?'

'He said . . . he said he might try to work on the boat, I think. I really don't remember.'

'Oh. That's funny.'

'What is?'

'I stopped by the dock on my way home. The harbour master said he hadn't seen Hooper all day.'

'Maybe he changed his mind.'

'He was probably shagging Daisy Wicker in some hotel room.'

Ellen heard the stream slow, then dwindle into droplets. Then she heard the toilet flush.

NINE

On Thursday morning Brody got a call summoning him to Vaughan's office for a noon meeting of the Board of Selectmen. He knew what the subject of the meeting was: opening the beaches for the Fourth of July week-end that would begin the day after tomorrow. By the time he left his office for the town hall, he had marshalled and examined every argument he could think of.

He knew his arguments were subjective, negative, based on intuition, caution, and an abiding, gnawing guilt. But Brody was convinced he was right. Opening the beaches would not be a solution or a conclusion. It would be a gamble that Amity – and Brody – could never really win. They would never know for certain that the shark had gone away. They would be living from day to day, hoping for a continuing draw. And one day, Brody was sure, they would lose.

The town hall stood at the head of Main Street, where Main dead-ended and was crossed by Water Street. The building was a crown at the top of the T formed by Main and Water Streets. It was an imposing, pseudo-Georgian affair – red brick with white trim and two white columns framing the entrance. A World War II howitzer sat on the lawn in front of the town hall, a memorial to the citizens of Amity who had served in the war.

The building had been given to the town in the late 1920s by an investment banker who had somehow convinced himself that Amity would one day be the hub of commerce on eastern Long Island. He felt that the town's public officials should work in a building befitting their destiny – not, as had been the case until then, conducting the town's business in a tiny suite of airless rooms above a saloon called the Mill. (In February, 1930, the distraught banker, who had proved no more adept at predicting his own destiny than Amity's, tried, unsuccessfully, to reclaim the building, insisting he had intended only to loan it to the town.)

The rooms inside the town hall were as preposterously grandiose as the exterior. They were huge and high-ceilinged, each with its own elaborate chandelier. Rather than pay to remodel the interior into small cubicles, successive Amity administrations had simply jammed more and more people into each room. Only the mayor was still permitted to perform his part-time duties in solitary splendour.

Vaughan's office was on the south-east corner of the second floor, overlooking most of the town, and, in the distance, the Atlantic Ocean.

Vaughan's secretary, a wholesome, pretty woman named Janet Sumner, sat at a desk outside the mayor's office. Though he saw her seldom, Brody was paternally fond of Janet, and he was idly mystified that – aged about twenty-six – she was still unmarried. He usually made a point of inquiring about her love life before he entered Vaughan's office. Today he said simply, 'Are they all inside?'

'All that's coming.' Brody started into the office, and Janet said, 'Don't you want to know who I'm going out with?'

He stopped, smiled, and said, 'Sure. I'm sorry. My mind's a mess today. So who is it?'

'Nobody. I'm in temporary retirement. But I'll tell you one thing.' She lowered her voice and leaned forward. 'I wouldn't mind playing footsie with that Mr Hooper.'

'Is he in there?'

Janet nodded.

'I wonder when he was elected selectman.'

'I don't know,' she said. 'But he sure is cute.'

'Sorry, Jan, he's spoken for.'

'By who?'

'Daisy Wicker.'

Janet laughed.

'What's funny? I just broke your heart.'

'You don't know about Daisy Wicker?'

'I guess I don't.'

Again Janet lowered her voice. 'She's queer. She's got a lady room mate and everything. She's not even AC-DC. She's just plain old DC.'

'I'll be damned,' said Brody. 'You sure do have an interesting job, Jan.' As he entered the office, Brody said to himself: Okay, so where the hell *was* Hooper yesterday?

As soon as he was inside the office, Brody knew he would be fighting alone. The only selectmen present were longtime friends and allies of Vaughan's: Tony Catsoulis, a builder who looked like a fire hydrant; Ned Thatcher, a frail old man whose family had owned the Abelard Arms Inn for three generations; Paul Conover, owner of Amity Liquors; and Rafe Lopez (pronounced *loaps*), a dark-skinned Portuguese elected to the board by, and a vocal defender of, the town's black community.

The four selectmen sat around a coffee table at one end of the immense room. Vaughan sat at his desk at the other end of the room. Hooper stood at a southerly window, staring out at the sea.

'Where's Albert Morris?' Brody said to Vaughan after perfunctorily greeting the others.

'He couldn't make it,' said Vaughan. 'I don't think he felt well.'

'And Fred Potter?'

'Same thing. There must be a bug going around.' Vaughan stood up. 'Well, I guess we're all here. Grab a chair and pull it over by the coffee table.'

God, he looks awful, Brody thought as he watched Vaughan drag a straight-back chair across the room. Vaughan's eyes were sunken and dark. His skin looked like mayonnaise.

Either he's got some fierce hangover, Brody decided, or else he hasn't slept in a month.

When everyone was seated, Vaughan said, 'You all know why we're here. And I guess it's safe to say that there's only one of us that needs convincing about what we should do.'

'You mean me,' said Brody.

Vaughan nodded. 'Look at it from our point of view, Martin. The town is dying. People are out of work. Stores that were going to open aren't. People aren't renting houses, let alone buying them. And every day we keep the beaches closed, we drive another nail into our own coffin. We're saying, officially, this town is unsafe: stay away from here. And people are listening.'

'Suppose you do open the beaches for the Fourth, Larry,' said Brody. 'And suppose someone gets killed.'

'It's a calculated risk, but I think – we think – it's worth taking.'

'Why?'

Vaughan said, 'Mr Hooper?'

'Several reasons,' said Hooper. 'First of all, nobody's seen the fish in a week.'

'Nobody's been in the water, either.'

'That's true. But I've been on the boat looking for him every day – every day but one.'

'I meant to ask you about that. Where were you yesterday?'

'It rained,' said Hooper. 'Remember?'

'So what did you do?'

'I just . . .' He paused momentarily, then said, 'I studied some water samples. And read.'

'Where? In your hotel room?'

'Part of the time, yeah. What are you driving at?'

'I called your hotel. They said you were out all afternoon.'

'So I was out!' Hooper said angrily. 'I don't have to report in every five minutes, do I?'

'No. But you're here to do a job, not go gallivanting around all those country clubs you used to belong to.'

'Listen, mister, you're not paying me. I can do whatever the fuck I want!'

Vaughan broke in. 'Come on. This isn't getting anybody anywhere.'

'Anyway,' said Hooper. I haven't seen a trace of that fish. Not a sign. Then there's the water. It's getting warmer every day. It's almost seventy now. As a rule – I know, rules are made to be broken – great whites prefer cooler water.'

'So you think he's gone farther north?'

'Or out deeper, into colder water. He could even have gone south. You can't predict what these things are going to do.'

'That's my point, said Brody. 'You can't predict it. So all you're doing is guessing.'

Vaughan said, 'You can't ask for a guarantee, Martin.'

'Tell that to Christine Watkins. Or the Kintner boy's mother.'

'I know, I know,' Vaughan said impatiently. 'But we have to do something. We can't sit around waiting for divine revelation. God isn't going to scribble across the sky. "The shark is gone." We have to weigh the evidence and make a decision.'

Brody nodded. 'I guess. So what else has the boy genius come up with?'

'What's the matter with you?' said Hooper. 'I was asked for my opinion.'

'Sure,' said Brody. 'Okay. What else?'

'What we've known all along. That there's no reason for that fish to hang around here. I haven't seen him. The Coast Guard hasn't seen him. No news has popped up from the bottom. No garbage scows are dumping stuff into the water. No extraordinary fish life is around. There's just no reason for him to be here.'

'But there never has been, has there? And he was here.'

'That's true. I can't explain it. I doubt if anyone can.'

'An act of God, then?'

'And there's no insurance against acts of God, is there, Larry?'

'I don't know what you're getting at, Martin,' said Vaughan. 'But we've got to make a decision. As far as I'm concerned, there's only one way to go.'

'The decision's been made,' said Brody.

'You could say that, yes.'

'And when someone else gets killed? Who's taking the blame this time? Who's going to talk to the husband or the mother or the wife and tell them, "We were just playing the odds, and we lost"?'

'Don't be so negative, Martin. When the time comes – *if* the time comes, and I'm betting it won't – we'll work that out then.'

'Now, goddamn it! I'm sick of taking all the shit for your mistakes.'

'Wait a minute, Martin.'

'I'm serious. If you want the authority for closing the beaches, then you take the responsibility, too.'

'What are you saying?'

'I'm saying that as long as I'm chief of police in this town, as long as I'm supposed to be responsible for public safety, those beaches will not be open.'

'I'll tell you this, Martin,' said Vaughan. 'If those beaches stay closed over the Fourth of July week-end, you won't have your job very long. And I'm not threatening. I'm telling you. We can still have a summer. But we have to tell people it's safe to come here. Twenty minutes after they hear you won't open the beaches, the people of this town will impeach you, or find a rail and run you out on it. Do you agree, gentlemen?'

'Fuckin' A,' said Catsoulis. 'I'll give 'em the rail myself.'

'My people got no work,' said Lopez. 'You don't let them work, you're not gonna work.'

Brody said flatly, 'You can have my job any time you want it.'

A buzzer sounded on Vaughan's desk. He stood up angrily and crossed the room. He picked up the phone. 'I told you we didn't want to be disturbed!' he snapped. There was a moment's silence, and he said to Brody, 'There's a call for you. Janet says it's urgent. You can take it here or outside.'

'I'll take it outside,' Brody said, wondering what could be urgent enough to call him out of a meeting with the selectmen. Another attack? He left the room and closed the door behind him. Janet handed him the phone on her desk, but before she could depress the flashing button to release it from 'hold' Brody said, 'Tell me: did Larry ever call Albert Morris and Fred Potter this morning?'

Janet looked away from him. 'I was told not to say anything about anything to anybody.'

'Tell me, Janet. I need to know.'

'Will you put in a good word for me with Golden Boy in there?'

'It's a deal.'

'No. The only ones I called were the four in there.'

'Push the button.' Janet pushed the button, and Brody said, 'Brody.'

Inside his office, Vaughan saw the light stop flashing, and he gently eased his finger off the receiver hook and placed his hand over the mouthpiece. He looked around the room, searching each face for a challenge. No one returned his gaze – not even Hooper, who had decided that the less he was involved in the affairs of Amity, the better off he would be.

'It's Harry, Martin,' said Meadows. 'I know you're in a meeting and I know you've got to get back to it. So just listen. I'll be brief. Larry Vaughan is up to his tail in hock.'

'I don't believe it.'

'Listen, I said! The fact that he's in debt doesn't mean anything. It's who he's in debt to that matters. A long time ago, maybe twenty-five years, before Larry had any money, his wife got sick. I don't remember what she had, but it was serious. And expensive. My memory's a little hazy on this, but I remember him saying afterwards that he had been helped out by a friend, gotten a loan to pull him through. It must have been for several thousand dollars. Larry told me the man's name. I wouldn't have thought anything about it, but Larry said something about the man being willing to help out people in trouble. I was young then, and I didn't have any money either. So I made a note of the name and stuck it away in my files. It never occurred to me to look it up again until you asked me to start snooping. The name was Tino Russo.'

'Get to the point, Harry.'

'I am. Now jump to the present. A couple of months ago, before this shark thing ever began, a company was formed called Caskata Estates. It's a holding company. At the beginning, it had no real assets. The first thing it bought was a big potato field just north of Scotch Road. When the summer didn't shape up well, Caskata began to buy a few more properties. It was all perfectly legitimate. The company obviously has cash behind it – somewhere – and it was taking advantage of the down market to pick up properties at low prices. But then – as soon as the first newspaper reports about the shark thing came out – Caskata really started buying. The lower real estate prices fell, the more they bought. All very quietly. Prices are so low now that it's almost like during the war, and Caskata's still buying. Very little money down. All short-term promissory notes. Signed by Larry Vaughan, who is listed as the president of Caskata. The executive vice-president of Caskata Estates is Tino Russo, who the *Times* has been listing for years as a second-echelon crumb in one of the five Mafia families in New York.'

Brody whistled through his teeth. 'And the sonofabitch has been moaning about how nobody's been buying anything from him. I still don't understand why he's being pressured to open the beaches.'

'I'm not sure. I'm not even sure he's still being pressured. He may be arguing out of personal desperation. I imagine he's way overextended. He couldn't buy anything more no matter how low the prices go. The only way he can get out without being ruined is if the market turns around and the prices go up. Then he can sell what he's bought and get the profit. Or Russo can get the profit, however the deal's worked out. If prices keep going down – in other words, if the town is still officially unsafe – his notes are going to come due. He can't possibly meet them. He's probably got over half a million out now in cash down payments. He'll lose his cash, and the properties will either revert to the original owners or else get picked up by Russo if he can raise the cash. I don't imagine Russo would want to take the risk. Prices might keep going down, and then he'd take a bath along with Vaughan. My guess is that Russo still has hopes of big profits, but the only way he has a chance of getting them is if Vaughan forces the beaches open. Then, if nothing happens – if the shark doesn't kill anybody else – before long prices will go up and Vaughan can sell out. Russo will take his cut – half the gross or whatever – and Caskata will be dissolved. Vaughan will get what's left, probably enough to keep him from being ruined. If the shark does kill someone else, then the only one who gets screwed is Vaughan. As far as I can tell, Russo doesn't have a nickel in cash in this outfit. It's all—'

'You're a goddamned liar, Meadows!' Vaughan's voice shrieked into the phone. 'You print one word of that crap and I'll sue you to death!' There was a click as Vaughan slammed down the phone.

'So much for the integrity of our elected officials,' said Meadows.

'What *are* you going to do, Harry? Can you print anything?'

'No, at least not yet. I can't document enough. You know as well as I do that the mob is getting more and more involved in Long Island – the construction business, restaurants, everything. But it's hard as hell to prove an actual illegality. In Vaughan's case, I'm not sure there's anything illegal going on, in the strict sense of the word. In a few days, with a little more digging, I should be able to put together a piece saying that Vaughan has been associating with a known mobster. I mean a piece that will hold up if Vaughan ever did try to sue.'

'It sounds to me like you've got enough now,' said Brody.

'I have the knowledge, but not the proof. I don't have the documents, or even copies of them. I've seen them, but that's all.'

'Do you think any of the selectmen are in on the deal? Larry loaded this meeting against me.'

'No. You mean Catsoulis and Conover. They're just old buddies who owe Larry a favour or two. If Thatcher's there, he's too old and too scared to say a word against Larry. And Lopez is straight. He's really concerned about jobs for his people.'

'Does Hooper know any of this? He's making a pretty strong case for opening the beaches.'

'No, I'm pretty sure he doesn't. I only wrapped it up myself a few minutes ago, and there are still a lot of loose threads.'

'What do you think I ought to do? I may have quit already. I offered them my job before I came out to take your call.'

'Christ, don't quit. First of all, we need you. If you quit, Russo will get together with Vaughan and handpick your successor. You may think all your troops are honest, but I'll bet Russo could find one who wouldn't mind exchanging a little integrity for a few dollars – or even just for a shot at the chief's job.'

'So where does that leave me?'

'If I were you, I'd open the beaches.'

'For God's sake, Harry, that's what they want! I might as well go on their payroll.'

'You said yourself that there's a strong argument for opening the beaches. I think Hooper's right. You're going to have to open them sometime, even if we never see that fish again. You might as well do it now.'

'And let the mob take their money and run.'

'What else *can* you do? You keep them closed, and Vaughan'll find a way to get rid of you and he'll open them himself. Then you'll be no use whatever. To anybody. At least this way, if you open the beaches and nothing happens, the town might have a chance. Then, maybe later, we can find a way to pin something on Vaughan. I don't know what, but maybe there'll be something.'

'Shit,' said Brody. 'All right, Harry, I'll think about it. But if I open them, I'm gonna do it my way. Thanks for the call.' He hung up and went into Vaughan's office.

Vaughan was standing at the southerly window, his back to the door. When he heard Brody walk in, he said, 'The meeting's over.'

'What do you mean, over?' said Catsoulis. 'We ain't decided a fuckin' thing.'

Vaughan spun around and said, 'It's over, Tony! Don't give me any trouble. It'll work out the way we want. Just give me a chance to have a little chat with the chief. Okay? Now everybody out.'

Hooper and the four selectmen left the office. Brody watched Vaughan as he ushered them out. He knew he should feel pity for Vaughan, but he couldn't suppress the contempt that flowed over him. Vaughan shut the door, walked over to the couch, and sat down heavily. He rested his elbows on his knees and rubbed his temples with his fingertips. 'We were friends, Martin,' he said. 'I hope we can be again.'

'How much of what Meadows said is true?'

'I won't tell you. I can't. Suffice it to say that a man once did a favour for me and now he wants me to repay the favour.'

'In other words, all of it.'

Vaughan looked up, and Brody saw that his eyes were red and wet. 'I swear to you, Martin, if I had any idea how far this would go, I'd never have gotten into it.'

'How much are you into him for?'

'The original amount was ten thousand. I tried to pay it back twice, a long time ago, but I could never get them to cash my cheques. They kept saying it was a gift, not to worry about it. But they never gave me back my marker. When they came to me a couple of months ago, I offered them a hundred thousand dollars – cash. They said it wasn't enough. They didn't want the money. They wanted me to make a few investments. Everybody'd be a winner, they said.'

'And how much are you out now?'

'God knows. Every cent I have. More than every cent. Probably close to a million dollars.' Vaughan took a deep breath. 'Can you help me, Martin?'

'The only thing I can do for you is put you in touch with the D.A. If you'd testify, you might be able to slap a loan-sharking rap on these guys.'

'I'd be dead before I got home from the D.A.'s office, and Eleanor would be left without anything. That's not the kind of help I meant.'

'I know,' Brody looked down at Vaughan, a huddled, wounded animal, and he did feel compassion for him. He began to doubt his own opposition to opening the beaches. How much of it was the residue of prior guilt, how much fear of another attack? How much was he indulging himself, playing it safe, and how much was prudent concern for the town? 'I'll tell you what, Larry. I'll open the beaches. Not to help you, because I'm sure if I didn't open them you'd find a way to get rid of me and open them yourself. I'll open the beaches because I'm not sure I'm right any more.'

'Thanks, Martin. I appreciate that.'

'I'm not finished. Like I said, I'll open them. But I'm going to post men on the beaches. And I'm going to have Hooper patrol in the boat. And I'm going to make sure every person who comes down there knows the danger.'

'You can't do that!' Vaughan said. 'You might as well leave the damn things closed.'

'I can do it, Larry, and I will.'

'What are you going to do? Post signs warning of a killer shark? Put an ad in the newspaper saying "Beaches Open – Stay Away"? Nobody's going to go to the beach if it's crawling with cops.'

'I don't know what I'm going to do. But something. I'm not going to make believe nothing ever happened.'

'All right, Martin.' Vaughan rose. 'You don't leave me much choice. If I got rid of you, you'd probably go down to the beach as a private citizen and run up and down yelling "Shark!" So all right. But be subtle – if not for my sake, for the town's.'

Brody left the office. As he walked down the stairs, he looked at his watch. It was past one o'clock, and he was hungry. He went down Water Street to Loeffler's, Amity's only delicatessen. It was owned by Paul Loeffler, a classmate of Brody's in high school.

As Brody pulled open the glass door, he heard Loeffler say, '. . . like a goddamn dictator, if you ask me. I don't know what's his problem.' When he saw Brody, Loeffler blushed. He had been a skinny kid in high school, but as soon as he had taken over his father's business, he had succumbed to the terrible temptations that surrounded him for twelve hours of every day of every week, and nowadays he looked like a pear.

Brody smiled. 'You weren't talking about *me*, were you, Paulie?'

'What makes you think that?' said Loeffler, his blush deepening.

'Nothing. Never mind. If you'll make me a ham and Swiss

on rye with mustard, I'll tell you something that will make you happy.'

'That I have to hear.' Loeffler began to assemble Brody's sandwich.

'I'm going to open the beaches for the Fourth.'

'That makes me happy.'

'Business bad?'

'Bad.'

'Business is always bad with you.'

'Not like this. If it doesn't get better soon, I'm gonna be the cause of a race riot.'

'What do you mean?'

'I'm supposed to hire two delivery boys for the summer. I'm committed. But I can't afford two. Let alone I don't have enough work for two, the way things are. So I can only hire one. One's white and one's black.'

'Which one are you hiring?'

'The black one. I figure he needs the money more. I just thank God the white one isn't Jewish.'

Brody arrived home at 5.10. As he pulled into the driveway, the back door to the house opened, and Ellen ran towards him. She had been crying, and she was still visibly upset.

'What's the matter?' he said.

'Thank God you're home. I tried to reach you at work, but you had already left. Come here. Quick.' She took him by the hand and led him past the back door to the shed where they kept the garbage cans. 'In there,' she said, pointing to a can. 'Look.'

Brody removed the lid from the can. Lying in a twisted heap atop a bag of garbage was Sean's cat – a big, husky tom named Frisky. The cat's head had been twisted completely around, and the yellow eyes overlooked its back.

'How the hell did that happen?' said Brody. 'A car?'

'No, a man.' Ellen's breath came in sobs. 'A man did it to

him. Sean was right there when it happened. The man got out of a car over by the kerb. He picked up the cat and twisted its head until the neck broke. Sean said it made a horrible snap. Then he dropped the cat on the lawn and got back in his car and drove away.'

'Did he say anything?'

'I don't know. Sean's inside. He's hysterical, and I don't blame him. Martin, what's *happening*?'

Brody slammed the top back on the can. 'God damn sonofa*bitch*!' he said. His throat felt tight, and he clenched his teeth, popping the muscles on both sides of his jaw. 'Let's go inside.'

Five minutes later, Brody marched out the back door. He tore the lid off the garbage can and threw it aside. He reached in and pulled out the cat's corpse. He took it to his car, pitched it through the open window, and climbed in. He backed out of the driveway and screeched away. A hundred yards down the road, in a burst of uncontrollable fury, he turned on his siren.

It took him only a couple of minutes to reach Vaughan's house, a large, Tudor-style stone mansion on Sprain Drive, just off Scotch Road. He got out of the car, dragging the dead cat by one of its hind legs, mounted the front steps, and rang the bell. He hoped Eleanor Vaughan wouldn't answer the door.

The door opened, and Vaughan said, 'Hello, Martin, I . . .'

Brody raised the cat and pushed it towards Vaughan's face. 'What about this, you cocksucker?'

Vaughan's eyes widened. 'What do you mean? I don't know what you're talking about?'

'One of your friends did this. Right in my front yard, right in front of my kid. They murdered my fucking cat! Did you tell them to do that?'

'Don't be crazy, Martin.' Vaughan seemed genuinely shocked. 'I'd never do anything like that. Never.'

Brody lowered the cat and said, 'Did you call your friends after I left?'

'Well ... yes. But just to say that the beaches would be open tomorrow.'

'That's all you said?'

'Yes. Why?'

'You lying fuck!' Brody hit Vaughan in the chest with the cat and let it fall to the floor. 'You know what the guy said after he strangled my cat? You know what he told my eight-year-old boy?'

'No. Of course I don't know. How would I know?'

'He said the same thing you did. He said: "Tell your old man this – 'Be subtle.'"'

Brody turned and walked down the steps, leaving Vaughan standing over the gnarled bundle of bone and fur.

TEN

Friday was cloudy, with scattered light showers, and the only people who swam were a young couple who took a quick dip early in the morning just as Brody's man arrived at the beach. Hooper patrolled for six hours and saw nothing. On Friday night Brody called the Coast Guard for a weather report. He wasn't sure what he hoped to hear. He knew he should wish for beautiful weather for the three-day holiday week-end. It would bring people to Amity and if nothing happened, if nothing was sighted, by Tuesday he might begin to believe the shark had gone. If nothing happened. Privately, he would have welcomed a three-day blow that would keep the beaches clear over the week-end. Either way, he begged his personal deities not to let anything happen.

He wanted Hooper to go back to Woods Hole. It was not just that Hooper was always there, the expert voice to contradict his caution. Brody sensed that somehow Hooper had come into his home. He knew Ellen had talked to Hooper since the party: young Martin had mentioned something about the possibility of Hooper taking them on a beach picnic to look for shells. Then there was that business on Wednesday. Ellen had said she was sick and she certainly had looked worn out when he came home. But where had Hooper been that day? Why had he been so evasive when Brody had asked him about it? For the first time in his married life, Brody was wondering, and the wondering filled him with an uncomfortable ambivalence – self-reproach for questioning Ellen, and fear that there might actually be something to wonder about.

The weather report was for clear and sunny, south-west

winds five to ten knots. Well, Brody thought, maybe that's for the best. If we have a good week-end and nobody gets hurt, maybe I can believe. And Hooper's sure to leave.

Brody had said he would call Hooper as soon as he talked to the Coast Guard. He was standing at the kitchen phone. Ellen was washing the supper dishes. Brody knew Hooper was staying at the Abelard Arms. He saw the phone book buried beneath a pile of bills, note pads, and comic books on the kitchen counter. He started to reach for it, then stopped. 'I have to call Hooper,' he said. 'You know where the phone book is?'

'It's six-five-four-three,' said Ellen.

'What is?'

'The Abelard. That's the number: six-five-four-three.'

'How do you know?'

'I have a memory for phone numbers. You know that. I always have.'

He did know it, and he cursed himself for playing stupid tricks. He dialled the number.

'Abelard Arms.' It was a male voice, young. The night clerk.

'Matt Hooper's room, please.'

'You don't happen to know the room number, sir?'

'No.' Brody cupped his hand over the mouthpiece and said to Ellen, 'You don't happen to know the room number, do you?'

She looked at him, and for a second she didn't answer. Then she shook her head.

The clerk said, 'Here it is. Four-oh-five.'

The phone rang twice before Hooper answered.

'This is Brody.'

'Yeah. Hi.'

Brody faced the wall, trying to imagine what the room looked like. He conjured visions of a small dark garret, a rumpled bed, stains on the sheets, the smells of rut. He felt, briefly, that he was going out of his mind. 'I guess we're on for tomorrow,' he said. 'The weather report is good.'

'Yeah, I know.'

'Then I'll see you down at the dock.'

'What time ?'

'Nine-thirty, I guess. Nobody's going to go swimming before then.'

'Okay. Nine-thirty.'

'Fine. Oh hey, by the way,' Brody said, 'how did things work out with Daisy Wicker ?'

'What ?'

Brody wished he hadn't asked the question. 'Nothing. I was just curious. You know, about whether you two hit it off.'

'Well . . . yeah, now that you mention it. Is that part of your job, to check up on people's sex life ?'

'Forget it. Forget I ever mentioned it.' He hung up the phone. Liar, he thought. What the hell is going on here ? He turned to Ellen. 'I meant to ask you, Matt said something about a beach picnic. When's that ?'

'No special time,' she said. 'It was just a thought.'

'Oh.' He looked at her, but she didn't return the glance. 'I think it's time you got some sleep.'

'Why do you say that ?'

'You haven't been feeling well. And that's the second time you've washed that glass.' He took a beer from the refrigerator. He yanked the metal tab and it broke off in his hand. 'Fuck!' he said, and he threw the full can into the waste-basket and marched out of the room.

Saturday noon, Brody stood on a dune overlooking the Scotch Road Beach, feeling half secret agent, half fool. He was wearing a polo shirt and a bathing suit: he had had to buy one specially for this assignment. He was chagrined at his white legs, nearly hairless after years of chafing in long pants.

He wished Ellen had come with him to make him feel less conspicuous, but she had begged off, claiming that since he wasn't going to be home over the week-end, this would be a good time to catch up on her housework. In a beach bag by Brody's side were a pair of binoculars, a walkie-talkie, two beers, and a cellophane-wrapped sandwich. Offshore, between a quarter and half a mile, the *Flicka* moved slowly eastward. Brody watched the boat and said to himself: At least I know where *he* is today.

The Coast Guard had been right: the day was splendid – cloudless and warm, with a light onshore breeze. The beach was now crowded. A dozen or so teen-agers were scattered about in their ritual rows. A few couples lay dozing – motionless as corpses, as if to move would disrupt the cosmic rhythms that generated a tan. A family was gathered around a charcoal fire in the sand, and the scent of grilling hamburger drifted into Brody's nose.

No one had yet gone swimming. Twice different sets of parents had led their children to the water's edge and allowed them to wade in the wavewash, but after a few minutes – bored or fearful – the parents had ordered the children back up the beach.

Brody heard footsteps crackling in the beach grass behind him, and he turned around. A man and a woman – in their late forties, probably, and both grossly overweight – were struggling up the dune, dragging two complaining children behind them. The man wore khakis, a T-shirt, and basketball sneakers. The woman wore a print dress that rode up her wrinkled thighs. In her hand she carried a pair of sandals. Behind them Brody saw a Winnebago camper parked on Scotch Road.

'Can I help you?' Brody said when the couple had reached the top of the dune.

'Is this the beach?' said the woman.

'What beach are you looking for? The public beach is—'

'This is it, awright,' said the man, pulling a map out of his pocket. He spoke with the unmistakable accent of the Queensborough New Yorker. 'We turned off Twenty-seven and followed this road here. This is it, awright.'

'So where's the shark?' said one of the children, a fat boy of about thirteen. 'I thought you said we were gonna see a shark.'

'Shut up,' said his father. He said to Brody: 'Where's this hotshot shark?'

'What shark?'

'The shark that's killed all them people. I seen it on TV – on three different channels. There's a shark that kills people. Right here.'

'There *was* a shark here,' said Brody. 'But it isn't here now. And with any luck, it won't come back.'

The man stared at Brody for a second and then snarled, 'You mean we drove all the way out here to see this shark and he's gone? That's not what the TV said.'

'I can't help that,' said Brody. 'I don't know who told you you were going to see that shark. They don't just come up on the beach and shake hands, you know.'

'Don't smart-mouth me, buddy.'

Brody stood up. 'Listen, mister,' he said, pulling his wallet from the belt of his bathing suit and opening it so the man could see his badge. 'I'm the chief of police in this town. I don't know who you are, or who you think you are, but you don't march on to a private beach in Amity and start behaving like a bum. Now state your business or beat it.'

The man stopped posturing. 'Sorry,' he said. 'It's just after all that goddamn traffic and the kids screaming in my ear, I thought at least we'd get a look at the shark. That's what we come all the way out here for.'

'You drove two and a half hours to see a shark? Why?'

'Something to do. Last week-end we went to Jungle Habitat. We thought maybe this week-end we'd go to the

Jersey Shore. But then we heard about the shark out here. The kids never seen a shark before.'

'Well, I hope they don't see one today, either.'

'Shit,' said the man.

'You said we'd see a shark!' whined one of the boys.

'Shut your mouth, Benny!' The man turned back to Brody. 'Is it okay if we have lunch here?'

Brody knew he could order the people down to the public beach, but without a resident's parking sticker they would have to park their camper more than a mile from the beach, so he said, 'I guess so. If somebody complains, you'll have to move, but I doubt anyone will complain today. Go ahead. But don't leave anything – not a gum wrapper or a matchstick – on the beach, or I'll slap a ticket on you for littering.'

'Okay.' The man said to his wife, 'You got the cooler?'

'I left it in the camper,' she said. 'I didn't know we'd be staying.'

'Shit.' The man trudged down the dune, panting. The woman and her two children walked twenty or thirty yards away and sat on the sand.

Brody looked at his watch: 12.15. He reached into the beach bag and took out the walkie-talkie. He pushed a button and said, 'You there, Leonard?' Then he released the button.

In a moment the reply came back, rasping through the speaker. 'I read you, Chief. Over.' Hendricks had volunteered to spend the week-end on the public beach, as the third point in the triangle of watch. ('You're getting to be a regular beach bum,' Brody had said when Hendricks volunteered. Hendricks had laughed and said, 'Sure, Chief. If you're going to live in a place like this, you might as well become a beautiful people.')

'What's up?' said Brody. 'Anything going on?'

'Nothing we can't handle, but there is a little problem. People keep coming up to me and trying to give me tickets. Over.'

'Tickets for what?'

'To get on to the beach. They say they bought special tickets in town that allow them to come on to the Amity beach. You should see the damn things. I got one right here. It says "Shark Beach. Admit One. Two-fifty." All I can figure is some sharpie is making a pretty fine killing selling people tickets they don't need. Over.'

'What's their reaction when you turn down their tickets?'

'First, they're mad as hell when I tell them they've been taken, that there's no charge for coming to the beach. Then they get even madder when I tell them that, ticket or no ticket, they can't leave their cars in the parking lot without a parking permit. Over.'

'Did any of them tell you who's selling the tickets?'

'Just some guy, they say. They met him on Main Street, and he told them they couldn't get on the beach without a ticket. Over

'I want to find out who the hell is selling those tickets, Leonard, and I want him stopped. Go to the phone booth in the parking lot and call headquarters and tell whoever answers that I want a man to go down to Main Street and arrest that bastard. If he comes from out of town, run him out of town. If he lives here, lock him up.'

'On what charge? Over.'

'I don't care. Think of something. Fraud. Just get him off the streets.'

'Okay, Chief.'

'Any other problems?'

'No. There are some more of those TV guys here with one of those mobile units, but they're not doing anything except interviewing people. Over.'

'About what?'

'Just the standard stuff. You know: Are you scared to go swimming? What do you think about the shark? All that crap. Over.'

'How long have they been there?'

'Most of the morning. I don't know how long they'll hang around, specially since no one's going in the water. Over.'

'As long as they're not causing any trouble.'

'Nope. Over.'

'Okay. Hey, Leonard, you don't have to say "over" all the time. I can tell when you're finished speaking.'

'Just procedure, Chief. Keeps things clear. Over and out.'

Brody waited a moment, then pushed the button again and said, 'Hooper, this is Brody. Anything out there?' There was no answer. 'This is Brody calling Hooper. Can you hear me?' He was about to call a third time, when he heard Hooper's voice.

'Sorry. I was out on the stern. I thought I saw something.'

'What did you see?'

'Nothing. I'm sure it was nothing. My eyes were playing tricks on me.'

'What did you *think* you saw?'

'I can't really describe it. A shadow, maybe. Nothing more. The sunlight can fool you.'

'You haven't seen anything else?'

'Not a thing. All morning.'

'Let's keep it that way. I'll check with you later.'

'Fine. I'll be in front of the public beach in a minute or two.'

Brody put the walkie-talkie back in the bag and took out his sandwich. The bread was cold and stiff from resting against the ice-filled plastic bag that contained the cans of beer.

By 2.30, the beach was almost empty. People had gone off to play tennis, to sail, to have their hair done. The only ones left on the beach were half a dozen teen-agers and the family from Queens.

Brody's legs had begun to sunburn – faint red blotches were surfacing on his thighs and the tops of his feet – so he covered them with his towel. He took the walkie-talkie out of the bag and called Hendricks. 'Anything happening, Leonard?'

'Not a thing, Chief. Over.'

'Anybody go swimming?'

'Nope. Wading, but that's about it. Over.'

'Same here. What do you hear about the ticket seller?'

'Nothing, but nobody's giving me tickets any more, so I guess somebody ran him off. Over.'

'What about the TV people?'

'They're gone. They left a few minutes ago. They wanted to know where you were. Over.'

'What for?'

'Beats me. Over.'

'Did you tell them?'

'Sure. I didn't see why not. Over.'

'Okay. I'll talk to you later.' Brody decided to take a walk. He pushed a finger into one of the pink blotches on his thigh. It turned stark white, then flushed angry red when he removed his finger. He stood, wrapped his towel around his waist to keep the sun from his legs, and, carrying the walkie-talkie, strolled towards the water.

He heard the sound of a car engine, and he turned and walked to the top of the dune. A white panel truck was parked on Scotch Road. The black lettering on its side said, 'WNBC-TV News.' The driver's door opened and a man got out and trudged through the sand towards Brody.

As the man drew closer, Brody thought he looked vaguely familiar. He was young, with long curly hair and a handle-bar moustache.

'Chief Brody?' he said when he was a few steps away.

'That's right.'

'They told me you'd be here. I'm Bob Middleton, Channel Four News.'

'Are you the reporter?'

'Yeah. The crew's in the truck.'

'I thought I'd seen you somewhere. What can I do for you?'

'I'd like to interview you.'

'About what?'

'The whole shark business. How you decided to open the beaches.'

Brody thought for a moment, then said to himself, What the hell: a little publicity couldn't hurt the town, now that the chances of anything happening – today, at least – are pretty slim. 'All right,' he said. 'Where do you want to do it?'

'Down on the beach. I'll get the crew. It'll take a few minutes to set up, so if you have something to do, feel free. I'll give a yell when we're ready.' Middleton trotted away towards the truck.

Brody had nothing special to do, but since he had started to take a walk, he thought he might as well take it. He walked down towards the water.

As he passed the group of teen-agers, he heard a boy say, 'What about it? Anybody got the guts? Ten bucks is ten bucks.'

A girl said, 'Come on, Limbo, lay off.'

Brody stopped about fifteen feet away, feigning interest in something offshore.

'What for?' said the boy. 'It's a pretty good offer. I don't think anybody's got the guts. Five minutes ago, you were all telling me there's no *way* that shark's still around here.'

Another boy said, 'If you're such hot shit, why don't you go in?'

'I'm the one making the offer,' said the first boy. 'Nobody's gonna pay *me* ten bucks to go in the water. Well, what do you say?'

There was a moment's silence, and then the other boy said, 'Ten bucks? Cash?'

'It's right here,' said the first boy, shaking a ten-dollar bill. 'How far out do I have to go?'

'Let's see. A hundred yards. That's a pretty good distance. Okay?'

'How do I know how far a hundred yards is?'

'Guess. Just keep swimming for a while and then stop. If it looks like you're a hundred yards out, I'll wave you back.'

'You've got a deal.' The boy stood up.

The girl said, 'You're crazy, Jimmy. Why do you want to go in the water? You don't need ten dollars.'

'You think I'm scared?'

'Nobody said anything about being scared,' said the girl. 'It's unnecessary, is all.'

'Ten bucks is never unnecessary,' said the boy, 'especially when your old man cuts off your allowance for blowing a little grass at your aunt's wedding.'

The boy turned and began to jog towards the water. Brody said, 'Hey!' and the boy stopped.

'What?'

Brody walked over to the boy. 'What are you doing?'

'Going swimming. Who are you?'

Brody took out his wallet and showed the boy his badge. 'Do you want to go swimming?' he said. He saw the boy look past him at his friends.

'Sure. Why not? It's legal, isn't it?'

Brody nodded. He didn't know whether the others were out of earshot, so he lowered his voice and said, 'Do you want me to order you not to?'

The boy looked at him, hesitated for a moment, then shook his head. 'No, man. I can use the ten bucks.'

'Don't stay in too long,' said Brody.

'I won't.' The boy scampered into the water. He flung himself over a small wave and began to swim.

Brody heard footsteps running behind him. Bob Middleton dashed past him and called out to the boy, 'Hey! Come back!' He waved his arms and called again.

The boy stopped swimming and stood up. 'What's the matter?'

'Nothing. I want to get some shots of you going into the water. Okay?'

'Sure, I guess so,' said the boy. He began to wade back towards shore.

Middleton turned to Brody and said, 'I'm glad I caught him before he got too far out. At least we'll get *somebody* swimming out here today.'

Two men came up beside Brody. One was carrying a 16 mm camera and a tripod. He wore combat boots, fatigue trousers, a khaki shirt, and a leather vest. The other man was shorter and older and fatter. He wore a rumpled grey suit and carried a rectangular box covered with dials and knobs. Around his neck was a pair of earphones.

'Right there's okay, Walter,' said Middleton. 'Let me know when you're ready.' He took a notebook from his pocket and began to ask the boy some questions.

The elderly man walked down to Middleton and handed him a microphone. He backed up to the cameraman, feeding wire off a coil in his hand.

'Anytime,' said the cameraman.

'I gotta get a level on the kid,' said the man with the earphones.

'Say something,' Middleton told the boy, and he held the microphone a few inches from the boy's mouth.

'What do you want me to say?'

'That's good,' said the man with the earphones.

'Okay,' said Middleton. 'We'll start tight, Walter, then go to a two-shot, okay? Give me speed when you're ready.'

The cameraman peered into the eyepiece, raised a finger, and pointed it at Middleton. 'Speed,' he said.

Middleton looked at the camera and said, 'We have been here on the Amity beach since early this morning, and as far as we know, no one has yet dared venture into the water.

There has been no sign of the shark, but the threat still lingers. I'm standing here with Jim Prescott, a young man who has just decided to take a swim. Tell me, Jim, do you have any worries about what might be swimming out there with you?'

'No,' said the boy. 'I don't think there's anything out there.'

'So you're not scared.'

'No.'

'Are you a good swimmer?'

'Pretty good.'

Middleton held out his hand. 'Well, good luck, Jim. Thanks for talking to us.'

The boy shook Middleton's hand. 'Yeah,' he said. 'What do you want me to do now?'

'Cut!' said Middleton. 'We'll take it from the top, Walter. Just a sec.' He turned to the boy. 'Don't ask that, Jim, okay? After I thank you, just turn around and head for the water.'

'Okay,' said the boy. He was shivering, and he rubbed his arms.

'Hey, Bob,' said the cameraman. 'The kid ought to dry off. He can't look wet if he isn't supposed to have been in the water yet.'

'Yeah, you're right,' said Middleton. 'Can you dry off, Jim?'

'Sure.' The boy jogged up to his friends and dried himself with a towel.

A voice beside Brody said, 'What's goin' on?' It was the man from Queens.

'Television,' said Brody. 'They want to film somebody swimming.'

'Oh yeah? I should of brought my suit.'

The interview was repeated, and after Middleton had thanked the boy, the boy ran into the water and began to swim.

Middleton walked back to the cameraman and said, 'Keep it going, Walter. Irv, you can kill the sound. We'll probably use this for B-roll.'

'How much do you want of this?' said the cameraman, tracking the boy as he swam.

'A hundred feet or so,' said Middleton. 'But let's stay here till he comes out. Be ready, just in case.'

Brody had become so accustomed to the far-off, barely audible hum of the *Flicka*'s engine that his mind no longer registered it as a sound. It was as integral a part of the beach as the wave sound. Suddenly the engine's pitch changed from a low murmur to an urgent growl. Brody looked beyond the swimming boy and saw the boat in a tight, fast turn – nothing like the slow, ambling sweeps Hooper made in his normal patrol. He put the walkie-talkie to his mouth and said, 'You see something, Hooper?' Brody saw the boat slow, then stop.

Middleton heard Brody speak. 'Give me sound, Irv,' he said. 'Get this, Walter.' He walked to Brody and said, 'Something going on, Chief?'

'I don't know,' said Brody. 'That's what I'm trying to find out.' He said into the walkie-talkie, 'Hooper?'

'Yes,' said Hooper's voice, 'but I still don't know what it is. It was that shadow again. I can't see it now. Maybe my eyes are getting tired.'

'You get that, Irv?' said Middleton. The sound man shook his head no.

'There's a kid swimming out there,' said Brody.

'Where?' said Hooper.

Middleton shoved the microphone at Brody's face, sliding it between his mouth and the mouthpiece of the walkie-talkie. Brody brushed it aside, but Middleton quickly jammed it back to within an inch of Brody's mouth.

'Thirty, maybe forty yards out. I think I better tell him to come in.' Brody tucked the walkie-talkie into the towel at his waist, cupped his hands around his mouth, and called, 'Hey out there! Come on in!'

'Jesus!' said the sound man. 'You damn near blew my ears out.'

The boy did not hear the call. He was swimming straight away from the beach.

The boy who had offered the ten dollars heard Brody's call, and he walked down to the water's edge. 'What's the trouble now?' he said.

'Nothing,' said Brody. 'I just think he'd better come in.'

'Who are you?'

Middleton stood between Brody and the boy, flipping the microphone back and forth between the two.

'I'm the police chief, kid,' Brody said. 'Now get your ass out of here!' He turned to Middleton. 'And you keep that fucking microphone out of my face, will you?'

'Don't worry, Irv,' said Middleton. 'We can edit that out.'

Brody said into the walkie-talkie, 'Hooper, he doesn't hear me. You want to toot in here and tell him to come ashore?'

'Sure,' said Hooper. 'I'll be there in a minute.'

The fish had sounded now, and was meandering a few feet above the sandy bottom, eighty feet below the *Flicka*. For hours, its sensory system had been tracking the strange sounds above. Twice the fish had risen to within a yard or two of the surface, allowing sight and smell and nerve canals to assess the creature passing noisily overhead. Twice it had sounded, compelled neither to attack nor move away.

Brody saw the boat, which had been facing westward, swing towards shore and kick up a shower of spray from the bouncing bow.

'Get the boat, Walter,' said Middleton.

Below, the fish sensed a change in the noise. It grew louder, then faded as the boat moved away. The fish turned, banking as smoothly as an aeroplane, and followed the receding sound.

The boy stopped swimming, raised his head, and looked

towards shore, treading water. Brody waved his arms and yelled, 'Come in!' The boy waved back and started for shore. He swam well, rolling his head to the left to catch a breath, kicking in rhythm with his arm strokes. Brody guessed he was sixty yards from shore and that it would take him a minute or more to reach the beach.

'What's goin' on?' said a voice next to Brody. It was the man from Queens. His two sons stood behind him, smiling eagerly.

'Nothing,' said Brody. 'I just don't want the boy to get out too far.'

'Is it the shark?' asked the father of the two boys.

'Hey, neat,' said the other boy.

'Never mind!' said Brody. 'Just get back up the beach.'

'Come on, Chief,' said the man. 'We drove all the way out here.'

'Beat it!' said Brody.

At fifteen knots, it took Hooper only thirty seconds to cover the couple of hundred yards and draw near the boy. He stopped a few yards away, letting the engine idle in neutral. He was just beyond the surf line, and he didn't dare go closer for fear of being caught in the waves.

The boy heard the engine, and he raised his head. 'What's the matter?' he said.

'Nothing,' said Hooper. 'Keep swimming.'

The boy lowered his head and swam. A swell caught him and moved him faster, and with two or three more strokes he was able to stand. The water was up to his shoulders, and he began to plod towards shore.

'Come on!' said Brody.

'I am,' said the boy. 'What's the problem, anyway?'

A few yards behind Brody, Middleton stood with the microphone in his hand. 'What are you on, Walter?' he said.

'The kid,' said the cameraman, 'and the cop. Both. A two-shot.'

'Okay. You running, Irv?'

The sound man nodded.

Middleton spoke into the microphone: 'Something is going on, ladies and gentlemen, but we don't know exactly what. All we know for sure is that Jim Prescott went swimming, and then suddenly a man on a boat out there saw something. Now Police Chief Brody is trying to get the boy to come ashore as fast as possible. It could be the shark, but we just don't know.'

Hooper put the boat in reverse, to back away from the waves. As he looked off the stern, he saw a silver streak moving in the grey-blue water. It seemed part of the wave-motion, but it moved independently. For a second, Hooper did not realize what he was seeing. And even when the realization struck, he did not see the fish clearly. He cried, 'Look out!'

'What is it?' yelled Brody.

'The fish! Get the kid out! Quick!'

The boy heard Hooper, and he tried to run. But in the chest-deep water his movements were slow and laboured. A swell knocked him sideways. He stumbled, then stood and leaned forward.

Brody ran into the water and reached out. A wave hit him in the knees and pushed him back.

Middleton said into the microphone, 'The man on the boat just said something about a fish. I don't know if he means a shark.'

'Is it the shark?' said the man from Queens, standing next to Middleton. 'I don't see it.'

Middleton said, 'Who are you?'

'Name's Lester Kraslow. You want to interview me?'

'Go away.'

The boy was moving faster now, pushing through the water with his chest and arms. He did not see the fin rise behind him, a sharp blade of brownish grey that hovered in the water.

'There it is!' said Kraslow. 'See it, Benny? Davey? It's right there.'

'I don't see nothin',' said one of his sons.

'There it is, Walter!' said Middleton. 'See it?'

'I'm zooming,' said the cameraman. 'Yeah, I've got it.'

'Hurry!' said Brody. He reached for the boy. The boy's eyes were wide and panicked. His nostrils flared, bubbling mucus and water. Brody's hand touched the boy's, and he pulled. He grabbed the boy around the chest, and together they staggered out of the water.

The fin dropped beneath the surface, and following the slope of the ocean floor, the fish moved into the deep.

Brody stood in the sand with his arm around the boy. 'Are you okay?' he said.

'I want to go home.' The boy shivered.

'I bet you do.' Brody started to walk the boy to where his friends were standing, but Middleton intercepted them.

'Can you repeat that for me?' said Middleton.

'Repeat what?'

'Whatever you said to the boy. Can we do that again?'

'Get out of my way!' Brody snapped. He took the boy to his friends, and said to the one who had offered the money, 'Take him home. And give him his ten dollars.' The boy nodded, pale and scared.

Brody saw his walkie-talkie wallowing in the wavewash. He retrieved it, wiped it free of water, pushed the 'talk' button, and said, 'Leonard, can you hear me?'

'I read you, Chief. Over.'

'The fish has been here. If you've got anybody in the water down there, get them out. Right away. And stay there till we get relief for you. Nobody goes near the water. The beach is officially closed.'

'Okay, Chief. Was anybody hurt? Over.'

'No, thank God. But almost.'

'Okay, Chief. Over and out.'

As Brody walked back to where he had left his beach bag, Middleton called to him. 'Hey, Chief, can we do that interview now?'

Brody stopped, tempted to tell Middleton to go fuck himself. Instead, he said, 'What do you want to know? You saw it as well as I did.'

'Just a couple of questions.'

Brody sighed and returned to where Middleton stood with his camera crew. 'All right,' he said, 'go ahead.'

'How much have you got on your roll, Walter?' said Middleton.

'About fifty feet. Make it brief.'

'Okay. Give me speed.'

'Speed.'

'Well, Chief Brody,' said Middleton, 'that was a lucky break, wouldn't you say?'

'It was very lucky. The boy might have died.'

'Would you say that's the same shark that killed the people?'

'I don't know,' said Brody. 'I guess it must be.'

'So where do you go from here?'

'The beaches are closed. For the time being, that's all I can do.'

'I guess you'd have to say that it isn't yet safe to swim here in Amity.'

'I'd have to say that, that's right.'

'What does that mean for Amity?'

'Trouble, Mr Middleton. We are in big trouble.'

'In retrospect, Chief, how do you feel about having opened the beaches today?'

'How do I *feel*? What kind of question is that? Angry, annoyed, confused. Thankful that nobody got hurt. Is that enough?'

'That's just fine, Chief,' Middleton said with a smile. 'Thank you, Chief Brody.' He paused, then said, 'Okay

Walter, that'll wrap it. Let's get home and start editing this mess.'

'What about a close?' said the cameraman. 'I've got about twenty-five feet left.'

'Okay,' said Middleton. 'Wait'll I think of something profound to say.'

Brody gathered up his towel and his beach bag and walked over the dune towards his car. When he got to Scotch Road, he saw the family from Queens standing beside their camper.

'Was that the shark that killed the people?' asked the father.

'Who knows?' said Brody. 'What's the difference?'

'Didn't look like much to me, just a fin. The boys was kind of disappointed.'

'Listen, you jerk,' Brody said. 'A boy almost got killed just now. Are you disappointed that didn't happen?'

'Don't give me that,' said the man. 'That thing wasn't even close to him. I bet the whole thing was a put-on for them TV guys.'

'Mister, get out of here. You and your whole goddamn brood. Get 'em out of here. Now!'

Brody waited while the man loaded his family and their gear into the camper. As he walked away, he heard the man say to his wife, 'I figured all the people would be snot-noses out here. I was right. Even the cops.'

At six o'clock, Brody sat in his office with Hooper and Meadows. He had already talked to Larry Vaughan, who called – drunk and in tears – and muttered wildly about the ruination of his life. The buzzer on Brody's desk rang, and he picked up the phone.

'Fellow named Bill Whitman to see you, Chief,' said Bixby. 'Says he's from the New York *Times*.'

'Oh, for . . . Okay, what the hell. Send him in.'

The door opened, and Whitman stood in the doorway. He said, 'Am I interrupting something?'

'Nothing much,' said Brody. 'Come on in. You remember Harry Meadows. This is Matt Hooper, from Woods Hole.'

'I remember Harry Meadows, all right,' said Whitman. 'It was thanks to him that I got my ass chewed from one end of Forty-third Street to the other by my boss.'

'Why was that?' said Brody.

'Mr Meadows conveniently forgot to tell me about the attack on Christine Watkins. But he didn't forget to tell his readers.'

'Must have slipped my mind,' said Meadows.

'What can we do for you?' said Brody.

'I was wondering,' said Whitman, 'if you're sure this is the same fish that killed the others.'

Brody gestured towards Hooper, who said, 'I can't be positive. I never saw the fish that killed the others, and I didn't really get a look at the one today. All I saw was a flash, sort of silvery grey. I know what it was, but I couldn't compare it to anything else. All I have to go on is probability, and in all probability it's the same fish. It's too far-fetched – for me, anyway – to believe that there are two big man-eating sharks off southern Long Island at the same time.'

Whitman said to Brody, 'What are you going to do, Chief? I mean, beyond closing the beaches, which I gather has already been done.'

'I don't know. What *can* we do? Christ, I'd rather have a hurricane. Or even an earthquake. At least after they happen, they're over and done with. You can look around and see what's been done and what has to be done. They're events, something you can handle. They have beginnings and ends. This is crazy. It's as if there was a maniac running around loose, killing people whenever he felt like it. You know who he is, but you can't catch him and you can't stop him. And what makes it worse, you don't know why he's doing it.'

Meadows said, 'Remember Minnie Eldridge.'

'Yeah,' said Brody. 'I'm beginning to think she may have something, after all.'

'Who's that?' said Whitman.

'Nobody. Just some nut.'

For a moment there was silence, an exhausted silence, as if everything that needed to be said had been said. Then Whitman said, 'Well?'

'Well what?' said Brody.

'There must be someplace to go from here, something to do.'

'I'd be happy to hear any suggestions. Personally, I think we're fucked. We're going to be lucky if there's a town left after this summer.'

'Isn't that a bit of an exaggeration?'

'I don't think so. Do you, Harry?'

'Not really,' said Meadows. 'The town survives on its summer people, Mr Whitman. Call it parasitic, if you will, but that's the way it is. The host animal comes every summer, and Amity feeds on it furiously, pulling every bit of sustenance it can before the host leaves again after Labour Day. Take away the host animal, and we're like dog ticks with no dog to feed on. We starve. At the least – the very least – next winter is going to be the worst in the history of this town. We're going to have so many people on the dole that Amity will look like Harlem.' He chuckled. 'Harlem-by-the-Sea.'

'What I'd give my ass to know,' said Brody, 'is why us? Why Amity? Why not East Hampton or Southampton or Quogue?'

'That,' said Hooper, 'is something we'll never know.'

'Why?' said Whitman.

'I don't want to sound like I'm making excuses for misjudging that fish,' said Hooper, 'but the line between the natural and the preternatural is very cloudy. Natural things occur, and for most of them there's a logical explanation.

But for a whole lot of things there's just no good or sensible answer. Say two people are swimming, one in front of the other, and a shark comes up from behind, passes right beside the guy in the rear, and attacks the guy in front. Why? Maybe they smelled different. Maybe the one in front was swimming in a more provocative way. Say the guy in back, the one who wasn't attacked, goes to help the one who was attacked. The shark may not touch him – may actually avoid him – while he keeps banging away at the guy he did hit. White sharks are supposed to prefer colder water. So why does one turn up off the coast of Mexico, strangled by a human corpse that he couldn't quite swallow? In a way, sharks are like tornadoes. They touch down here, but not there. They wipe out this house but suddenly veer away and miss the house next door. The guy in the house that's wiped out says, "Why me?" The guy in the house that's missed says, "Thank God."'

'All right,' said Whitman. 'But what I still don't get is why the shark can't be caught.'

'Maybe it can be,' said Hooper. 'But I don't think by us. At least not with the equipment we have here. I suppose we could try chumming again.'

'Yeah,' said Brody. 'Ben Gardner can tell us all about chumming.'

'Do you know anything about some fellow named Quint?' said Whitman.

'I've heard the name,' Brody said. 'Did you ever look into the guy, Harry?'

'I read what little there was. As far as I know, he's never done anything illegal.'

'Well,' said Brody, 'maybe it's worth a call.'

'You're joking,' said Hooper. 'You'd really do business with this guy?'

'I'll tell you what, Hooper. At this point, if someone came in here and said he was Superman and he could piss that shark away from here, I'd say fine and dandy. I'd even hold his dick for him.'

'Yeah, but . . .'

Brody cut him off. 'What do you say, Harry? You think he's in the phone book?'

'You really are serious,' said Hooper.

'You bet your sweet ass. You got any better ideas?'

'No, it's just . . . I don't know. How do we know the guy isn't a phony or a drunk or something?'

'We'll never know till we try.' Brody took a phone book from the top drawer of his desk, and opened it to the Qs. He ran his finger down the page. 'Here it is. "Quint." That's all it says. No first name. But it's the only one on the page. Must be him.' He dialled the number.

'Quint,' said a voice.

'Mr Quint, this is Martin Brody. I'm the chief of police over in Amity. We have a problem.'

'I've heard.'

'The shark was around again today.'

'Anybody get et?'

'No, but one boy almost did.'

'Fish that big needs a lot of food,' said Quint.

'Have you seen the fish?'

'Nope. Looked for him a couple times, but I couldn't spend too much time looking. My people don't spend their money for looking. They want action.'

'How did you know how big it is?'

'I hear tell. Sort of averaged out the estimates and took off about eight feet. That's still a piece of fish you got there.'

'I know. What I'm wondering is whether you can help us.'

'I know. I thought you might call.'

'Can you?'

'That depends.'

'On what?'

'On how much you're willing to spend, for one thing.'

203

'We'll pay whatever the going rate is. Whatever you charge by the day. We'll pay you by the day until we kill the thing.'

'I don't think so,' said Quint. 'I think this is a premium job.'

'What does that mean?'

'My everyday rate's two hundred a day. But this is special. I think you'll pay double.'

'Not a chance.'

'Good-bye.'

'Wait a minute! Come on, man. Why are you holding me up?'

'You got no place else to go.'

'There are other fishermen.'

Brody heard Quint laugh – a short, derisive bark. 'Sure there are,' said Quint. 'You already sent one. Send another one. Send half a dozen more. Then when you come back to me again, maybe you'll even pay triple. I got nothing to lose by waiting.'

'I'm not asking for any favours,' Brody said. 'I know you've got a living to make. But this fish is killing people. I want to stop it. I want to save lives. I want your help. Can't you at least treat me the way you treat regular clients?'

'You're breaking my heart,' said Quint. 'You got a fish needs killing, I'll try to kill it for you. No guarantees, but I'll do my best. And my best is worth four hundred dollars a day.'

Brody sighed. 'I don't know that the selectmen will give me the money.'

'You'll find it somewhere.'

'How long do you think it'll take to catch the fish?'

'A day, a week, a month. Who knows? We may never find him. He may go away.'

'Don't I wish,' said Brody. He paused. 'Okay,' he said finally. 'I guess we don't have any choice.'

'No, you don't.'

'Can you start tomorrow?'

'Nope. Monday's the earliest. I got a party tomorrow.'

'A party? What do you mean, a dinner party?'

Quint laughed again, the same piercing bark. 'A charter party,' he said. 'You don't do much fishing.'

Brody blushed. 'No, that's right. Can't you cancel them? If we're paying all that money, it seems to me we deserve a little special service.'

'Nope. They're regular customers. I couldn't do that to them or I'd lose their business. You're just a one-shot deal.'

'Suppose you run into the big fish tomorrow. Will you try to catch him?'

'That would save you a lot of money, wouldn't it? We won't see your fish. We're going due east. Terrific fishing due east. You oughta try it sometime.'

'You had it all figured out, right?'

'There's one more thing,' said Quint. 'I'm gonna need a man with me. I lost my mate, and I wouldn't feel comfortable taking on that big fish without an extra pair of hands.'

'Lost your mate? What, overboard?'

'No, he quit. He got nerves. Happens to most people after a while in this work. They get to thinking too much.'

'But it doesn't happen to you.'

'No. I know I'm smarter'n the fish.'

'And that's enough, just being smarter?'

'Has been so far. I'm still alive. What about it? You got a man for me?'

'You can't find another mate?'

'Not this quick, and not for this kind of work.'

'Who are you going to use tomorrow?'

'Some kid. But I won't take him out after a big white.'

'I can understand that,' said Brody, beginning to doubt the wisdom of approaching Quint for help. He added casually, 'I'll be there, you know.' He was shocked by the words as soon as he said them, appalled at what he had committed himself to do.

'You? Ha!'

Brody smarted under Quint's derision. 'I can handle myself,' he said.

'Maybe. I don't know you. But you can't handle a big fish if you don't know nothing about fishing. Can you swim?'

'Of course. What has that got to do with anything?'

'People fall overboard, and sometimes it takes a while to swing around and get to 'em.'

'Don't worry about me.'

'Whatever you say. But I still need a man who knows something about fishing. Or at least about boats.'

Brody looked across his desk at Hooper. The last thing he wanted was to spend days on a boat with Hooper, especially in a situation in which Hooper would outrank him in knowledge, if not authority. He could send Hooper alone and stay ashore himself. But that, he felt, would be capitulating, admitting finally and irrevocably his inability to face and conquer the strange enemy that was waging war on his town.

Besides, maybe – over the course of a long day on a boat – Hooper might make a slip that would reveal what he had been doing last Wednesday, the day it rained. Brody was becoming obsessed with finding out where Hooper was that day, for whenever he allowed himself to consider the various alternatives, the one on which his mind always settled was the one he most dreaded. He wanted to *know* that Hooper was at the movies, or playing backgammon at the Field Club, or smoking dope with some hippie, or laying some Girl Scout. He didn't care what it was, as long as he could know that Hooper had not been with Ellen. Or that he had been. In that case ... ? The thought was still too wretched to cope with.

He cupped his hand over the mouthpiece and said to Hooper, 'Do you want to come along? He needs a mate.'

'He doesn't even have a mate? What a half-assed operation.'

'Never mind that. Do you want to come or not?'

'Yes,' said Hooper. 'I'll probably live to regret it, but yes. I want to see that fish, and I guess this is my only chance.'

Brody said to Quint, 'Okay, I've got your man.'

'Does he know boats?'

'He knows boats.'

'Monday morning, six o'clock. Bring whatever you want to eat. You know how to get here?'

'Route 27 to the turnoff for Promised Land, right?'

'Yeah. It's called Cranberry Hole Road. Straight into town. About a hundred yards past the last houses, take a left on a dirt road.'

'Is there a sign?'

'No, but it's the only road around here. Leads right to my dock.'

'Yours the only boat there?'

'Only one. It's called the *Orca*.'

'All right. See you Monday.'

'One more thing,' said Quint. 'Cash. Every day. In advance.'

'Okay, but how come?'

'That's the way I do business. I don't want you falling overboard with my money.'

'All right,' said Brody. 'You'll have it.' He hung up and said to Hooper, 'Monday, six AM, okay?'

'Okay.'

Meadows said, 'Do I gather from your conversation that you're going, too, Martin?'

Brody nodded. 'It's my job.'

'I'd say it's a bit beyond the call.'

'Well, it's done now.'

'What's the name of his boat?' asked Hooper.

'I think he said *Orca*,' said Brody. 'I don't know what it means.'

'It doesn't *mean* anything. It *is* something. It's a killer whale.'

207

Meadows, Hooper, and Whitman rose to go. 'Good luck,' said Whitman. 'I kind of envy you your trip. It should be exciting.'

'I can do without excitement,' said Brody. 'I just want to get the damn thing over with.'

At the door, Hooper turned and said, 'Thinking of orca reminds me of something. You know what Australians call great white sharks?'

'No,' said Brody, not really interested. 'What?'

'White death.'

'You had to tell me, didn't you?' Brody said as he closed the door behind them.

He was on his way out when the night desk man stopped him and said, 'You had a call before, Chief, while you were inside. I didn't think I should bother you.'

'Who was it?'

'Mrs Vaughan.'

'*Mrs* Vaughan!' As far as Brody could remember, he had never in his life talked to Eleanor Vaughan on the telephone.

'She said not to disturb you, that it could wait.'

'I'd better call her. She's so shy that if her house was burning down, she'd call the fire department and apologize for bothering them and ask if there was a chance they could stop by the next time they were in the neighbourhood.' As he walked back into his office, Brody recalled something Vaughan had told him about Eleanor: whenever she wrote a cheque for an even-dollar amount, she refused to write 'and 00/100.' She felt it would be an insult, as if she were suggesting that the person who cashed the cheque might try to steal a few cents.

Brody dialled the Vaughans' home number, and Eleanor Vaughan answered before the phone had rung once. She's been sitting right by the phone, Brody thought. 'Martin Brody, Eleanor. You called.'

'Oh yes. I do hate to bother you, Martin. If you'd rather—'

'No, it's perfectly okay. What's on your mind?'

'It's . . . well, the reason I'm calling *you* is that I know Larry talked with you earlier. I thought you might know if . . . if anything's wrong.'

Brody thought: She doesn't know anything, not a thing. Well, I'm damned if I'm going to tell her. 'Why? What do you mean?'

'I don't know how to say this exactly, but . . . well Larry doesn't drink much, you know. Very rarely, at least at home.'

'And?'

'This evening, when he came home, he didn't say anything. He just went into his study and – I think, at least – he drank almost a whole bottle of whisky. He's asleep now, in a chair.'

'I wouldn't worry about it, Eleanor. He's probably got things on his mind. We all tie one on now and then.'

'I know. It's only . . . something *is* wrong. I can tell. He hasn't acted like himself for several days now. I thought that perhaps . . . you're his friend. Do you know what it could be?'

His friend, Brody thought. That's what Vaughan had said, too, but he had known better. 'We used to be friends,' he had said. 'No, Eleanor, I don't,' he lied. 'I'll talk to him about it, though, if you like.'

'Would you, Martin? I'd appreciate that. But . . . please . . . don't tell him I called you. He's never wanted me to meddle in his affairs.'

'I won't. Don't worry. Try to get some sleep.'

'Will he be all right in the chair?'

'Sure. Just take off his shoes and throw a blanket over him. He'll be fine.'

Paul Loeffler stood behind the counter of his delicatessen and looked at his watch. 'It's quarter to nine,' he said to his wife, a plump, pretty woman named Rose, who was arranging boxes of butter in a refrigerator. 'What do you say we cheat and close up fifteen minutes early?'

'After a day like today I agree,' said Rose. 'Eighteen pounds of bologna! Since when have we ever moved eighteen pounds of bologna in one day?'

'And the Swiss cheese,' said Loeffler. 'When did we ever run out of Swiss cheese before? A few more days like this I could use. Roast beef, liverwurst, everything. It's like everybody from Brooklyn Heights to East Hampton stopped by for sandwiches.'

'Brooklyn Heights, my eye. Pennsylvania. One man said he had come all the way from Pennsylvania. Just to see a fish. They don't have fish in Pennsylvania?'

'Who knows?' said Loeffler. 'It's getting to be like Coney Island.'

'The public beach must look like a dump.'

'It's worth it. We deserve one or two good days.'

'I heard the beaches are closed again,' said Rose.

'Yeah. Like I always say, when it rains it pours.'

'What are you talking about?'

'I don't know. Let's close up.'

Part 3

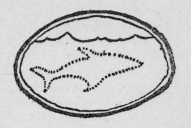

ELEVEN

The sea was as flat as gelatine. There was no whisper of wind to ripple the surface. The sun sucked shimmering waves of heat from the water. Now and then, a passing tern would plunge for food, and rise again, and the wavelets from its dive became circles that grew without cease.

The boat sat still in the water, drifting imperceptibly in the tide. Two fishing rods, in rod-holders at the stern, trailed wire line into the oily slick that spread westward behind the boat. Hooper sat at the stern, a twenty-gallon garbage pail at his side. Every few seconds, he dipped a ladle into the pail and spilled it overboard into the slick.

Forward, in two rows that peaked at the bow, lay ten wooden barrels the size of quarter kegs of beer. Each was wrapped in several thicknesses of three-quarter-inch hemp, which continued in a hundred-foot coil beside the barrel. Tied to the end of each rope was the steel head of a harpoon.

Brody sat in the swivelled fighting chair bolted to the deck, trying to stay awake. He was hot and sticky. There had been no breeze at all during the six hours they had been sitting and waiting. The back of his neck was already badly sunburned, and every time he moved his head the collar of his uniform shirt raked the tender skin. His body odour rose to his face and, blended with the stench of the fish guts and blood being ladled overboard, nauseated him. He felt poached.

Brody looked up at the figure on the flying bridge: Quint. He wore a white tee-shirt, faded blue-jean trousers, white socks, and a pair of greying Top-Sider sneakers. Brody guessed Quint was about fifty, and though surely he had once been twenty and would one day be sixty, it was impossible to imagine what he would look like at either of those ages. His present age seemed the age he should always be, should always have been. He was about six feet four and very lean – perhaps 180 or 190 pounds. His head was totally bald – not shaven, for there were no telltale black specks on his scalp, but as bald as if he had never had any hair – and when, as now, the sun was high and hot, he wore a Marine Corps fatigue cap. His face, like the rest of him, was hard and sharp. It was ruled by a long, straight nose. When he looked down from the flying bridge, he seemed to aim his eyes – the darkest eyes Brody had ever seen – along the nose as if it were a rifle barrel. His skin was permanently browned and creased by wind and salt and sun. He gazed off the stern, rarely blinking, his eyes fixed on the slick.

A trickle of sweat running down Brody's chest made him stir. He turned his head, wincing at the sting in his neck, and tried to stare at the slick. But the reflection of the sun on the water hurt his eyes, and he turned away. 'I don't see how you do it, Quint,' he said. 'Don't you ever wear sunglasses ?'

Quint looked down and said, 'Never.' His tone was completely neutral, neither friendly nor unfriendly. It did not invite conversation.

But Brody was bored, and he wanted to talk. 'How come ?'

'No need to. I see things the way they are. That's better.'

Brody looked at his watch. It was a little after two : three or four more hours before they would give up for the day and go home. 'Do you have a lot of days like this ?' The excitement and anticipation of the early morning had long passed, and Brody was sure they would not sight the fish that day.

'Like what ?'

'Like this. When you sit all day long and nothing happens.'

'Some.'

'And people pay you even though they never catch a thing.'

'Those are the rules.'

'Even if they never get a bite?'

Quint nodded. 'That doesn't happen too often. There's generally something that'll take a bait. Or something we can stick.'

'Stick?'

'With an iron.' Quint pointed to the harpoons on the bow.

Hooper said, 'What kinds of things do you stick, Quint?'

'Anything that swims by.'

'Really? I don't—'

Quint cut him off. 'Something's taking one of the baits.'

Shading his eyes with his hand, Brody looked off the stern, but as far as he could see, the slick was undisturbed, the water flat and calm. 'Where?' he said.

'Wait a second,' said Quint. 'You'll see.'

With a soft metallic hiss, the wire on the starboard fishing rod began to feed overboard, knifing into the water in a straight silver line.

'Take the rod,' Quint said to Brody. 'And when I tell you, throw the brake and hit him.'

'Is it the shark?' said Brody. The possibility that at last he was going to confront the fish – the beast, the monster, the nightmare – made Brody's heart pound. His mouth was sticky-dry. He wiped his hands on his trousers, took the rod out of the holder, and stuck it in the swivel between his legs.

Quint laughed – a short, sour yip. 'That thing? No. That's just a little fella. Give you some practice for when your fish finds us.' Quint watched the line for a few more seconds, then said, 'Hit it!'

Brody pushed the small lever on the reel forward, leaned down, then pulled back. The tip of the rod bent into an arc. With his right hand, Brody began to turn the crank to reel in the fish, but the reel did not respond. The line kept speeding out.

'Don't waste your energy,' said Quint.

Hooper who had been sitting on the transom, stood up and said, 'Here, I'll tighten down the drag.'

'You will not!' said Quint. 'You leave that rod alone.'

Hooper looked up, bewildered and slightly hurt.

Brody noticed Hooper's pained expression, and he thought: What do you know? It's about time.

After a moment, Quint said, 'You tighten the drag down too far and you'll tear the hook out of his mouth.'

'Oh,' said Hooper.

'I thought you was supposed to know something about fishing.'

Hooper said nothing. He turned and sat down on the transom.

Brody held on to the rod with both hands. The fish had gone deep and was moving slowly from side to side, but it was no longer taking line. Brody reeled – leaning forward and cranking quickly as he picked up slack, hauling backward with the muscles in his shoulders and back. His left wrist ached, and the fingers in his right hand began to cramp from cranking. 'What the hell have I got here?' he said.

'A blue,' said Quint.

'He must weigh half a ton.'

Quint laughed. 'Maybe a hundred fifty pounds.'

Brody hauled and leaned, hauled and leaned, until finally he heard Quint say, 'You're getting there. Hold it.' He stopped reeling.

With a smooth, unhurried motion, Quint swung down the ladder from the flying bridge. He had a rifle in his hand, an old army M-1. He stood at the gunwale and looked down. 'You want to see the fish?' he said. 'Come look.'

Brody stood, and reeling to take up the slack as he walked, he moved to the side of the boat. In the dark water the shark was acrylic blue. It was about eight feet long, slender, with long pectoral fins. It swam slowly from side to side, no longer struggling.

'He's beautiful, isn't he?' said Hooper.

Quint flicked the rifle's safety to 'off', and when the shark moved its head to within a few inches of the surface, he squeezed off three quick shots. The bullets made clean round holes in the shark's head, drawing no blood. The shark shuddered and stopped moving.

'He's dead,' said Brody.

'Shit,' said Quint. 'He's stunned, maybe, but that's all.' Quint took a glove from one of his hip pockets, slipped his right hand into it, and grabbed the wire line. From a sheath at his belt he took a knife. He lifted the shark's head clear of the water and bent over the gunwale. The shark's mouth was open two or three inches wide. Its right eye, partly covered by a shield of flesh, gazed blankly at Quint. Quint jammed the knife into the shark's mouth and tried to pry it open farther, but the shark bit down, holding the blade in its small triangular teeth. Quint pulled and twisted until the knife came free. He put it back in its sheath and took a pair of wire cutters from his pocket.

'I guess you're paying me enough so I can afford to lose a hook and a little leader,' he said. He touched the wire cutters to the leader and was about to snip it. 'Wait a minute,' he said, putting the cutters back in his pocket and taking out his knife. 'Watch this. This always gives the folks a boot.' Holding the leader in his left hand, he hoisted most of the shark out of the water. With a single swift motion he slit the shark's belly from the anal fin to just below the jaw. The flesh pulled apart, and bloody entrails – white and red and blue – tumbled into the water like laundry falling from a basket. Then Quint cut the leader with the wire snips, and the shark slid overboard. As soon as its head was beneath the water, the shark began to thrash in the cloud of blood and innards, biting any morsel that passed into its maw. The body twitched as the shark swallowed, and pieces of intestines passed out the hole in the belly, to be eaten again.

'Now watch,' said Quint. 'If we're lucky, in a minute other blues'll come around, and they'll help him eat himself. If we get enough of them, there'll be a real feeding frenzy. That's quite a show. The folks like that.'

Brody watched, spellbound, as the shark continued to nibble at the floating guts. In a moment he saw a flash of blue rise from below. A small shark – no more than four feet long – snapped at the body of the disembowelled fish. Its jaws closed on a bit of flapping flesh. Its head shook violently from side to side, and its body trembled, snakelike. A piece of flesh tore away, and the smaller shark swallowed it. Soon another shark appeared, and another, and the water began to roil. Flecks of blood mingled with the drops of water that splashed on the surface.

Quint took a gaff from beneath the gunwale. He leaned overboard, holding the gaff poised like an axe. Suddenly he lunged and jerked backwards. Impaled on the gaff hook, squirming and snapping, was a small shark. Quint took the knife from its sheath, slashed the shark's belly, and released it. 'Now you'll see something,' he said.

Brody couldn't tell how many sharks there were in the explosion of water. Fins crisscrossed on the surface, tails whipped the water. Amid the sounds of splashes came an occasional grunt as fish slammed into fish. Brody looked down at his shirt and saw that it was spattered with water and blood.

The frenzy continued for several minutes, until only three large sharks remained, cruising back and forth beneath the surface.

The men watched in silence until the last of the three had vanished.

'Jesus,' said Hooper.

'You don't approve,' said Quint.

'That's right. I don't like to see things die for people's amusement.' Quint snickered, and Hooper said, 'Do you?'

'It ain't a question of liking it or not. It's what feeds me.'

Quint reached into an ice chest and took out another hook and leader. The hook had been baited before they left the dock – a squid skewered and tied to the shaft and barb of the hook. Using pliers, Quint attached the leader to the end of the wire line. He dropped the bait overboard, fed out thirty yards of line, and let it drift into the slick.

Hooper resumed his routine of ladling chum into the water. Brody said, 'Anybody want a beer?' Both Quint and Hooper nodded, so he went below and took three cans from a cooler. As he left the cabin, Brody noticed two old, cracked, and curling photographs thumbtacked to the bulkhead. One showed Quint standing hip-deep in a pile of big, strange-looking fish. The other was a picture of a dead shark lying on a beach. There was nothing else in the photograph to compare the fish to, so Brody couldn't determine its size.

Brody left the cabin, gave the others their beers, and sat down in the fighting chair. 'I saw your pictures down there,' he said to Quint. 'What are all those fish you're standing in?'

'Tarpon,' said Quint. 'That was a while back, when I did some fishing in Florida. I never seen anything like it. We must have got thirty, forty tarpon – big tarpon – in four nights' fishing.'

'And you kept them?' said Hooper. 'You're supposed to throw them back.'

'Customers wanted 'em. For pictures, I guess. Anyway, they don't make bad chum, chopped up.'

'What you're saying is, they're more use dead than alive.'

'Sure. Same with most fish. And a lot of animals, too. I never did try to eat a live steer.' Quint laughed.

'What's the other picture?' said Brody. 'Just a shark?'

'Well, not *just* a shark. It was a big white – about fourteen, fifteen feet. Weighed over three thousand pounds.'

'How did you catch it?'

'Ironed it. But I tell you' – Quint chuckled – 'for a while there it was a question of who was gonna catch who.'

'What do you mean?'

'Damn thing attacked the boat. No provocation, no nothing. We were sitting out here minding our own business, when whamo! It felt like we was hit by a freight train. Knocked my mate right on his ass, and the customer started screaming bloody murder that we were sinking. Then the bastard hit us again. I put an iron in him and we chased him – Christ, we must have chased him half-way across the Atlantic.'

'How could you follow him?' Brody asked. 'Why didn't he go deep?'

'Couldn't. Not with that barrel following him. They float. He dragged it down for a little while, but before too long the strain got to him and he came to the surface. So we just kept following the barrel. After a couple hours we got another two irons in him, and he finally came up, real quiet, and we throwed a rope round his tail and towed him to shore. And all the time that customer's going bullshit, 'cause he's sure we're sinking and gonna get et up.

'You know the funniest thing? When we got the fish back and we was all tied up safe and sound and not likely to sink, that dumb fuck of a customer comes up to me and offers me five hundred bucks if I'll say he caught the fish on hook and line. Iron holes all over it, and he wants me to swear he caught it on hook and line! Then he starts giving me some song and dance about how I ought to cut my fee in half because I didn't give him a chance to catch the fish on hook and line. I told him that if I had let him try, I'd be out one hook, three hundred yards of wire line, probably one reel and one rod, and definitely one fish. Then he says what about all the valuable publicity I'll be getting from a trip *he's* paying for. I told him he could give me the money and keep the publicity and try to spread it on a cracker for himself and his wife.'

'I wondered about that hook-and-line business,' said Brody.

'What do you mean?'

'What you were saying. You wouldn't try to catch the fish we're after on a hook and line, would you?'

'Shit, no. From what I hear, the fish that's been bothering you makes the one we got look like a pup.'

'Then how come the lines are out?'

'Two reasons. First, a big white might just take a little squid bait like that. It'd cut the line pretty quick, but at least we'd know he was around. It's a useful telltale. The other reason is, you never know what a chum slick will bring around. Even if your fish doesn't show up, we might run into something else that'll take the bait.'

'Like what?'

'Who knows? Maybe something useful. I've had swordfish taking a drifting squid, and with all the federal bullshit about mercury no one's catching them commercially any more, so you can get two fifty a pound for broadbill in Montauk. Or maybe just something that'll give you a boot in the ass to catch, like a mako. If you're paying four hundred bucks, you might as well have some fun for your money.'

'Suppose the big white did come around,' said Brody. 'What would be the first thing you'd do?'

'Try to keep him interested enough so he'd stick around till we could get at him. It's no big trick; they're pretty stupid fish. It depends on how he finds us. If he pulls the same crap the other one did and attacks the boat, we'll just start pumping irons into him as fast as we can, then pull away from him and let him wear himself down. If he takes one of the lines, there'll be no way to stop him if he wants to run. But I'll try to turn him towards us – tighten the drag way down and take the risk of tearing loose. He'll probably bend the hook out pretty quick, but we might get him close enough for an iron. And once I've got one iron in him, it's only a matter of time.

'Most likely, the way he'll come will be following his nose –

right up the slick, either on the surface or just below. And that's where we'll have a little trouble. The squid isn't enough to keep him interested. Fish that size'll suck a squid right down and not even know he's et it. So we'll have to give him something special that he can't turn down, something with a big ol' hook in it that'll hold him at least until we can stick him once or twice.'

'If the hook's too obvious,' said Brody, 'won't he avoid the bait altogether?'

'No. These things don't have the brains of a dog. They eat anything. If they're feeding, you could throw a bare hook down at 'em and they'll take it if they see it. A friend of mine had one come up once and try to eat the outboard motor off his dinghy. He only spat it out 'cause he couldn't get it down in one swallow.'

From the stern, where he was ladling chum, Hooper said, 'What's something special, Quint?'

'You mean that special treat he can't turn down?' Quint smiled and pointed to a green plastic garbage can nestled in a corner amidships. 'Take a look for yourself. It's in that can. I've been saving it for a fish like the one we're after. On anything else it'd be a waste.'

Hooper walked over to the can, flipped the metal clasps off the sides, and lifted the top. His shock at what he saw made him gasp. Floating vertically in the can full of water, its lifeless head swaying gently with the motion of the boat, was a tiny bottle-nosed dolphin, no more than two feet long. Sticking out from a puncture on the underside of the jaw was the eye of a huge shark hook, and from a hole in the belly the barbed hook itself curled forward. Hooper clutched the sides of the can and said, 'A baby.'

'Even better,' Quint said with a grin. 'Unborn.'

Hooper gazed into the can for a few more seconds, then slammed the top back on and said, 'Where did you get it?'

'Oh, I guess about six miles from here, due east. Why?'

'I mean how did you get it?'

'How do you think? From the mother.'

'You killed her.'

'No.' Quint laughed. 'She jumped into the boat and swallowed a bunch of sleeping pills.' He paused, waiting for a laugh, and when none came he said, 'You can't rightly buy them, you know.'

Hooper stared at Quint. He was furious, outraged. But he said only, 'You know they're protected.'

'When I fish, son, I catch what I want.'

'But what about laws? Don't—'

'What's your line of work, Hooper?'

'I'm an ichthyologist. I study fish. That's why I'm here. Didn't you know that?'

'When people charter my boat, I don't ask questions about them. But okay, you study fish for a living. If you had to work for a living – I mean the kind of work where the amount of money you make depends on the amount of sweat you put in – you'd know more about what laws really mean. Sure, those porpoise are protected. But that law wasn't put in to stop Quint from taking one or two for bait. It was meant to stop big-time fishing for them, to stop nuts from shooting them for sport. So I'll tell you what, Hooper: you can bitch and moan all you want. But don't tell Quint he can't catch a few fish to help him make a living.'

'Look, Quint, the point is that these dolphins are in danger of being wiped out, extinguished. And what you're doing speeds up the process.'

'Don't give me that horseshit! Tell the tuna boats to stop snaring porpoise in their nets. Tell the Jap long-liners to stop hookin' 'em. They'll tell you to go take a flying fuck at the moon. They got mouths to feed. Well, so do I. Mine.'

'I get your message,' said Hooper. 'Take it while you can, and if after a while there's nothing left, why, we'll just start taking something else. It's so stupid!'

'Don't overstep, son,' said Quint. His voice was flat, tone-less, and he looked directly into Hooper's eyes.

'What?'

'Don't go calling me stupid.'

Hooper hadn't intended to give offence, and he was sur-prised to find offence taken. 'I didn't mean that, for God's sake. I just meant . . .'

On his perch midway between the two men, Brody decided it was time to stop the argument. 'Let's drop it, Hooper, okay?' he said. 'We're not out here to have a debate on ecology.'

'What do you know about ecology, Brody?' said Hooper. 'I bet all it means to you is someone telling you you can't burn leaves in your back yard.'

'Listen, you. I don't need any of your two-bit, rich-kid bullshit.'

'So that's it! "Rich-kid bullshit." That rich-kid stuff really burns your ass, doesn't it?'

'Listen, damn you! We're out here to stop a fish from killing people, and if using one porpoise will help us save God knows how many lives, that seems to me a pretty good bargain.'

Hooper smirked and said to Brody, 'So now you're an expert on saving lives, are you? Let's see. How many could have been saved if you'd closed the beaches after the . . .'

Brody was on his feet moving at Hooper before he con-sciously knew he had left his chair. 'You shut your mouth!' he said. Reflexively, he dropped his right hand to his hip. He stopped short when he felt no holster at his side, scared by the sudden realization that if he had had a pistol he might have used it. He stood facing Hooper, who glowered back at him.

A quick, sharp laugh from Quint broke the thread of ten-sion. 'What a pair of assholes,' he said. 'I seen that coming since you came aboard this morning.'

TWELVE

The second day of the hunt was as still as the first. When they left the dock at six in the morning, a light south-west breeze was blowing, promising to cool the day. The passage around Montauk Point was choppy. But by ten the breeze had died, and the boat lay motionless on the glassy sea, like a paper cup in a puddle. There were no clouds, but the sun was dulled by a heavy haze. Driving to the dock, Brody had heard on the radio that the pollution in New York City had reached a crisis stage – something about an air inversion. People were falling sick and of those who were sick already, or very old, some were dying.

Brody had dressed more sensibly today. He wore a white short-sleeved shirt with a high collar, light cotton trousers, white socks, and sneakers. He had brought a book along to pass the time, a sex mystery borrowed from Hendricks, called *The Deadly Virgin*.

Brody did not want to have to fill time with conversation, conversation that might lead to a repeat of yesterday's scene with Hooper. It had embarrassed him – Hooper, too, he thought. Today they seldom spoke to one another, directing most of their comments at Quint. Brody did not trust himself to feign civility with Hooper.

Brody had observed that in the mornings, Quint was quiet – tight and reserved. Words had to be wrung from him. But as the day wore on, he loosened up and became more and more loquacious. As they had left the dock that morning, for instance, Brody had asked Quint how he knew what spot to pick to wait for the fish.

'Don't,' said Quint.

'You don't know?'

Quint moved his head once from left to right, then back again.

'Then how do you choose a place?'

'Just choose one.'

'What do you look for?'

'Nothing.'

'You don't go by the tide?'

'Well, yeah.'

'Does it matter whether the water's deep or shallow?'

'Some.'

'How so?'

For a moment, Brody thought Quint would refuse to answer. He stared straight ahead, eyes fixed on the horizon. Then he said, as if it were a supreme effort, 'Big fish like that probably won't be in too shallow water. But you never know.'

Brody knew he should drop the subject and leave Quint in peace, but he was interested, so he asked another question. 'If we find that fish, or if he finds us, it'll be luck, won't it?'

'Sort of.'

'Like a needle in a haystack.'

'Not quite.'

'Why not?'

'If the tide's running good, we can put out a slick that'll cover ten mile and more by the end of the day.'

'Would it be better if we stayed the night out here?'

'What for?' said Quint.

'To keep the slick going. If we can spread ten miles in a day, we could make it more than twenty miles long if we stayed out all night.'

'If a slick gets too big, it's no good.'

'Why?'

'Gets confusing. If you stayed out here a month, you could cover the whole fuckin' ocean. Not much sense in that.'

226

Quint smiled, apparently at the thought of a chum slick covering the whole ocean.

Brody gave up and read *The Deadly Virgin*.

By noon, Quint had opened up. The lines had been in the slick for over four hours. Though no one had specifically assigned him the task, Hooper had taken up the chum ladle as soon as they began to drift, and now he sat at the stern, methodically scooping and dumping. At about ten o'clock a fish had taken the starboard line and had caused a few seconds of excitement. But it turned out to be a five-pound bonito that could barely get its mouth around the hook. At ten-thirty, a small blue shark took the port line. Brody reeled it in. Quint brought it to gaff, slit its stomach open, and released it. The shark nibbled feebly at a few pieces of itself, then slipped into the deep. No other sharks came around to feed.

At a little after eleven, Quint spied the scythed dorsal fin of a swordfish coming towards them up the slick. They waited silently, begging the fish to take a bait, but it ignored both squid and cruised aimlessly sixty yards off the stern. Quint jigged one of the baits – tugging the line to make the squid move and seem alive – but the swordfish wasn't impressed. Finally, Quint decided to harpoon the fish. He turned on his engine, told Brody and Hooper to reel in the lines, and drove the boat in a wide circle. One harpoon dart was already attached to the throwing pole, and a line-covered barrel stood ready at the bow. Quint explained the pattern of attack: Hooper would drive the boat. Quint would stand at the end of the pulpit in the bow, holding the harpoon over his right shoulder. As they came upon the fish, Quint would point the harpoon left or right, depending on which way he wanted the boat to turn. Hooper would turn the boat until the harpoon was again pointing straight ahead. It was like following a compass heading. If all went well, they would be able to creep up on the fish, and Quint could plunge the iron off his right shoulder – a throw of about twelve feet, almost straight down. Brody would stand at the barrel, making sure the line was kept clear as the fish sounded.

All did go well until the last moment. Moving slowly, with the engine sound barely above a murmur, the boat closed on the fish, which lay resting on the surface. The boat had a sensitive helm, and Hooper was able to follow Quint's directions precisely. Then somehow, the fish sensed the presence of the boat. Just as Quint raised his arm to cast the iron, the fish lurched forward, thrust its tail, and darted for the bottom. Quint threw, yelling, 'Prick!' and missed by six feet.

Now they were back at the head of the slick again.

'You asked yesterday if we have many days like this,' Quint said to Brody. 'It's not often we string two of them together. We should of at least had a bunch of blue sharks by now.'

'Is it the weather?'

'Could be. Makes people feel shitty enough. Maybe fish, too.'

They ate lunch – sandwiches and beer – and when they were finished, Quint checked to see if his carbine was loaded. Then he ducked into the cabin and returned, holding a machine Brody had never seen before. 'Still got your beer can?' Quint asked.

'Sure,' said Brody. 'What do you want it for?'

'I'll show you.' The device looked like a potato-masher hand grenade – a metal cylinder with a handle at one end. Quint pushed the beer can down into the cylinder, turned it till there was a click, and took a ·22 blank cartridge from his shirt pocket. He slipped the blank into a small hole at the base of the cylinder, then turned the handle until there was another click. He handed the device to Brody. 'See that lever there?' he said, pointing to the top of the handle. 'Point the thing up to the sky, and when I tell you, push that lever.'

Quint picked up the M-1, released the safety, raised the rifle to his shoulder, and said, 'Now.'

Brody flipped the lever. There was a sharp, high report, a mild kick, and the beer can was launched from his hand straight up into the air. It spun, and in the bright sunlight it shone like a sparkler. At the height of its track – the split-second point when it hung suspended in air – Quint fired. He aimed low, to catch the can as it started down, and he hit its bottom. There was a loud *whang*, and the can cart-wheeled down into the water. It did not sink immediately, but floated at a cockeyed angle, bobbing on the surface.

'Want to try?' said Quint.

'You bet,' said Brody.

'Remember to try to catch it right at the top and lead it a little bit low. If you go for it in full rise or full fall, you've got to lead by a whole lot, and it's much harder. If you miss it, drop your sights, lead it again, and squeeze off another round.'

Brody exchanged the launcher for the M-1 and stationed himself at the gunwale. As soon as Quint had reloaded the launcher, Brody shouted, 'Now!' and Quint released the can. Brody fired once. Nothing. He tried again at the top of the arc. Nothing. And he led it by too much as it fell. 'Boy, that's a bitch,' he said.

'Takes some getting used to,' said Quint. 'See if you can hit it now.'

The can floated upright in the still water, fifteen or twenty yards from the boat. Half of it was exposed above water. Brody aimed – consciously a hair low – and squeezed the trigger. There was a metallic *plop* as the bullet hit the can at the water line. The can vanished.

'Hooper?' said Quint. 'There's one can left, and we can always drink more beer.'

'No thanks,' said Hooper.

'What's the problem?'

'Nothing. I just don't want to shoot, that's all.'

Quint smiled. 'You worried about the cans in the water? That's an awful lot of tin we're dropping into the ocean.

Probably rust and sink to the bottom and clutter up everything down there.'

'That's not it,' said Hooper, careful not to rise to Quint's bait. 'It's nothing. I just don't feel like it.'

'Afraid of guns?'

'Afraid? No.'

'Ever shot one?'

Brody was fascinated to see Quint press, and pleased to see Hooper squirm, but he didn't know why Quint was doing it. Maybe Quint got ornery when he was bored and wasn't catching fish.

Hooper didn't know what Quint was doing either, but he didn't like it. He felt he was being set up to be knocked down. 'Sure,' he said. 'I've shot guns before.'

'Where? In the service?'

'No. I . . .'

'Were you in the service?'

'No.'

'I didn't think so.'

'What's that supposed to mean?'

'Christ, I'd even bet you're still a virgin.'

Brody looked at Hooper's face to see his response, and for a split second he caught Hooper looking at him.

Then Hooper looked away, his face beginning to redden. He said, 'What's on your mind, Quint? What are you getting at?'

Quint leaned back in his chair and grinned. 'Not a thing,' he said. 'Just making a little friendly conversation to pass the time. Mind if I take your beer can when you're through? Maybe Brody'd like to take another shot.'

'No, I don't mind,' said Hooper. 'But get off my back, will you?'

For the next hour they sat in silence. Brody dozed in the fighting chair, a hat pulled down over his face to protect it from the sun. Hooper sat at the stern, ladling and occasionally shaking his head to keep awake. And Quint sat on the flying bridge, watching the slick, his Marine Corps cap tilted back on his head.

Suddenly Quint said – his voice flat, soft, matter-of-fact – 'We've got a visitor.'

Brody snapped awake. Hooper stood up. The starboard line was running out, smoothly and very fast.

'Take the rod,' Quint said. He removed his cap and dropped it on to the bench.

Brody took the rod out of the holder, fit it between his legs, and held on.

'When I tell you,' said Quint, 'you throw that brake and hit him.' The line stopped running. 'Wait. He's turning. He'll start again. Don't want to hit him now or he'll spit the hook.' But the line lay dead in the water, limp and unmoving. After several moments, Quint said, 'I'll be goddamned. Keel it in.'

Brody cranked the line in. It came easily, too easily. There was not even the mild resistance of the bait.

'Hold the line with a couple fingers or it'll snarl,' said Quint. 'Whatever that was took the bait gentle as you please. Must have kissed it off the line.'

The line came clear of the water and hung at the tip of the rod. There was no hook, no bait, no leader. The wire had been neatly severed. Quint hopped down from the flying bridge and looked at it. He felt the end, ran his fingers around the edges of the break, and gazed out over the slick.

'I think we've just met your friend,' he said.

'What?' said Brody.

Hooper jumped down off the transom and said excitedly, 'You've got to be kidding. That's terrific.'

'That's just a guess,' said Quint. 'But I'd bet on it. This wire's been chewed clean through. One try. No hesitation. No other marks on it. The fish probably didn't even know he had

231

it in his mouth. He just sucked the bait in and closed his mouth and that did it.'

'So what do we do now?' said Brody.

'We wait and see if he takes the other one, or if he surfaces.'

'What about using the porpoise?'

'When I know it's him,' said Quint. 'When I get a look at him and know the bastard's big enough to be worth it, then I'll give him the porpoise. They're garbage-eating machines, these fish, and I don't want to waste a prize bait on some little runt.'

They waited. There was no movement on the surface of the water. No birds dived, no fish jumped. The only sound was the liquid plop of the chum Hooper ladled overboard. Then the port line began to run.

'Leave it in the holder,' said Quint. 'No sense in getting ready if he's going to chew through this one too.'

Adrenalin was pumping through Brody's body. He was both excited and afraid, awed by the thought of what was swimming below them, a creature whose power he could not imagine. Hooper stood at the port gunwale, transfixed by the running line.

The line stopped and went limp.

'Shit,' said Quint. 'He done it again.' He took the rod out of the holder and began to reel. The severed line came aboard exactly as had the other one. 'We'll give him one more chance,' said Quint, 'and I'll put on a tougher leader. Not that that'll stop him if it's the fish I think it is.' He reached into the ice chest for another bait and removed the wire leader. From a drawer in the cockpit he took a four-foot length of three-eighths-inch chain.

'That looks like a dog's leash,' said Brody.

'Used to be,' said Quint. He wired one end of the chain to the eye of the baited hook, the other to the wire line.

'Can he bite through that?'

'I imagine so. Take him a little longer, maybe, but he'd do

it if he wanted to. All I'm trying to do is goose him a little and bring him to the surface.'

'What's next if this doesn't work?'

'Don't know yet. I suppose I could take a four-inch shark hook and a length of no-shit chain and drop it overboard with a bunch of bait on it. But if he took it, I wouldn't know what to do with him. He'd tear out any cleat I've got on board, and until I see him I'm not going to take a chance and wrap chain around anything important.' Quint flipped the bait hook overboard and fed out a few yards of line. 'Come on, you bugger,' he said. 'Let's have a look at you.'

The three men watched the port line. Hooper bent down, filled his ladle with chum, and tossed it into the slick. Something caught his eye and made him turn to the left. What he saw sucked from him a throaty grunt, unintelligible but enough to draw the eyes of the other two men.

'Jesus Christ!' said Brody.

No more than ten feet off the stern, slightly to the starboard, was the flat, conical snout of the fish. It stuck out of the water perhaps two feet. The top of the head was a sooty grey, pocked with two black eyes. At each side of the end of the snout, where the grey turned to cream white, were the nostrils – deep slashes in the armoured hide. The mouth was open not quite half-way, a dim, dark cavern guarded by huge, triangular teeth.

Fish and men confronted each other for perhaps ten seconds. Then Quint yelled, 'Get an iron!' and, obeying himself, he dashed forward and began to fumble with a harpoon. Brody reached for the rifle. Just then, the fish slid quietly backward into the water. The long, scythed tail flicked once – Brody shot at it and missed – and the fish disappeared.

'He's gone,' said Brody.

'Fantastic!' said Hooper. 'That fish is everything I thought. And more. He's fantastic! The head must have been four feet across.'

'Could be,' said Quint, walking aft. He deposited two harpoon barbs, two barrels, and two coils of rope in the stern. 'In case he comes back,' he said.

'Have you ever seen a fish like that, Quint?' said Hooper. His eyes were bright, and he felt ebullient, vibrant.

'Not quite,' said Quint.

'How long, would you say?'

'Hard to tell. Twenty feet. Maybe more. I don't know. With them things, it don't make much difference over six feet. Once they get to six feet, they're trouble. And this sonofabitch is trouble.'

'God, I hope he comes back,' said Hooper.

Brody felt a chill, and he shuddered. 'That was very strange,' he said, shaking his head. 'He looked like he was grinning.'

'That's what they look like when their mouths are open,' said Quint. 'Don't make him out to be more than he is. He's just a dumb garbage bucket.'

'How can you say that?' said Hooper. 'That fish is a beauty. It's the kind of thing that makes you believe in a god. It shows you what nature can do when she sets her mind to it.'

'Horseshit,' said Quint, and he climbed the ladder to the flying bridge.

'Are you going to use the porpoise?' said Brody.

'No need. We got him on the surface once. He'll be back.'

As Quint spoke, a noise behind Hooper made him turn. It was a swishing noise, a liquid hiss. 'Look,' said Quint. Heading straight for the boat, thirty feet away, was a triangular dorsal fin more than a foot high, knifing the water and leaving a rippled wake. It was followed by a towering tail that swatted left and right in tight cadence.

'It's attacking the boat!' cried Brody. Involuntarily, he backed into the seat of the fighting chair and tried to draw away.

Quint came down from the flying bridge, cursing. 'No fucking warning this time,' he said. 'Hand me that iron.'

The fish was almost at the boat. It raised its flat head, gazed vacantly at Hooper with one of its black eyes, and passed under the boat. Quint raised the harpoon and turned back to the port side. The throwing pole struck the fighting chair, and the dart dislodged and fell to the deck.

'Cock*sucker*!' shouted Quint. 'Is he still there?' He reached down, grabbed the dart, and stuck it back on the end of the pole.

'Your side, your side!' yelled Hooper. 'He's passed this side already.'

Quint turned back in time to see the grey-brown shape of the fish as it pulled away from the boat and began to dive. He dropped the harpoon and, in a rage, snatched up the rifle and emptied the clip into the water behind the fish. 'Bastard!' he said. 'Give me some warning next time.' Then he put the rifle down and laughed. 'I suppose I should be grateful,' he said. 'At least he didn't attack the boat.' He looked at Brody and said, 'Gave you a bit of a start.'

'More 'n a bit,' said Brody. He shook his head, as if to reassemble his thoughts and sort out his visions. 'I'm still not sure I believe it.' His mind was full of images of a torpedo shape streaking upward in the blackness and tearing Christine Watkins to pieces; of the boy on the raft, unknowing, unsuspecting, until suddenly seized by a nightmare creature, and of the nightmares he knew would come to him, dreams of violence and blood and a woman screaming at him that he killed her son. 'You can't tell me that thing's a fish,' he said. 'It's more like one of those things they make movies about. You know, the monster from twenty million fathoms.'

'It's a fish, all right,' said Hooper. He was still visibly excited. 'And what a fish! Damn near *megalodon*.'

'What are you talking about?' said Brody.

'That's an exaggeration,' said Hooper, 'but if there's

something like this swimming around, what's to say *megalodon* isn't? What do you say, Quint?'

'I'd say the sun's got to you,' said Quint.

'No, really. How big do you think these fish grow?'

'I'm no good at guessing. I'd put that fish at twenty feet, so I'd say they grow to twenty feet. If I see one tomorrow that's twenty-five feet, I'll say they grow to twenty-five feet. Guessing is bullshit.'

'How big *do* they grow?' Brody asked, wishing immediately that he hadn't said anything. He felt that the question subordinated him to Hooper.

But Hooper was too caught up in the moment, too flushed and happy, to be patronizing. 'That's the point,' he said. 'Nobody knows. There was one in Australia that got snarled in some chains and drowned. He was measured at thirty-six feet, or so said the reports.'

'That's almost twice as big as this one,' said Brody. His mind, barely able to comprehend the fish he had seen, could not grasp the immensity of the one Hooper described.

Hooper nodded. 'Generally, people seem to accept thirty feet as a maximum size, but the figure is fancy. It's like what Quint says. If they see one tomorrow that's sixty feet, they'll accept sixty feet. The really terrific thing, the thing that blows your mind, is imagining – and it could be true – that there are great whites way down in the deep that are a hundred feet long.'

'Oh bullshit,' said Quint.

'I'm not saying it's so,' said Hooper. 'I'm saying it could be so.'

'Still bullshit.'

'Maybe. Maybe not. Look, the Latin name for this fish is *Carcharodon carcharias*, okay? The closest ancestor we can find for it is something called *Carcharodon megalodon*, a fish that existed maybe thirty or forty thousand years ago. We have fossil teeth from *megalodon*. They're six inches long.

That would put the fish at between eighty and a hundred feet. And the teeth are exactly like the teeth you see in great whites today. What I'm getting at is, suppose the two fish are really one species. What's to say *megalodon* is really extinct? Why should it be? Not lack of food. If there's enough down there to support whales, there's enough to support sharks that big. Just because we've never seen a hundred-foot white doesn't mean they couldn't exist. They'd have no reason to come to the surface. All their food would be way down in the deep. A dead one wouldn't float to shore, because they don't have flotation bladders. Can you imagine what a hundred-foot white would look like? Can you imagine what it could do, what kind of power it would have?'

'I don't want to,' said Brody.

'It would be like a locomotive with a mouth full of butcher knives.'

'Are you saying this is just a baby?' Brody was beginning to feel lonely and vulnerable. A fish as large as what Hooper was describing could chew the boat to splinters.

'No, this is a mature fish,' said Hooper. 'I'm sure of it. But it's like people. Some people are five feet tall, some people are seven feet tall. Boy, what I'd give to have a look at a big *megalodon*.'

'You're out of your mind,' said Brody.

'No, man, just think of it. It would be like finding the Abominable Snowman.'

'Hey, Hooper,' said Quint, 'do you think you can stop the fairy tales and start throwing chum overboard? I'd kind of like to catch a fish.'

'Sure,' said Hooper. He returned to his post at the stern and began to ladle chum into the water.

'You think he'll come back?' said Brody.

'I don't know,' said Quint. 'You never know what these bastards are going to do.' From a pocket he took a note pad and a pencil. He extended his left arm and pointed it towards

237

shore. He closed his right eye and sighted down the index finger of his left hand, then scribbled something on the pad. He moved his hand a couple of inches to the left, sighted again, and made another note. Anticipating a question from Brody, Quint said, 'Taking bearings. I want to see where we are, so if he doesn't show up for the rest of today, I'll know where to come tomorrow.'

Brody looked towards shore. Even shading his eyes and squinting, all he could see was a dim grey line of land. 'What are you taking them on?'

'Lighthouse on the point and the water tower in town. They line up different ways depending where you are.'

'You can see them?' Brody strained his eyes, but he saw nothing more distinct than a lump in the line.

'Sure. You could too, if you'd been out here for thirty years.'

Hooper smiled and said, 'Do you really think the fish will stay in one place?'

'I don't know,' said Quint. 'But this is where we found him this time, and we didn't find him anywhere else.'

'And he sure as hell stayed around Amity,' said Brody.

'That's because he had food,' said Hooper. There was no irony in his voice, no taunt. But the remark was like a needle stabbing into Brody's brain.

They waited for three more hours, but the fish never returned. The tide slackened, carrying the slick ever slower.

At a little after five, Quint said, 'We might as well go in. It's enough to piss off the Good Humour man.'

'Where do you think he went?' said Brody. The question was rhetorical; he knew there was no answer.

'Anywhere,' said Quint. 'When you want 'em, they're never around. It's only when you don't want 'em, and don't expect 'em, that they show up. Contrary fuckers.'

'And you don't think we should spend the night, to keep the slick going.'

'No. Like I said, if the slick gets too big, it's no good. We don't have any food out here. And last but not least, you're not paying me for a twenty-four-hour day.'

'If I could get the money, would you do it?'

Quint thought for a moment. 'Nope. It's tempting, though, 'cause I don't think there's much chance anything would happen at night. The slick would be big and confusing, and even if he came right up alongside and looked at us, we wouldn't know he was there unless he took a bite out of us. So it'd be taking your money just to let you sleep on board. But I won't do it, for two reasons. First off, if the slick did get too big, it would screw us up for the next day. Second, I like to get this boat in at night.'

'I guess I can't blame you,' said Brody. 'Your wife must like it better, too, having you home.'

Quint said flatly, 'Got no wife.'

'Oh. I'm sorry.'

'Don't be. I never saw the need for one.' Quint turned and climbed the ladder to the flying bridge.

Ellen was fixing the children's supper when the doorbell rang. The boys were watching television in the living-room, and she called to them, 'Would somebody please answer the door?'

She heard the door open, heard some words exchanged, and, a moment later, saw Larry Vaughan standing in the kitchen door. It had been less than two weeks since she had last seen him, yet the change in his appearance was so startling that she couldn't help staring at him. As always, he was dressed perfectly – a two-button blue blazer, button-down shirt, grey slacks, and Gucci loafers. It was his face that had changed. He had lost weight, and like many people who have no excess on their bodies, Vaughan showed the loss in his face. His eyes had receded in their sockets, and their colour seemed to Ellen lighter than normal – a nasty grey. His skin looked grey, too, and appeared to droop at the cheekbones.

His lips were moist, and he licked them every few seconds.

Embarrassed when she found herself staring, Ellen lowered her eyes and said, 'Larry. Hello.'

'Hello, Ellen. I stopped by to . . .' Vaughan backed up a few steps and peered into the living-room. 'First of all, do you suppose I could have a drink?'

'Of course. You know where everything is. Help yourself. I'd get it for you, but my hands are covered with chicken.'

'Don't be silly. I can find everything.' Vaughan opened the cupboard where the liquor was kept, took out a bottle, and poured a glass full of gin. 'As I started to say, I stopped by to say farewell.'

Ellen stopped shuffling pieces of chicken in the frying-pan and said, 'You're going away? For how long?'

'I don't know. Perhaps for good. There's nothing here for me any more.'

'What about your business?'

'That's gone. Or it soon will be.'

'What do you mean, gone? A business doesn't just go away.'

'No, but I won't own it any more. What few assets there are will belong to my . . . partners.' He spat the word and then, as if to cleanse his mouth of its unpleasant residue, took a long swallow of gin. 'Has Martin told you about our conversation?'

'Yes.' Ellen looked down at the frying-pan and stirred the chicken.

'I imagine you don't think very highly of me any more.'

'It's not up to me to judge you, Larry.'

'I never wanted to hurt anybody. I hope you believe that.'

'I believe it. How much does Eleanor know?'

'Nothing, poor dear. I want to spare her, if I can. That's one reason I want to move away. She loves me, you know, and I'd hate to take that love away . . . from either of us.' Vaughan leaned against the sink. 'You know something?

240

Sometimes I think – and I've thought this from time to time over the years – that you and I would have made a wonderful couple.'

Ellen reddened. 'What do you mean?'

'You're from a good family. You know all the people I had to fight to get to know. We would have fit together and fit in Amity. You're lovely and good and strong. You would have been a real asset to me. And I think I could have given you a life you would have loved.'

Ellen smiled. 'I'm not as strong as you think, Larry. I don't know what kind of . . . asset I would have been.'

'Don't belittle yourself. I only hope Martin appreciates the treasure he has.' Vaughan finished his drink and put the glass in the sink. 'Anyway, no point in dreaming.' He walked across the kitchen, touched Ellen's shoulder, and kissed the top of her head. 'Good-bye, dear,' he said. 'Think of me once in a while.'

Ellen looked at him. 'I will.' She kissed his cheek. 'Where are you going?'

'I don't know. Vermont, maybe, or New Hampshire. I might sell land to the ski-ing crowd. Who knows? I might even take up the sport myself.'

'Have you told Eleanor?'

'I told her we might be moving. She just smiled and said, "Whatever you wish."'

'Are you leaving soon?'

'As soon as I chat with my lawyers about my . . . liabilities.'

'Send us a card so we'll know where you are.'

'I will. Good-bye.' Vaughan left the room, and Ellen heard the screen door close behind him.

When she had served the children their supper, Ellen went upstairs and sat on her bed. 'A life you would have loved,' Vaughan had said. What would a life with Larry Vaughan have been like? There would have been money, and acceptance. She would never have missed the life she led as a girl, for it would never have ended. There would have been no craving for renewal and self-confidence and confirmation of her femininity, no need for a fling with someone like Hooper.

But no. She might have been driven to it by boredom, like so many of the women who spent their weeks in Amity while their husbands were in New York. Life with Larry Vaughan would have been life without challenge, a life of cheap satisfactions.

As she pondered what Vaughan had said, she began to recognize the richness of her life: a relationship with Brody more rewarding than any Larry Vaughan would ever experience; an amalgam of minor trials and tiny triumphs that, together, added up to something akin to joy. And as her recognition grew, so did a regret that it had taken her so long to see the waste of time and emotion in trying to cling to her past. Suddenly she felt fear – fear that she was growing up too late, that something might happen to Brody before she could savour her awareness. She looked at her watch: 6.20. He should have been home by now. Something has happened to him, she thought. Oh please, God, not him.

She heard the door open downstairs. She jumped off the bed, ran into the hall and down the stairs. She wrapped her arms around Brody's neck and kissed him hard on the mouth.

'My God,' he said when she let him go. 'That's quite a welcome.'

THIRTEEN

'You're not putting that thing on my boat,' said Quint.

They stood on the dock in the brightening light. The sun had cleared the horizon, but it lay behind a low bank of clouds that touched the eastern sea. A gentle wind blew from the south. The boat was ready to go. Barrels lined the bow; rods stood straight in their holders, leaders snapped into eyelets on the reels. The engine chugged quietly, sputtering bubbles as tiny waves washed against the exhaust pipe, coughing diesel fumes that rose and were carried away by the breeze.

At the end of the dock a man got into a pickup truck and started the engine, and the truck began to move slowly off down the dirt road. The words stencilled on the door of the truck read: Woods Hole Oceanographic Institute.

Quint stood with his back to the boat, facing Brody and Hooper, who stood on each side of an aluminium cage. The cage was slightly over six feet tall and six feet wide and four feet deep. Inside, there was a control panel; on top were two cylindrical tanks. On the floor of the cage were a scuba tank, a regulator, a face mask, and a wet suit.

'Why not?' said Hooper. 'It doesn't weigh much, and I can lash it down out of the way.'

'Take up too much room.'

'That's what I said,' said Brody. 'But he wouldn't listen.'

'What the hell is it anyway?' said Quint.

'It's a shark cage,' said Hooper. 'Divers use them to protect themselves when they're swimming in the open ocean. I had it sent down from Woods Hole – in that truck that just left.'

'And what do you plan to do with it?'

'When we find the fish, or when the fish finds us, I want to go down in the cage and take some pictures. No one's ever been able to photograph a fish this big before.'

'Not a chance,' said Quint. 'Not on my boat.'

'Why not?'

'It's foolishness, that's why. A sensible man knows his limits. That's beyond your limits.'

'How do you know?'

'It's beyond any man's limits. A fish that big could eat that cage for breakfast.'

'But *would* he? I don't think so. I think he might bump it, might even mouth it, but I don't think he'd seriously try to eat it.'

'He would if he saw something as juicy as you inside.'

'I doubt it.'

'Well, forget it.'

'Look, Quint, this is a chance of a lifetime. Not just for me. I wouldn't have thought of doing it until I saw the fish yesterday. It's unique, at least in this hemisphere. And even though people have filmed great whites before, no one's ever filmed a twenty-foot white swimming in the open ocean. Never.'

'He said forget it,' said Brody. 'So forget it. Besides, I don't want the responsibility. We're out here to kill that fish, not make a home movie about it.'

'What responsibility? You're not responsible for me.'

'Oh yes I am. The town of Amity is paying for this trip, so what I say goes.'

Hooper said to Quint, 'I'll pay you.'

Quint smiled. 'Oh yeah? How much?'

'Forget it,' said Brody. 'I don't care what Quint says. *I* say you're not bringing that thing along.'

Hooper ignored him and said to Quint, 'A hundred dollars. Cash. In advance, the way you like it.' He reached into his back pocket for his wallet.

'I said no!' said Brody.

'What do you say, Quint? A hundred bucks. Cash. Here it is.' He counted five twenties and held them out to Quint.

'I don't know.' Then Quint reached for the money and said, 'Shit, I don't suppose it's my business to keep a man from killing himself if he wants to.'

'You put that cage on the boat,' Brody said to Quint, 'and you don't get your four hundred.' If Hooper wants to kill himself, Brody thought, let him do it on his own time.

'And if the cage doesn't go,' said Hooper, 'I don't go.'

'Fuck yourself,' said Brody. 'You can stay here, for all I care.'

'I don't think Quint would like that. Right, Quint? You want to go out and take on that fish with just you and the chief? You feel good about that?'

'We'll find another man,' said Brody.

'Go ahead,' Hooper snapped. 'Good luck.'

'Can't do it,' said Quint. 'Not on this short notice.'

'Then the hell with it!' said Brody. 'We'll go tomorrow. Hooper can go back to Woods Hole and play with his fish.'

Hooper was angry – angrier, in fact, than he knew, for before he could stop himself, he had said, 'That's not all I might ... Oh, forget it.'

For several seconds, a leaden silence fell over the three men. Brody stared at Hooper, unwilling to believe what he had heard, uncertain how much substance there was in the remark and how much empty threat. Then suddenly he was overcome by rage. He reached Hooper in two steps, grabbed both sides of his collar, and rammed his fists into Hooper's throat. 'What was that?' he said. 'What did you say?'

Hooper could hardly breathe. He clawed at Brody's fingers. 'Nothing!' he said, choking. 'Nothing!' He tried to back away, but Brody gripped him tighter.

'What did you mean by that?'

'Nothing, I tell you! I was angry. It was something to say.'

'Where were you last Wednesday afternoon?'

'Nowhere!' Hooper's temples were throbbing. 'Let me go! You're choking me!'

'Where were you?' Brody twisted his fists tighter.

'In a motel! Now let me go!'

Brody eased his grip. 'With who?' he said, praying to himself, God, don't let it be Ellen; let his alibi be a good one.

'Daisy Wicker.'

'Liar!' Brody tightened his grip again, and he felt tears begin to squeeze from his eyes.

'What do you mean?' said Hooper, struggling to free himself.

'Daisy Wicker's a goddamn lesbian! What were you doing, knitting?'

Hooper's thoughts were fogging. Brody's knuckles were cutting off the flow of blood to his brain. His eyelids flickered and he began to lose consciousness. Brody released him and pushed him down to the dock, where he sat, sucking air.

'What do you say to that?' said Brody. 'Are you such a hotshot you can fuck a lesbian?'

Hooper's mind cleared quickly, and he said, 'No. I didn't find it out until . . . until it was too late.'

'What do you mean? You mean she went with you to a motel and then turned you down? No dyke is gonna go to any motel with you.'

'She did!' said Hooper, desperately trying to keep pace with Brody's questions. 'She said she wanted . . . that it was time she tried it straight. But then she couldn't go through with it. It was awful.'

'You're bullshitting me!'

'I'm not! You can check with her yourself.' Hooper knew it was a weak excuse. Brody could check it out with no trouble. But it was all he could think of. He could stop on the way home that evening and call Daisy Wicker from a phone booth, beg her to corroborate his story. Or he could simply never return to Amity – turn north and take the ferry from Orient Point and be out of the state before Brody could reach Daisy Wicker.

'I will check,' said Brody. 'You can count on it.'

Behind him, Brody heard Quint laugh and say, 'That's the funniest thing I ever did hear. Tried to lay a lesbian.'

Brody tried to read Hooper's face, searching for anything that might betray a lie. But Hooper kept his eyes fixed on the dock.

'Well, what do you say?' said Quint. 'We going today or not? Either way, Brody, it'll cost you.'

Brody felt shaken. He was tempted to cancel the trip, return to Amity and discover the truth about Hooper and Ellen. But suppose the worst was true. What could he do then? Confront Ellen? Beat her? Walk out on her? What good would that do? He had to have time to think. He said to Quint, 'We'll go.'

'With the cage?'

'With the cage. If this asshole wants to kill himself, let him.'

'Okay by me,' said Quint. 'Let's get this circus on the road.'

Hooper stood and walked to the cage. 'I'll get in the boat,' he said hoarsely. 'If you two can push it over to the edge of the dock and lean it towards me, then one of you come down into the boat with me, we can carry it over into the corner.'

Brody and Quint slid the cage across the wooden boards, and Brody was surprised at how light it was. Even with the diving gear inside, it couldn't have weighed more than two hundred pounds. They tipped it towards Hooper, who grabbed two of the bars and waited until Quint joined him in the cockpit. The two men easily carried the cage a few feet and pushed it into a corner under the overhang that supported the flying bridge. Hooper secured it with two pieces of rope.

Brody jumped aboard and said, 'Let's go.'

'Aren't you forgetting something?' said Quint.

'What?'

'Four hundred dollars.'

Brody took an envelope from his pocket and handed it to Quint. 'You're going to die a rich man, Quint.'

'That's my aim. Uncleat the stern line, will you?' Quint uncleated the bow and midships spring lines and tossed them on to the dock, and when he saw that the stern line was clear, too, he pushed the throttle forward and guided the boat out of the slip. He turned right and pushed the throttle forward, and the boat moved swiftly through the calm sea – past Hicks Island and Goff Point, around Shagwong and Montauk points. Soon the lighthouse on Montauk Point was behind them, and they were cruising south by south-west in the open ocean.

Gradually, as the boat fell into the rhythm of the long ocean swells, Brody's fury dulled. Maybe Hooper was telling the truth. It was possible. A person wouldn't make up a story that was so easy to check. Ellen had never cheated on him before, he was sure of that. She never even flirted with other men. But, he told himself, there's always a first time. And once again the thought made his throat tighten. He felt jealous and injured, inadequate and outraged. He hopped down from the fighting chair and climbed up to the flying bridge.

Quint made room on the bench for Brody, and Brody sat down next to him. Quint chuckled. 'You boys almost had a no-shit punch-up back there.'

'It was nothing.'

'Looked like something to me. What is it, you think he's been poking your wife?'

Confronted with his own thoughts stated so brutally, Brody was shocked. 'None of your damn business,' he said.

'Whatever you say. But if you ask me, he ain't got it in him.'

'Nobody asked you.' Anxious to change the subject, Brody said, 'Are we going back to the same place?'

'Same place. Won't be too long now.'

'What are the chances the fish will still be there?'

'Who knows? But it's the only thing we can do.'

'You said something on the phone the other day about being smarter than fish. Is that all there is to it? Is that the only secret of success?'

'That's all there is. You just got to outguess 'em. It's no trick. They're stupid as sin.'

'You've never found a smart fish?'

'Never met one yet.'

Brody remembered the leering, grinning face that had stared up at him from the water. 'I don't know,' he said. 'That fish sure looked mean yesterday. Like he meant to be mean. Like he knew what he was doing.'

'Shit, he don't know nothing.'

'Do they have different personalities?'

'Fish?' Quint laughed. 'That's giving them more credit than they're due. You can't treat 'em like people, even though I guess some people are as dumb as fish. No. They do different things sometimes, but after a while you get to know everything they *can* do.'

'It's not a challenge, then. You're not fighting an enemy.'

'No. No more'n a plumber who's trying to unstick a drain. Maybe he'll cuss at it and hit it with a wrench. But down deep he don't think he's fighting some*body*. Sometimes I run into an ornery fish that gives me more trouble than other ones, but I just use different tools.'

'There are fish you can't catch, aren't there?'

'Oh sure, but that don't mean they're smart or sneaky or anything. It only means they're not hungry when you try to catch 'em, or they're too fast for you, or you're using the wrong bait.'

Quint fell silent for a moment, then spoke again. 'Once,' he said, 'a shark almost caught *me*. It was about twenty years ago. I had a fair-size blue shark to gaff and he gave a big yank and hauled me overboard with him.'

'What did you do?'

'I come up over that transom so fast I don't think my feet touched anything between water and deck. I was lucky. I fell over the stern, where it's fairly low down, near the water. If I'd of fallen over amidships, I don't know what I would've done. Anyway, I was out of that water before the fish even knew I was in it. He was busy trying to shake the gaff.'

'Suppose you fell over with this fish. Is there anything you could do?'

'Sure. Pray. It'd be like falling out of an aeroplane without a parachute and hoping you'll land in a haystack. The only thing that'd save you would be God, and since He pushed you overboard in the first place, I wouldn't give a nickel for your chances.'

'There's a woman in Amity who thinks that's why we're having trouble,' said Brody. 'She thinks it's some sort of divine retribution.'

Quint smiled. 'Might be. He made the damn thing, I suppose. He can tell it what to do.'

'You serious?'

'No, not really. I don't put much stock in religion.'

'So why do you think people have been killed?'

'Bad luck.' Quint pulled back on the throttle. The boat slowed and settled in the swells. 'We'll try to change it.' He took a piece of paper from his pocket, unfolded it, read the notes, and sighting along his outstretched arm, checked his bearings. He turned the ignition key, and the engine died. There was a weight, a thickness, to the sudden silence. 'Okay, Hooper,' he said. 'Start chuckin' the shit overboard.'

Hooper took the top off the chum bucket and began to ladle the contents into the sea. The first ladleful spattered on the still water, and slowly the oily smear spread westward.

By ten o'clock a breeze had come up – not strong, but fresh enough to ripple the water and cool the men, who sat and watched and said nothing. The only sound was the regular splash as Hooper poured chum off the stern.

Brody sat in the fighting chair, struggling to stay awake. He yawned, then recalled that he had left the half-read copy of *The Deadly Virgin* in a magazine rack below. He stood, stretched, and went down the three steps into the cabin. He found the book and started topside again, when his eye caught the ice chest. He looked at his watch and said to himself, the hell with it; there's no time out here.

'I'm going to have a beer,' he called. 'Anybody want one?'

'No,' said Hooper.

'Sure,' said Quint. 'We can shoot at the cans.'

Brody took two beers from the chest, removed the metal tabs, and started to climb the stairs. His foot was on the top step when he heard Quint's flat, calm voice say, 'There he is.'

At first, Brody thought Quint was referring to him, but then he saw Hooper jump off the transom and heard him whistle and say, 'Wow! He sure is!'

Brody felt his pulse speed up. He stepped quickly on to the deck and said, 'Where?'

'Right there,' said Quint. 'Dead off the stern.'

It took Brody's eyes a moment to adjust, but then he saw the fin – a ragged, brownish-grey triangle that sliced through the water, followed by the scythed tail sweeping left and right with short, spasmodic thrusts. The fish was at least thirty yards behind the boat, Brody guessed. Maybe forty. 'Are you sure it's him?' he said.

'It's him,' said Quint.

'What are you going to do?'

'Nothing. Not till we see what he does. Hooper, you keep ladling that shit. Let's bring him in here.'

Hooper lifted the bucket up on to the transom and scooped the chum into the water. Quint walked forward and fastened a harpoon head to the wooden shaft. He picked up a barrel and put it under one arm. He held the coiled rope over his other

251

arm and clutched the harpoon in his hand. He carried it all aft and set it on the deck.

The fish cruised back and forth in the slick, seeming to search for the source of the bloody miasma.

'Reel in those lines,' Quint said to Brody. 'They won't do any good now we've got him up.'

Brody brought in the lines one by one and let the squid bait fall to the deck. The fish moved slightly closer to the boat, still cruising slowly.

Quint set the barrel on the transom to the left of Hooper's bucket and arranged the rope beside it. Then he climbed up on the transom and stood, his right arm cocked, holding the harpoon. 'Come on,' he said. 'Come on in here.'

But the fish would come no closer than fifty feet from the boat.

'I don't get it,' said Quint. 'He should come in and take a look at us. Brody, take the cutters out of my back pocket and clip off those squid bait and throw 'em overboard. Maybe some food'll bring him in. And splash the hell out of the water when you throw 'em. Let him know something's there.'

Brody did as he was told, slapping and roiling the water with a gaff, always keeping the fin in sight, for he imagined the fish suddenly appearing from the deep and seizing him by the arm.

'Throw some other ones while you're at it,' said Quint. 'They're in the chest there. And throw those beers over, too.'

'The beers? What for?'

'The more we can get in the water, the better. Don't make no difference what it is, so long as it gets him interested enough to want to find out.'

Hooper said, 'What about the porpoise?'

'Why, Mr Hooper,' said Quint, 'I thought you didn't approve.'

'Never mind that,' Hooper said, his eyes bright with excitement. 'I want to see that fish!'

'We'll see,' said Quint. 'If I have to use it, I will.'

The squid had drifted back towards the shark, and one of the beers bobbled on the surface as it slowly faded aft of the boat. But still the fish stayed away.

They waited – Hooper ladling, Quint poised on the transom, Brody standing by one of the rods.

'Shit,' said Quint. 'I guess I got no choice.' He set the harpoon down and jumped off the transom. He flipped the top off the garbage can next to Brody, and Brody saw the lifeless eyes of the tiny porpoise as it swayed in the briny water. The sight repelled him, and he turned away.

'Well, little fella,' said Quint. 'The time has come.' From the lazaret he took a length of dog-leash chain and snapped one end of it into the hook eye protruding from beneath the porpoise's jaw. To the other end of the chain he tied a length of three-quarter-inch hemp. He uncoiled several yards of the rope, cut it, and made it fast to a cleat on the starboard gunwale.

'I thought you said the shark could pull out a cleat,' said Brody.

'It might just,' said Quint. 'But I'm betting I can get an iron in him and cut the rope before he pulls it taut enough to yank the cleat.' Quint took hold of the dog chain and lifted the porpoise clear of the garbage can. He carried it over to the starboard gunwale and set it down. He climbed on to the transom and pulled the porpoise after him. He took the knife from the sheath at his belt. With his left hand he held the porpoise out in front of him. Then, with his right, he cut a series of shallow slashes in the porpoise's belly. A rank, dark liquid oozed from the animal and fell in droplets on the water. Quint tossed the porpoise into the water, let out six feet of line, then put the rope under his foot on the transom and stepped down hard. The porpoise floated just beneath the surface of the water, less than six feet from the boat.

'That's pretty close,' said Brody.

'Has to be,' said Quint. 'I can't get a shot at him if he's thirty feet away.'

'Why are you standing on the rope?'

'To keep the little fella where he is. I don't want to cleat it down that close to the boat. If he took it and didn't have any running room, he could thrash around and beat us to pieces.' Quint hefted the harpoon and looked at the shark's fin.

The fish moved closer, still cruising back and forth but closing the gap between itself and the boat by a few feet with every passage. Then it stopped, twenty or twenty-five feet away, and for a second seemed to lie motionless in the water, aimed directly at the boat. The tail dropped beneath the surface; the dorsal fin slid backward and vanished; and the great head reared up, mouth open in a slack, savage grin, eyes black and abysmal.

Brody stared in mute horror, sensing that this was what it must be like to try to stare down the devil.

'Hey, fish!' Quint called. He stood on the transom, legs spread, his hand curled around the shaft of the harpoon that rested on his shoulder. 'Come see what we've got for you!'

For another moment the fish hung in the water, watching. Then, soundlessly, the head slid back and disappeared.

'Where'd he go?' said Brody.

'He'll be coming now,' said Quint. 'Come, fish,' he purred. 'Come, fish. Come get your supper.' He pointed the harpoon at the floating porpoise.

Suddenly the boat lurched violently to the side. Quint's legs skidded out from under him, and he fell on his back on the transom. The harpoon dart separated from the shaft and clattered to the deck, Brody tumbled sideways, grabbed the back of the chair, and twirled around as the chair swivelled. Hooper spun backward and slammed into the port gunwale.

The rope attached to the porpoise tautened and shivered. The knot by which it was secured to the cleat tightened so hard that the rope flattened and its fibres popped. The wood

under the cleat began to crack. Then the rope snapped backward, went slack, and curled in the water beside the boat.

'I'll be fucked!' said Quint.

'It was like he knew what you were trying to do,' said
Brody, 'like he knew there was a trap set for him.'

'Goddamn it! I never have seen a fish do that before.'

'He knew if he knocked you down he could get to the
porpoise.'

'Shit, he was just aiming for the porpoise, and he missed.'

Hooper said, 'Aiming from the opposite side of the boat?'

'Well, it don't make no never-mind,' said Quint. 'Whatever
he did, it worked.'

'How do you think he got off the hook?' said Brody. 'He
didn't pull the cleat out.'

Quint walked over to the starboard gunwale and began to
pull in the rope. 'He either bit right through the chain, or
else . . . uh-huh, that's what I figured.' He leaned over the
gunwale and grabbed the chain. He pulled it aboard. It was
intact, the clip still attached to the eye of the hook. But the
hook itself had been destroyed. The steel shaft no longer
curled. It was nearly straight, marked by two small bumps
where once it had been tempered into a curve.

'Jesus Christ!' said Brody. 'He did that with his mouth?'

'Bent it out nice as you please,' said Quint. 'Probably
didn't slow him down for more than a second or two.'

Brody felt light-headed. His fingertips tingled. He sat down
in the chair and drew several deep breaths, trying to stifle the
fear that was mounting inside him.

'Where do you suppose he's gone?' said Hooper, standing
at the stern and looking at the water.

'He's around here somewhere,' said Quint. 'I imagine he'll
be back. That porpoise wasn't any more to him than an
anchovy is to a bluefish. He'll be looking for more food.' He
reassembled the harpoon, recoiled the rope, and set them on
the transom. 'We're just gonna have to wait. And keep

chumming. I'll tie up some more squid and hang 'em overboard.'

Brody watched Quint as he wrapped twine around each squid and dropped it overboard, attached to the boat at cleats, rod-holders, and almost anything else around which he could tie a knot. When a dozen squid had been placed at various points and various depths around the boat, Quint climbed to the flying bridge and sat down.

Hoping to be contradicted, Brody said, 'That sure does seem to be a smart fish.'

'Smart or not, I wouldn't know,' said Quint. 'But he's doing things I've never seen a fish do before.' He paused, then said – as much to himself as to Brody – 'but I'm gonna get that fucker. That's one thing for sure.'

'How can you be sure?'

'I know it, that's all. Now leave me be.'

It was a command, not a request, and though Brody wanted to talk – about anything, even the fish itself, as long as he could steer his mind away from the image of the beast lurking in the water below him – he said nothing more. He looked at his watch: 11.05.

They waited, expecting at any moment to see the fin rise off the stern and cut back and forth through the water. Hooper ladled chum, which sounded to Brody, every time it hit the water, like diarrhoea.

At eleven-thirty, Brody was startled by a sharp resonant *snap*. Quint leaped down the ladder, across the deck, and on to the transom. He picked up the harpoon and held it at his shoulder, scanning the water around the stern.

'What the hell was that?' said Brody.

'He's back.'

'How do you know? What was that noise?'

'Twine snapping. He took one of the squid.'

'Why would it snap? Why wouldn't he chew right through it?'

'He probably never bit down on it. He sucked it in, and the twine came tight behind his teeth when he closed his mouth. He went like this, I imagine' – Quint jerked his head to the side – 'and the line parted.'

'How could we hear it snap if it snapped under water?'

'It didn't snap under water, for Christ sake! It snapped right there.' Quint pointed to a few inches of limp twine hanging from a cleat amidships.

'Oh,' said Brody. As he looked at the remnant, he saw another piece of twine – a few feet farther up the gunwale – go limp. 'There's another one,' he said. He stood and walked to the gunwale and pulled in the line. 'He must be right underneath us.'

Quint said, 'Anybody care to go swimming?'

'Let's put the cage overboard,' said Hooper.

'You're kidding,' said Brody.

'No, I'm not. It might bring him out.'

'With you in it?'

'Not at first. Let's see what he does. What do you say, Quint?'

'Might as well,' said Quint. 'Can't hurt just to put it in the water, and you paid for it.' He put down the harpoon, and he and Hooper walked to the cage.

They tipped the cage on to its side, and Hooper opened the top hatch and crawled through it. He removed the scuba tank, regulator, face mask, and neoprene wet suit, and set them on the deck. They tipped the cage upright again and slid it across the deck to the starboard gunwale. 'You got a couple of lines?' said Hooper. 'I want to make it fast to the boat.' Quint went below and returned with two coils of rope. They tied one to an after cleat, one to a cleat amidships, then secured the ends to the bars on top to the cage. 'Okay,' said Hooper. 'Let's put her over.' They lifted the cage, tipped it backward, and pushed it overboard. It sank until the ropes stopped it, a few feet beneath the surface. There it rested, rising and falling slowly in the swells. The three men stood at the gunwale, looking into the water.

'What makes you think this'll bring him up?' said Brody.

'I didn't say "up",' said Hooper, 'I said "out". I think he'll come out and have a look at it, to see whether he wants to eat it.'

'That won't do us any damn good,' said Quint. 'I can't stick him if he's twelve feet under water.'

'Once he comes out,' said Hooper, 'maybe he'll come up. We're not having any luck with anything else.'

But the fish did not come out. The cage lay quietly in the water, unmolested.

'There goes another squid,' said Quint, pointing forward. 'He's there, all right.' He leaned overboard and shouted, 'Goddamn you, fish! Come out where I can have a shot at you.'

After fifteen minutes, Hooper said, 'Oh well,' and went below. He reappeared moments later, carrying a movie camera in a waterproof housing, and what looked to Brody like a walking stick with a thong at one end.

'What are you doing?' Brody said.

'I'm going down there. Maybe that'll bring him out.'

'You're out of your goddamn mind. What are you going to do if he does come out?'

'First, I'm going to take some pictures of him. Then I'm going to try to kill him.'

'With what, may I ask?'

'This.' Hooper held up the stick.

'Good thinking,' Quint said with a derisive cackle. 'If that doesn't work you can tickle him to death.'

'What is that?' said Brody.

'Some people call it a bang stick. Others call it a power head. Anyway, it's basically an underwater gun.' He pulled both ends of the stick, and it came apart in two pieces. 'In here,' he said, pointing to a chamber at the point where the

258

stick had come apart, 'you put a twelve-gauge shotgun shell.' He took a shotgun shell from his pocket and pushed it into the chamber, then rejoined the two ends of the stick. 'Then, when you get close enough to the fish, you jab it at him and the shell goes off. If you hit him right – in the brain's the only sure place – you kill him.'

'Even a fish that big?'

'I think so. If I hit him right.'

'And if you don't? Suppose you miss by just a hair.'

'That's what I'm afraid of.'

'I would be, too,' said Quint. 'I don't think I'd like five thousand pounds of pissed-off dinosaur trying to eat me.'

'That's not my worry,' said Hooper. 'What concerns me is that if I miss, I might drive him off. He'd probably sound, and we'd never know if he died or not.'

'Until he ate someone else,' said Brody.

'That's right.'

'You're fucking crazy,' said Quint.

'Am I, Quint? You're not having much success with this fish. We could stay here all month and let him eat your bait right out from under us.'

'He'll come up,' said Quint. 'Mark my words.'

'You'll be dead of old age before he comes up, Quint. I think this fish has you all shook. He's not playing by the rules.'

Quint looked at Hooper and said evenly, 'You telling me my business, boy?'

'No. But I am telling you I think this fish is more than you can handle.'

'That right, boy? You think you can do better'n Quint?'

'Call it that if you want. I think I can kill the fish.'

'Fine and dandy. You're gonna get your chance.'

Brody said, 'Come on. We can't let him go in that thing.'

'What are *you* bitchin' about?' said Quint. 'From what I seen, you just as soon he went down there and never come up. At least that'd stop him from—'

259

'Shut your mouth!' Brody's emotions were jumbled. Part of him didn't care whether Hooper lived or died – might even relish the prospect of Hooper's death. But such vengeance would be hollow – and quite possibly, unmerited. Could he really wish a man dead? No. Not yet.

'Go on,' Quint said to Hooper. 'Get in that thing.'

'Right away.' Hooper removed his shirt, sneakers, and trousers, and began to pull the neoprene suit over his legs. 'When I'm inside,' he said, forcing his arms into the rubber sleeves of the jacket, 'stand up here and keep an eye. Maybe you can use the rifle if he gets close enough to the surface.' He looked at Quint. 'You can be ready with the harpoon . . . if you want to.'

'I'll do what I'll do,' said Quint. 'You worry about yourself.'

When he was dressed, Hooper fitted the regulator on to the neck of the air tank, tightened the wing nut that held it in place, and opened the air valve. He sucked two breaths from the tank to make sure it was feeding air. 'Help me put this on, will you?' he said to Brody.

Brody lifted the tank and held it while Hooper slipped his arms through the straps and fastened a third strap around his middle. He put the face mask on his head. 'I should have brought weights,' said Hooper.

Quint said, 'You should have brought brains.'

Hooper put his right wrist through the thong at the end of the power head, picked up the camera with his right hand, and said, 'Okay.' He walked to the gunwale. 'If you'll each take a rope and pull, that'll bring the cage to the surface. Then I'll open the hatch and go in through the top, and you can let the ropes go. It'll hang by the ropes. I won't use the flotation tanks unless one of the ropes breaks.'

'Or gets chewed through,' said Quint.

Hooper looked at Quint and smiled. 'Thanks for the thought.'

Quint and Brody pulled on the ropes, and the cage rose in

the water. When the hatch broke the surface, Hooper said, 'Okay, right there.' He spat in the face mask, rubbed the saliva around on the glass, and fitted the mask over his face. He reached for the regulator tube, put the mouthpiece in his mouth, and took a breath. Then he bent over the gunwale, unlatched the top of the hatch and flipped it open. He started to put a knee on the gunwale, but stopped. He took the mouthpiece out of his mouth and said, 'I forgot something.' His nose was enclosed in the mask, so his voice sounded thick and nasal. He walked across the deck and picked up his trousers. He rummaged through the pockets until he found what he was looking for. He unzipped his wet-suit jacket.

'What's that?' said Brody.

Hooper held up a shark's tooth, rimmed in silver. It was a duplicate of the one he had given Ellen. He dropped it inside his wet suit and zipped up the jacket. 'Can't be too careful,' he said, smiling. He crossed the deck again, put his mouthpiece in his mouth, and kneeled on the gunwale. He took a final breath and dived overboard through the open hatch. Brody watched him go, wondering if he really wanted to know the truth about Hooper and Ellen.

Hooper stopped himself before he hit the bottom of the cage. He curled around and stood up. He reached out to the top of the hatch and pulled it closed. Then he looked up at Brody, put the thumb and index finger of his left hand together in the okay sign, and ducked down.

'I guess we can let go,' said Brody. They released the ropes and let the cage descend until the hatch was about four feet beneath the surface.

'Get the rifle,' said Quint. 'It's on the rack below. It's all loaded.' He climbed on to the transom and lifted the harpoon to his shoulder.

Brody went below, found the rifle, and hurried back on deck. He opened the breach and slid a cartridge into the chamber. 'How much air does he have?' he said.

'I don't know,' said Quint. 'However much he has, I doubt he'll live to breathe it.'

'Maybe you're right. But you said yourself you never know what these fish will do.'

'Yeah, but this is different. This is like putting your hand in a fire and hoping you won't get burned. A sensible man don't *do* it.'

Below, Hooper waited until the bubbly froth of his descent had dissipated. There was water in his mask, so he tilted his head backward, pressed on the top of the faceplate, and blew through his nose until the mask was clear. He felt serene. It was the pervasive sense of freedom and ease that he always felt when he dived. He was alone in blue silence speckled with shafts of sunlight that danced through the water. The only sounds were those he made breathing – a deep, hollow noise as he breathed in, a soft thudding of bubbles as he exhaled. He held his breath, and the silence was complete. Without weights, he was too buoyant, and he had to hold on to the bars to keep his tank from clanging against the hatch overhead. He turned around and looked up at the hull of the boat, a grey body that sat above him, bouncing slowly. At first, the cage annoyed him. It confined him, restricted him, prevented him from enjoying the grace of underwater movement. But then he remembered why he was there, and he was grateful.

He looked for the fish. He knew it couldn't be sitting beneath the boat, as Quint had thought. It could not 'sit' anywhere, could not rest or stay still. It had to move to survive.

Even with the bright sunlight, the visibility in the murky water was poor – no more than forty feet. Hooper turned slowly around, trying to pierce the edge of gloom and grasp any sliver of colour or movement. He looked beneath the boat, where the water turned from blue to grey to black. Nothing. He looked at his watch, calculating that if he controlled his breathing, he could stay down for at least half an hour more.

Carried by the tide, one of the small white squid slipped between the bars of the cage and, tethered by twine, fluttered in Hooper's face. He pushed it out of the cage.

He glanced downward, started to look away, then snapped his eyes down again. Rising at him from the darkling blue – slowly, smoothly – was the shark. It rose with no apparent effort, an angel of death gliding towards an appointment foreordained.

Hooper stared, enthralled, impelled to flee but unable to move. As the fish drew nearer, he marvelled at its colours: the flat brown-greys seen on the surface had vanished. The top of the immense body was a hard ferrous grey, bluish where dappled with streaks of sun. Beneath the lateral line, all was creamy, ghostly white.

Hooper wanted to raise his camera, but his arm would not obey. In a minute, he said to himself, in a minute.

The fish came closer, silent as a shadow, and Hooper drew back. The head was only a few feet from the cage when the fish turned and began to pass before Hooper's eyes – casually, as if in proud display of its incalculable mass and power. The snout passed first, then the jaw, slack and smiling, armed with row upon row of serrate triangles. And then the black, fathomless eye, seemingly riveted upon him. The gills rippled – bloodless wounds in the steely skin.

Tentatively, Hooper stuck a hand through the bars and touched the flank. It felt cold and hard, not clammy but smooth as vinyl. He let his fingertips caress the flesh – past the pectoral fins, the pelvic fin, the thick, firm genital claspers – until finally (the fish seemed to have no end) they were slapped away by the sweeping tail.

The fish continued to move away from the cage. Hooper heard faint popping noises, and he saw three straight spirals of angry bubbles speed from the surface, then slow and stop, well above the fish. Bullets. Not yet, he told himself. One more pass for pictures. The fish began to turn, banking, the rubbery pectoral fins changing pitch.

The fish rammed through the space between the bars.

'What the hell is he doing down there?' said Brody. 'Why didn't he jab him with the gun?'

Quint didn't answer. He stood on the transom, harpoon clutched in his fist, peering into the water. 'Come up, fish,' he said. 'Come to Quint.'

'Do you see it?' said Brody. 'What's it doing?'

'Nothing. Not yet, anyway.'

The fish had moved off to the limit of Hooper's vision – a spectral silver-grey blur tracing a slow circle. Hooper raised his camera and pressed the trigger. He knew the film would be worthless unless the fish moved in once more, but he wanted to catch the beast as it emerged from the darkness.

Through the viewfinder he saw the fish turn towards him. It moved fast, tail thrusting vigorously, mouth opening and closing as if gasping for breath. Hooper raised his right hand to change the focus. Remember to change it again, he told himself, when it turns.

But the fish did not turn. A shiver travelled the length of its body as it closed on the cage. It struck the cage head on, the snout ramming between two bars and spreading them. The snout hit Hooper in the chest and knocked him backward. The camera flew from his hands, and the mouthpiece shot from his mouth. The fish turned on its side, and the pounding tail forced the great body farther into the cage. Hooper groped for his mouthpiece but couldn't find it. His chest was convulsed with the need for air.

'It's attacking!' screamed Brody. He grabbed one of the tether ropes and pulled, desperately trying to raise the cage.

'God damn your fucking soul!' Quint shouted.

'Throw it! Throw it!'

'I can't throw it! I gotta get him on the surface! Come up, you devil! You prick!'

The fish slid backward out of the cage and turned sharply to the right in a tight circle. Hooper reached behind his head, found the regulator tube, and followed it with his hand until he located the mouthpiece. He put it in his mouth and, forgetting to exhale first, sucked for air. He got water, and he gagged and choked until at last the mouthpiece cleared and he drew an agonized breath. It was then that he saw the wide gap in the bars and saw the giant head lunging through it. He raised his hands above his head, grasping at the escape hatch.

The fish rammed through the space between the bars, spreading them still farther with each thrust of its tail. Hooper, flattened against the back of the cage, saw the mouth reaching, straining for him. He remembered the power head, and he tried to lower his right arm and grab it. The fish thrust again, and Hooper saw with the terror of doom that the mouth was going to reach him.

The jaws closed around his torso. Hooper felt a terrible pressure as if his guts were compacted. He jabbed his fist into the black eye. The fish bit down, and the last thing Hooper saw before he died was the eye gazing at him through a cloud of his own blood.

'He's got him!' cried Brody. 'Do something!'

'The man is dead,' Quint said.

'How do you know? We may be able to save him.'

'He is dead.'

Holding Hooper in its mouth, the fish backed out of the cage. It sank a few feet, chewing, swallowing the viscera that were squeezed into its gullet. Then it shuddered and thrust forward with its tail, driving itself and prey upward in the water.

'He's coming up!' said Brody.

'Grab the rifle!' Quint cocked his hand for the throw.

The fish broke water fifteen feet from the boat, surging upward in a shower of spray. Hooper's body protruded from each side of the mouth, head and arms hanging limply down one side, knees, calves, and feet from the other.

In the few seconds while the fish was clear of the water, Brody thought he saw Hooper's glazed eyes staring open through his face mask. As if in contempt and triumph, the fish hung suspended for an instant, challenging mortal vengeance.

Simultaneously, Brody reached for the rifle and Quint cast the harpoon. The target was huge, a field of white belly, and the distance was not too great for a successful throw above water. But as Quint threw, the fish began to slide down in the water, and the iron went high.

For another instant, the fish remained on the surface, its head out of water, Hooper hanging from its mouth.

'Shoot!' Quint yelled. 'For Christ sake, shoot!'

Brody shot without aiming. The first two shots hit the water in front of the fish. The third, to Brody's horror, struck Hooper in the neck.

'Here, give me the goddamn thing!' said Quint, grabbing the rifle from Brody. In a single, quick motion he raised the rifle to his shoulder and squeezed off two shots. But the fish, with a last, vacant gaze, had already begun to slip beneath the surface. The bullets plopped harmlessly into the swirl where the head had been.

The fish might never have been there. There was no noise, save the whisper of a breeze. From the surface the cage seemed undamaged. The water was calm. The only difference was that Hooper was gone.

'What do we do now?' said Brody. 'What in the name of God can we do now? There's nothing left. We might as well go back.'

'We'll go back,' said Quint. 'For now.'

'For now? What do you mean? There's nothing we can do. The fish is too much for us. It's not real, not natural.'

'Are you beaten, man?'

'I'm beaten. All we can do is wait until God or nature or

266

whatever the hell is doing this to us decides we've had enough. It's out of man's hands.'

'Not mine,' said Quint. 'I am going to kill that thing.'

'I'm not sure I can get any more money after what happened today.'

'Keep your money. This is no longer a matter of money.'

'What do you mean?' Brody looked at Quint, who was standing at the stern, looking at the spot where the fish's head had been, as if he expected it to reappear at any moment clutching the shredded corpse in its mouth. He searched the sea, craving another confrontation.

Quint said to Brody, 'I am going to kill that fish. Come if you want. Stay home if you want. But I am going to kill that fish.'

As Quint spoke, Brody looked into his eyes. They seemed as dark and bottomless as the eye of the fish. 'I'll come,' said Brody. 'I don't guess I have any choice.'

'No,' said Quint. 'We have no choice.' He took his knife from its sheath and handed it to Brody. 'Here. Cut that cage loose and let's get out of here.'

When the boat was tied up at the dock, Brody walked towards his car. At the end of the dock there was a phone booth, and he stopped beside it prompted by his earlier resolve to call Daisy Wicker. But he suppressed the impulse and moved on to his car. What's the point? he thought. If there was anything, it's over now.

Still, as he drove towards Amity, Brody wondered what Ellen's reaction had been when the Coast Guard had called her with the news of Hooper's death. Quint had radioed the Coast Guard before they started in, and Brody had asked the duty officer to phone Ellen and tell her that he, at least, was all right.

By the time Brody arrived home, Ellen had long since finished crying. She had wept mechanically, angrily, grieving not so much for Hooper as in hopelessness and bitterness at yet another death. She had been sadder at the disintegration of Larry Vaughan than she was now, for Vaughan had been a dear and close friend. Hooper had been a 'lover' in only the most shallow sense of the word. She had not *loved* him. She had used him, and though she was grateful for what he had given her, she felt no obligation to him. She was sorry he was dead, of course, just as she would have been sorry to hear that his brother, David, had died. In her mind they were both now relics of her distant past.

She heard Brody's car pull into the driveway, and she opened the back door. Lord, he looks whipped, she thought as she watched him walk towards the house. His eyes were red and sunken, and he seemed slightly hunched as he walked. She kissed him at the door and said, 'You look like you could use a drink.'

'That I could.' He went into the living-room and flopped into a chair.

'What would you like?'

'Anything. Just so long as it's strong.'

She went into the kitchen, filled a glass with equal portions of vodka and orange juice, and brought it to him. She sat on the arm of his chair and ran her hand over his head. She smiled and said, 'There's your bald spot. It's been so long since I touched your bald spot that I'd forgotten it was there.'

'I'm surprised there's any hair left at all. Christ, I'll never be as old as I feel today.'

'I'll bet. Well, it's over now.'

'I wish it was,' said Brody. 'I truly do wish it was.'

'What do you mean? It is over, isn't it? There's nothing more you can do.'

'We're going out tomorrow. Six o'clock.'

'You're kidding.'

'I wish I was.'

'Why?' Ellen was stunned. 'What do you think you can do?'

'Catch the fish. And kill it.'

'Do you believe that?'

'I'm not sure. But Quint believes it. God, how he believes it.'

'Then let him go. Let him get killed.'

'I can't.'

'Why not?'

'It's my job.'

'It is *not* your job!' She was furious, and scared, and tears began to well behind her eyes.

Brody thought for a moment and said, 'No, you're right.'

'Then *why*?'

'I don't think I can tell you. I don't think I know.'

'Are you trying to prove something?'

'Maybe. I don't know. I didn't feel this way before. After Hooper was killed, I was ready to give it up.'

'What changed your mind?'

'Quint, I guess.'

'You mean you're letting him tell you what to do?'

'No. He didn't tell me anything. It's a feeling. I can't explain it. But giving up isn't an answer. It doesn't put an end to anything.'

'Why is an end so important?'

'Different reasons, I think. Quint feels that if he doesn't kill the fish, everything he believes in is wrong.'

'And you?'

Brody tried to smile. 'Me, I guess I'm just a screwed-up cop.'

'Don't joke with me!' Ellen cried, and tears spilled out of her eyes. 'What about me and the children? Do you want to get killed?'

'No, God no. It's just . . .'

'You think it's all your fault. You think you're responsible.'

'Responsible for what?'

'For that little boy and the old man. You think killing the shark will make everything all right again. You want revenge.'

Brody sighed. 'Maybe I do. I don't know. I feel ... I believe that the only way this town can be alive again is if we kill that thing.'

'And you're willing to get killed trying to—'

'Don't be stupid! I'm not willing to get killed. I'm not even willing – if that's the word you want to use – to go out in that goddamn boat. You think I like it out there? I'm so scared every minute I'm out there I want to puke.'

'Then *why go*?' She was pleading with him, begging. 'Can't you ever think of anybody but yourself?'

Brody was shocked at the suggestion of selfishness. It had never occurred to him that he was being selfish, indulging a personal need for expiation. 'I love you,' he said. 'You know that ... no matter what.'

'Sure you do,' she said bitterly. 'Oh, sure you do.'

They ate dinner in silence. When they were finished, Ellen picked up the dishes, washed them, and went upstairs. Brody walked around the living-room, turning out lights. Just as he reached for the switch to turn off the hall light, he heard a tap on the front door. He opened it and saw Meadows.

'Hey, Harry,' he said. 'Come on in.'

'No,' said Meadows. 'It's too late. I just wanted to drop this by.' He handed Brody a manila envelope.

'What is it?'

'Open it and see. I'll talk to you tomorrow.' Meadows turned and walked down the path to the kerb, where his car was parked, lights on and motor running.

Brody shut the door and opened the envelope. Inside was a proof of the editorial page of the next day's *Leader*. The first two editorials had been circled in red grease pencil. Brody read:

In the past three weeks, Amity has suffered through one horrible tragedy after another. Its citizens, and its friends, have been struck down by a savage menace that no one can deter, no one can explain.

Yesterday another human life was cut short by the Great White Shark. Matt Hooper, the young oceanographer from Woods Hole, was killed as he tried to kill the beast single-handedly.

People may debate the wisdom of Mr Hooper's daring attempt. But call it brave or foolhardy, there can be no debate about the motive that sent him on his fatal mission. He was trying to help Amity, spending his own time and money in an effort to restore peace to this despairing community.

He was a friend, and he gave his life so that we, his friends, might live.

... AND A VOTE OF THANKS

Ever since the marauding shark first came to Amity, one man has spent his every waking minute trying to protect his fellow citizens. That man is Police Chief Martin Brody.

After the first attack, Chief Brody wanted to inform the public of the danger and close the beaches. But a chorus of less prudent voices, including that of the editor of this newspaper, told him he was wrong. Play down the risk, we said, and it will disappear. It was we who were wrong.

Some in Amity were slow to learn the lesson. When, after repeated attacks, Chief Brody insisted on keeping the beaches closed, he was vilified and threatened. A few of his most vocal critics were men motivated not by public-spiritedness but personal greed. Chief Brody persisted, and, once again, he was proven right.

Now Chief Brody is risking his life on the same expedition that took the life of Matt Hooper. We must all offer our prayers for his safe return . . . and our thanks for his extraordinary fortitude and integrity.

Brody said aloud, 'Thank *you*, Harry.'

Around midnight, the wind began to blow hard from the north-east, whistling through the screens and soon bringing a driving rain that splashed on the bedroom floor. Brody got out of bed and shut the window. He tried to go back to sleep, but his mind refused to rest. He got up again, put on his bathrobe, went downstairs to the living-room, and turned on the television. He switched channels until he found a movie – *Weekend at the Waldorf*, with Fred Astaire and Ginger Rogers. Then he sat down in a chair and promptly slipped into a fitful doze.

He awoke at five, to the whine of the television test pattern, turned off the set, and listened for the wind. It had moderated and seemed to be coming from a different quarter, but it still carried rain. He debated calling Quint, but thought, no, no use: we'll be going even if this blows up into a gale. He went upstairs and quietly dressed. Before he left the bedroom, he looked at Ellen, who had a frown on her sleeping face. 'I do love you, you know,' he whispered, and he kissed her brow. He started down the stairs and then, impulsively, went and looked in the boys' bedrooms. They were all asleep.

FOURTEEN

When he drove up to the dock, Quint was waiting for him – a tall, impassive figure whose yellow oilskins shone under the dark sky. He was sharpening a harpoon dart on a carborundum stone.

'I almost called you,' Brody said as he pulled on his slicker. 'What does this weather mean?'

'Nothing,' said Quint. 'It'll let up after a while. Or even if it doesn't, it don't matter. He'll be there.'

Brody looked up at the scudding clouds. 'Gloomy enough.'

'Fitting,' said Quint, and he hopped aboard the boat.

'Is it just us?'

'Just us. You expecting somebody else?'

'No. But I thought you liked an extra pair of hands.'

'You know this fish as well as any man, and more hands won't make no difference now. Besides, it's nobody else's business.'

Brody stepped from the dock on to the transom, and was about to jump down to the deck when he noticed a canvas tarpaulin covering something in a corner. 'What's that?' he said, pointing.

'Sheep.' Quint turned the ignition key. The engine coughed once, caught, and began to chug evenly.

'What for?' Brody stepped down on to the deck. 'You going to sacrifice it?'

Quint barked a brief, grim laugh. 'Might at that,' he said. 'No, it's bait. Give him a little breakfast before we have at him. Undo my stern line.' He walked forward and cast off the bow and spring lines.

As Brody reached for the stern line, he heard a car engine.

A pair of headlights sped along the road, and there was a squeal of rubber as the car stopped at the end of the pier. A man jumped out of the car and ran towards the *Orca*. It was Bill Whitman.

'I almost missed you,' he said, panting.

'What do you want?' said Brody.

'I want to come along. Or, rather, I've been ordered to come along.'

'Tough shit,' said Quint. 'I don't know who you are, but nobody's coming along. Brody, cast off the stern line.'

'Why not?' said Whitman. 'I won't get in the way. Maybe I can help. Look, man, this is news. If you're going to catch that fish, I want to be there.'

'Fuck yourself,' said Quint.

'I'll charter a boat and follow you.'

Quint laughed. 'Go ahead. See if you can find someone foolish enough to take you out. Then try to find us. It's a big ocean. Throw the line, Brody!'

Brody tossed the stern line on to the dock. Quint pushed the throttle forward, and the boat eased out of the slip. Brody looked back and saw Whitman walking down the pier towards his car.

The water off Montauk was rough, for the wind – from the south-east now – was at odds with the tide. The boat lurched through the waves, its bow pounding down and casting a mantle of spray. The dead sheep bounced in the stern.

When they reached the open sea, heading south and slightly west, their motion was eased. The rain had slackened to a drizzle, and with each moment there were fewer white-caps tumbling from the top of waves.

They had been around the point only fifteen minutes when Quint pulled back on the throttle and slowed the engine.

Brody looked towards shore. In the growing light he could see the water tower clearly – a black point rising from the grey

274

strip of land. The lighthouse beacon still shone. 'We're not out as far as we usually go,' he said.

'No.'

'We can't be more than a couple of miles offshore.'

'Just about.'

'So why are you stopping?'

'I got a feeling.' Quint pointed to the left, to a cluster of lights farther down the shore. 'That's Amity there.'

'So?'

'I don't think he'll be so far out today. I think he'll be somewhere between here and Amity.'

'Why?'

'Like I said, it's a feeling. There's not always a why to these things.'

'Two days in a row we found him farther out.'

'Or he found us.'

'I don't get it, Quint. For a man who says there's no such thing as a smart fish, you're making this one out to be a genius.'

'I wouldn't go that far.'

Brody bristled at Quint's sly, enigmatic tone. 'What kind of game are you playing?'

'No game. If I'm wrong, I'm wrong.'

'And we try somewhere else tomorrow.' Brody half hoped Quint would be wrong, that there would be a day's reprieve.

'Or later today. But I don't think we'll have to wait that long.' Quint cut the engine, went to the stern, and lifted a bucket of chum on to the transom. 'Start chummin',' he said, handing Brody the ladle. He uncovered the sheep, tied a rope around its neck, and lay it on the gunwale. He slashed its stomach and flung the animal overboard, letting it drift twenty feet from the boat before securing the rope to an after cleat. Then he went forward, unlashed two barrels, and carried them, and their coils of ropes and harpoon darts, back to the stern. He set the barrels on each side of the transom, each next to its own rope, and slipped one dart on to the wooden throwing shaft. 'Okay,' he said. 'Now let's see how long it takes.'

The sky had lightened to full, grey daylight, and in ones and twos the lights on the shore flicked off.

The stench of the mess Brody was ladling overboard made his stomach turn, and he wished he had eaten something – anything – before he left home.

Quint sat on the flying bridge, watching the rhythms of the sea.

Brody's butt was sore from sitting on the hard transom, and his arm was growing weary from the dipping and empty-ing of the ladle. So he stood up, stretched, and facing off the stern, tried a new scooping motion with the ladle.

Suddenly he saw the monstrous head of the fish – not five feet away, so close he could reach over and touch it with the ladle – black eyes staring at him, silver-grey snout pointing at him, gaping jaw grinning at him. 'Oh God!' Brody said, wondering in his shock how long the fish had been there before he had stood up and turned around. 'There he is!'

Quint was down the ladder and at the stern in an instant. As he jumped on to the transom, the fish's head slipped back into the water and, a second later, slammed into the transom. The jaws closed on the wood, and the head shook violently from side to side. Brody grabbed a cleat and held on, unable to look away from the eyes. The boat shuddered and jerked each time the fish moved its head. Quint slipped and fell to his knees on the transom. The fish let go and dropped beneath the surface, and the boat lay still again.

'He was waiting for us!' yelled Brody.

'I know,' said Quint.

'How did he—'

'It don't matter,' said Quint. 'We've got him now.'

'*We've* got *him*? Did you see what he did to the boat?'

'Give it a mighty good shake, didn't he?'

The rope holding the sheep tightened, shook for a moment, then went slack.

Quint stood and picked up the harpoon. 'He's took the sheep. It'll be minutes before he comes back.'

'How come he didn't take the sheep first?'

'He got no manners,' Quint cackled. 'Come on, you motherfucker. Come and get your due.'

Brody saw fever in Quint's face – a heat that lit up his dark eyes, an intensity that drew his lips back from his teeth in a crooked smile, an anticipation that strummed the sinews in his neck and whitened his knuckles.

The boat shuddered again, and there was a dull, hollow thump.

'What's he doing?' said Brody.

Quint leaned over the side and shouted, 'Come out from under there, you cocksucker! Where are your guts? You'll not sink me before I get you!'

'What do you mean, sink us?' said Brody. 'What's he doing?'

'He's trying to chew a hole in the bottom of the fucking boat, that's what! Look in the bilge. Come out, you God-forsaken sonofabitch!' Quint raised high his harpoon.

Brody knelt and raised the hatch cover over the engine room. He peered into the dark, oily hole. There was water in the bilges, but there always was, and he saw no new hole through which water could pour. 'Looks okay to me,' he said. 'Thank God.'

The dorsal fin and tail surfaced ten yards to the right of the stern and began to move again towards the boat. 'There you come,' said Quint, cooing. 'There you come.' He stood, legs spread, left hand on his hip, right hand extended to the sky, grasping the harpoon. When the fish was a few feet from the boat and heading straight on, Quint cast his iron.

The harpoon struck the fish in front of the dorsal fin. And then the fish hit the boat, knocking the stern sideways and sending Quint tumbling backward. His head struck the foot-rest of the fighting chair, and a trickle of blood ran down his neck. He jumped to his feet and cried, 'I got you! I got you, you miserable prick!'

The rope attached to the iron dart snaked overboard as the fish sounded, and when it reached the end, the barrel popped off the transom, fell into the water, and vanished.

'He took it down with him!' said Brody.

'Not for long,' said Quint. 'He'll be back, and we'll throw another into him, and another, and another, until he quits. And then he's ours!' Quint leaned on the transom, watching the water.

Quint's confidence was contagious, and Brody now felt ebullient, gleeful, relieved. It was a kind of freedom, a freedom from the mist of death. He yelled, 'Hot shit!' Then he noticed the blood running down Quint's neck, and he said, 'Your head's bleeding.'

'Get another barrel,' said Quint. 'Bring it back here. And don't fuck up the coil. I want it to go over smooth as cream.'

Brody ran forward, unlashed a barrel, slipped the coiled rope over his arm, and carried the gear to Quint.

'There he comes,' said Quint, pointing to the left. The barrel came to the surface and bobbed in the water. Quint pulled the string attached to the wooden shaft and brought it aboard. He fixed the shaft to the new dart and raised the harpoon above his head. 'He's coming up!'

The fish broke water a few yards from the boat. Like a rocket lifting off, snout, jaw, and pectoral fins rose straight from the water. Then the smoke-white belly, pelvic fin, and huge, salami-like claspers.

'I see your cock, you bastard!' cried Quint, and he threw a second iron, leaning his shoulder and back into the throw. The iron hit the fish in the belly, just as the great body began to fall forward. The belly smacked the water with a thunder-ous boom, sending a blinding fall of spray over the boat.

'He's done!' said Quint as the second rope uncoiled and tumbled overboard.

The boat lurched once, and again, and there was the distant sound of crunching.

'Attack me, will you ?' said Quint. 'You'll take no man with you, uppity fuck!' Quint ran forward and started the engine. He pushed the throttle forward, and the boat moved away from the bobbing barrels.

'Has he done any damage ?' said Brody.

'Some. We're riding a little heavy aft. He probably poked a hole in us. It's nothing to worry about. We'll pump her out.'

'That's it, then,' Brody said happily.

'What's what ?'

'The fish is as good as dead.'

'Not quite. Look.'

Following the boat, keeping pace, were the two red wood barrels. They did not bob. Dragged by the great force of the fish, each cut through the water, pushing a wave before it and leaving a wake behind.

'He's chasing us ?' said Brody.

Quint nodded.

'Why ? He can't still think we're food.'

'No. He means to make a fight of it.'

For the first time, Brody saw a frown of disquiet on Quint's face. It was not fear, nor true alarm, but rather a look of uneasy concern – as if, in a game, the rules had been changed without warning, or the stakes raised. Seeing the change in Quint's mood, Brody was afraid.

'Have you ever had a fish do this before ?' he asked.

'Not like this, no. I've had 'em attack the boat, like I told you. But most times, once you get an iron in 'em, they stop fighting you and fight against that thing stickin' in 'em.'

Brody looked astern. The boat was moving at moderate speed, turning this way and that in response to Quint's random turning of the wheel. Always the barrels kept up with them.

'Fuck it,' said Quint. 'If it's a fight he wants, it's a fight he'll get.' He throttled down to idling speed, jumped down from the flying bridge and up on to the transom. He picked up the harpoon. Excitement had returned to his face. 'Okay, shit-eater!' he called. 'Come and get it!'

The barrels kept coming, ploughing through the water – thirty yards away, then twenty-five, then twenty. Brody saw the flat plain of grey pass along the starboard side of the boat, six feet beneath the surface. 'He's here!' he cried. 'Heading forward.'

'Shit!' said Quint, cursing his misjudgement of the length of the ropes. He detached the harpoon dart from the shaft, snapped the twine that held the shaft to a cleat, hopped down from the transom, and ran forward. When he reached the bow, he bent down and tied the twine to a forward cleat, un-lashed a barrel, and slipped its dart on to the shaft. He stood at the end of the pulpit, harpoon raised.

The fish had already passed out of range. The tail surfaced twenty feet in front of the boat. The two barrels bumped into the stern almost simultaneously. They bounced once, then rolled off the stern, one on each side, and slid down the sides of the boat.

Thirty yards in front of the boat, the fish turned. The head raised out of the water, then dipped back in. The tail, stand-ing like a sail, began to thrash back and forth. 'Here he comes!' said Quint.

Brody raced up the ladder to the flying bridge. Just as he got there, he saw Quint draw his right arm back and rise up on tiptoes.

The fish hit the bow head on, with a noise like a muffled explosion. Quint cast his iron. It struck the fish atop the head, over the right eye, and it held fast. The rope fed slowly overboard as the fish backed off.

'Perfect!' said Quint. 'Got him in the head that time.'

There were three barrels in the water now, and they skated across the surface. Then they disappeared.

'God *damn*!' said Quint. 'That's no normal fish that can sound with three irons in him and three barrels to hold him up.'

The boat trembled, seeming to rise up, then dropped back. The barrels popped up, two on one side of the boat, one on the other. Then they submerged again. A few seconds later, they reappeared twenty yards from the boat.

'Go below,' said Quint, as he readied another harpoon. 'See if that prick done us any dirt up forward.'

Brody swung down into the cabin. It was dry. He pulled back the threadbare carpet, saw a hatch, and opened it. A river of water was flowing aft beneath the floor of the cabin. We're sinking, he told himself, and the memories of his childhood nightmares leaped into his mind. He went topside and said to Quint, 'It doesn't look good. There's a lot of water under the cabin floor.'

'I better go take a look. Here.' Quint handed Brody the harpoon. 'If he comes back while I'm below, stick this in him for good measure.' He walked aft and went below.

Brody stood on the pulpit, holding the harpoon, and he looked at the floating barrels. They lay practically still in the water, twitching now and then as the fish moved about below. How do you die? Brody said silently to the fish. He heard an electric motor start.

'No sweat,' said Quint, walking forward. He took the harpoon from Brody. 'He's banged us up, all right, but the pumps should take care of it. We'll be able to tow him in.'

Brody dried his palms on the seat of his pants. 'Are you really going to tow him in?'

'I am. When he dies.'

'And when will that be?'

'When he's ready.'

'And until then?'

'We wait.'

Brody looked at his watch. It was eight-thirty.

For three hours they waited, tracking the barrels as they moved, ever more slowly, on a random path across the surface of the sea. At first they would disappear every ten or fifteen minutes, resurfacing a few dozen yards away. Then their submergences grew rarer until by eleven, they had not gone under for nearly an hour. By eleven-thirty, the barrels were wallowing in the water.

The rain had stopped, and the wind had subsided to a comfortable breeze. The sky was an unbroken sheet of grey.

'What do you think?' said Brody. 'Is he dead?'

'I doubt it. But he may be close enough to it for us to throw a rope 'round his tail and drag him till he drowns.'

Quint took a coil of rope from one of the barrels in the bow. He tied one end to an after cleat. The other end he tied into a noose.

At the foot of the gin pole was an electric winch. Quint switched it on to make sure it was working, then turned it off again. He gunned the engine and moved the boat towards the barrels. He drove slowly, cautiously prepared to veer away if the fish attacked. But the barrels lay still.

Quint idled the engine when he came alongside the barrels. He reached overboard with a gaff, snagged a rope, and pulled a barrel aboard. He tried to untie the rope from the barrel but the knot had been soaked and strained. So he took his knife from the sheath at his belt and cut the rope. He stabbed the knife into the gunwale, freeing his left hand to hold the rope, his right to shove the barrel to the deck.

He climbed on to the gunwale, ran the rope through a pulley at the top of the gin pole and down the pole to the winch. He took a few turns around the winch, then flipped the starter switch. As soon as the slack in the rope was taken up the boat heeled hard to starboard, dragged down by the weight of the fish.

'Can that winch handle him?' said Brody.

'Seems to be. It'd never haul him out of the water, but I bet it'll bring him up to us.' The winch was turning slowly, humming, taking a full turn every three or four seconds. The rope quivered under the strain, scattering drops of water on Quint's shirt.

Suddenly the rope started coming too fast. It fouled on the winch, coiling in snarls. The boat snapped upright.

'Rope break?' said Brody.

'Shit no!' said Quint, and now Brody saw fear in his face. 'The sonofabitch is coming up!' He dashed to the controls and threw the engine into forward. But it was too late.

The fish broke water right beside the boat, with a great rushing whoosh of noise. It rose vertically, and in an instant of horror Brody gasped at the size of the body. Towering overhead, it blocked out the light. The pectoral fins hovered like wings, stiff and straight, and as the fish fell forward, they seemed to be reaching out to Brody.

The fish landed on the stern of the boat with a shattering crash, driving the boat beneath the waves. Water poured in over the transom. In seconds, Quint and Brody were standing in water up to their hips.

The fish lay there, its jaw not three feet from Brody's chest. The body twitched, and in the black eye, as big as a baseball, Brody thought he saw his own image reflected.

'God damn your black soul!' screamed Quint. 'You sunk my boat!' A barrel floated into the cockpit, the rope writhing like a gathering of worms. Quint grabbed the harpoon dart at the end of the rope and, with his hand, plunged it into the soft white belly of the fish. Blood poured from the wound and bathed Quint's hands.

The boat was sinking. The stern was completely submerged, and the bow was rising.

The fish rolled off the stern and slid beneath the waves. The rope, attached to the dart Quint had stuck into the fish, followed.

Suddenly, Quint lost his footing and fell backward into the water. 'The knife!' he cried, lifting his left leg above the surface, and Brody saw the rope coiled around Quint's foot.

Brody looked to the starboard gunwale. The knife was there, embedded in the wood. He lunged for it, wrenched it free, and turned back, struggling to run in the deepening water. He could not move fast enough. He watched in helpless terror as Quint, reaching towards him with grasping fingers, eyes wide and pleading, was pulled slowly down into the dark water.

For a moment there was silence, except for the sucking sound of the boat slipping gradually down. The water was up to Brody's shoulders, and he clung desperately to the gin pole. A seat cushion popped to the surface next to him, and Brody grabbed it. ('They'd hold you up all right,' Brody remembered Hendricks saying, 'if you were an eight-year-old boy.')

Brody saw the tail and dorsal fin break the surface twenty yards away. The tail waved once left, once right, and the dorsal fin moved closer. 'Get away, damn you!' Brody yelled.

The fish kept coming, barely moving, closing in. The barrels and skeins of rope trailed behind.

The gin pole went under, and Brody let go of it. He tried to kick over to the bow of the boat, which was almost vertical now. Before he could reach it, the bow raised even higher, then quickly and soundlessly slid beneath the surface.

Brody clutched the cushion, and he found that by holding it in front of him, his forearms across it, and by kicking constantly, he could stay afloat without exhausting himself.

The fish came closer. It was only a few feet away, and Brody could see the conical snout. He screamed, an ejaculation of hopelessness, and closed his eyes, waiting for an agony he could not imagine.

Nothing happened. He opened his eyes. The fish was nearly touching him, only a foot or two away, but it had stopped. And then, as Brody watched, the steel-grey body began to recede downward into the gloom. It seemed to fall away, an apparition evanescing into darkness.

Brody put his face into the water and opened his eyes. Through the stinging saltwater mist he saw the fish sink in a slow and graceful spiral, trailing behind it the body of Quint – arms out to the sides, head thrown back, mouth open in mute protest.

The fish faded from view. But, kept from sinking into the deep by the bobbing barrels, it stopped somewhere beyond the reach of light, and Quint's body hung suspended, a shadow twirling slowly in the twilight.

Brody watched until his lungs ached for air. He raised his head, cleared his eyes, and sighted in the distance the black point of the water tower. Then he began to kick towards shore.

Ed McBain

Axe 40p

'A high level of sharp, credible dialogue and ingenious puzzlement'
Sunday Times

January brought a sunless lack of cheer to the 87th Precinct. There would be no happy new year for George Lasser. An axe had split his skull wide open. It was pretty goddamn gory.
Then someone killed a cop.
Before, only an eighty-year-old janitor was dead.
Now it was a cop.
It looked like being a lousy month for Detectives Hawes and Carella . . .

Ed McBain's *87th Precinct* mysteries are 'the best of today's procedural school of police stories – wholly satisfactory'
New York Times

Other *87th Precinct* novels available in Pan include:
Fuzz
Jigsaw
Shotgun
80 Million Eyes
Sadie When She Died
He Who Hesitates
Ten Plus One

Arthur Hailey

More record-breaking bestsellers from the acclaimed master of blockbusting epic fiction.

Wheels 60p

The most incisive piece of fiction ever written about the US auto industry. 'All a bestseller's elements abound – sex, intrigue, glamour and ruthless high-power executives making million-dollar decisions' CHICAGO SUN-TIMES

Airport 50p

Non-stop reading excitement as Arthur Hailey probes the hidden nerve-centre that controls a great modern airport. 'Supercharged' CHICAGO SUN-TIMES

In High Places 50p

A spellbinding tale of the passions that seethe behind the prim facade of government offices as politicians in power fight to stay there – bartering, backstabbing, browbeating, bribing with honours, money or women . . .

Flight Into Danger 35p

As the airliner droned westward through the Canadian night, the fierce, unheralded terror struck. The peaceful, happy evening became a hideous nightmare. And hundreds of miles away, on solid ground at Vancouver Airport, everyone watched and prayed. Silent. Helpless . . .

Selected bestsellers

- ☐ **Let Sleeping Vets Lie** James Herriot 50p
- ☐ **Jaws** Peter Benchley
- ☐ **Slay-Ride** Dick Francis 45p
- ☐ **The Tower** Richard Martin Stern 50p
  (filmed as *The Towering Inferno*)
- ☐ **Open Season** David Osborn 50p
- ☐ **The Man with the Golden Gun** Ian Fleming 40p
- ☐ **Gold** Wilbur Smith 40p
- ☐ **Airport** Arthur Hailey 50p
- ☐ **Mandingo** Kyle Onstott 50p
- ☐ **Royal Flash** George MacDonald Fraser 40p
- ☐ **The Poseidon Adventure** Paul Gallico 60p
- ☐ **Penmarric** Susan Howatch 75p
- ☐ **Lady of Quality** Georgette Heyer 50p
- ☐ **The Frightened Bride** Barbara Cartland 40p
- ☐ **Fuzz** Ed McBain 30p
- ☐ **Jonathan Livingston Seagull** Richard Bach 50p
- ☐ **The Spy Who Came In from the Cold** John le Carré 40p
- ☐ **Princess of Celle** Jean Plaidy 60p
- ☐ **Bury My Heart at Wounded Knee** Dee Brown 95p
- ☐ **The Little Prince** Antoine de Saint-Exupéry 35p
- ☐ **The Maltese Falcon** Dashiell Hammett 45p

All these books are available at your bookshop or newsagent;
or can be obtained direct from the publisher
Just tick the titles you want and fill in the form below

Pan Books Cavaye Place London SW10 9PG
Send purchase price plus 15p for the first book and 5p for
each additional book, to allow for postage and packing

Name (block letters) _____

Address _____

_____

While every effort is made to keep prices low, it is sometimes
necessary to increase prices at short notice. Pan Books reserve the
right to show on covers new retail prices which may differ from
those advertised in the text or elsewhere